BEING
FRANK

National Library of New Zealand Cataloguing-in-Publication Data
Endacott, Frank.
Being Frank: the Frank Endacott story/Frank Endacott with John Coffey.
ISBN: 1-86958-922-X
1. Endacott, Frank. 2. Rugby League football — New Zealand.
3. Rugby football coaches — New Zealand — Biography. I.Coffey, John (John Oliver), 1946-
II. Title.
796.3338092 — dc21

ISBN 1-86958-922-X

© 2002 — Design and format Hodder Moa Beckett Publishers Limited
Published in 2002 by Hodder Moa Beckett Publishers Limited
[a member of the Hodder Headline Group]
4 Whetu Place, Mairangi Bay, Auckland

Designed and produced by Hodder Moa Beckett
Printed in China by Midas Printing (Asia) Ltd.

This book is dedicated to my wife, Joan,

for all the wonderful support she has

given me over the years.

Contents

Acknowledgements

The author and publishers thank those organisations and individuals who have contributed to this book, in particular Photosport; News Media, Auckland; the Mad Butcher and the *Wigan Observer*.

Foreword I

By Dave Hadfield, rugby league correspondent,
Independent, England

There were some long faces in the British media the day Wigan announced that they were sacking Frank Endacott. There are plenty of good people in rugby league, but few of us had ever dealt with anyone quite as affable as Frank. We like our Kiwis in British rugby league and they like it here. That is shown by the number who make their home permanently in the UK. Frank's stay was shorter, but he enjoyed every minute of it – and we enjoyed having him here. That's why we were all so sorry to see him go.

Players have to be a little more circumspect in what they say publicly – they have a new coach to get along with – but I know how upset many of them were when Frank got the bullet. As for the supporters, I don't think there's a single one of them who, were they to have the good fortune to bump into him socially, wouldn't want to buy him a beer. That says a lot about what a popular bloke he is on these shores. But the fact that he is The Nicest Chap in Rugby League obscures something else almost as important. After all, he didn't achieve what he did in the game simply by being everyone's pal. Frank Endacott has been a pretty remarkable rugby league coach as well.

The results that Canterbury and New Zealand achieved under his stewardship speak for themselves. With the two Warriors – Auckland and Wigan – his club career fell foul of bosses lacking the vital ingredient for lasting success: a bit of patience. I don't think there was a player with any of those teams who didn't want to play for Frank. That simple factor is downplayed by some of the most technical coaches, but it is surely always the first essential.

The thing that shone through watching Frank at work was the sense of sheer pleasure. There was hardly a training session or a match day throughout his career that he didn't enjoy. That's a wonderful gift and when I see some other coaches to whom the whole business seems like a form of slow torture, I wish there were more who shared it.

Everyone will have their favourite memory of Frank and his relish for the game. My own came not among any of the elite athletes to whom he has imparted his knowledge, but with a bunch of amateurs that I asked him to come and coach. He laid on an inspiring session, which was more about the philosophy of the game than merely about the technicalities. When it was over, we had a bit of a question-and-answer segment, out there on the training paddock. The talk went on for quite a while. In fact, I realised it was time to move on when I looked up and saw it had gone dark and Frank Endacott was still rhapsodising about the game he loves.

That's the bloke for you.

Dave Hadfield
Bolton, March 2002

Foreword II

By Steve Mascord, rugby league writer,
Sydney Morning Herald, Australia

I'm not quite sure who came up with 'Happy Frank'. The first person this reporter remembers using the moniker was Michael Donaldson, the New Zealand Press Association's Sydney correspondent.

Michael was not just a rugby league writer and, indeed, not even a fulltime sports reporter. He spent most of his time trailing around politicians, trade union officials, and third-rate entertainers, and was probably used to being treated with anything from indifference to outright rudeness. And here was this man who remembered him by name, greeted him with a broad smile and a firm handshake when the Kiwis were in town and — later — every second week, when the Auckland Warriors crossed the ditch. It must have helped Michael distinguish between weekdays and weekends.

As rugby league writer with the *Sydney Morning Herald*, I had tried to bestow the nickname 'Brutally Frank' on Endacott. That was the thing about him: he was happy, but he was honest. When the Kiwis hosted rugby league media from three countries at Wilderspool, Warrington, in 1995, at the beginning of the World Cup, Endacott was asked why much-decorated former All Black Craig Innes wasn't in the side. Not even pausing to contemplate his answer, he said it was Innes' defence. And why was Henry Paul not in the starting team? Because he was undisciplined with the ball and could lose you a match. Innes' defence and Paul's flair with the football would eventually become legion among rugby league fans but at the time Endacott didn't think they were ready and wasn't afraid to say so — with tape recorders and cameras whirring.

BEING FRANK

Then came the Super League war, a period when honesty and the 13-a-side game were like oil and water. Endacott held off signing for either side but vehemently stood up for Kiwi rugby league at every turn. At one stage, the ARL accused Endacott of offering players $5000 not to play in a 'rebel' test for the so-called All Golds against the ARL Australians. 'This is the first time I've heard of it, although no allegation would surprise me at the moment,' Endacott said. 'I don't need to offer players money, they just don't want to play.'

In 1997, before the Anzac test, Endacott said to me, 'Sometimes people make the mistake of thinking that because you respect people and you're approachable that you are soft. People can think that at their own peril. I can be a hard bastard but I can't see any use being a hard bastard for no reason.' In many ways, Frank's hardness allowed him to keep a smile on his face while those about him were fast losing interest in a sport increasingly beset by greed and selfishness. It was a low ebb for the game, but for a little while things looked good for Frank. He succeeded John Monie as coach of the Auckland Warriors but was still the same jolly character, remembering the names attached to the multitude of hands he had to shake each day. He forged an unlikely but enduring relationship with Kiwi skipper Matthew Ridge, whose temperament couldn't have been more different from his.

Frank was at his happiest, of course, when his Kiwis were beating Australia and they began to do it regularly. Only an ounce of luck prevented them ending Australia's two-decade purple patch against all comers in the unforgettable 1999 Tri-Nations final. Endacott became the most successful Kiwi coach of all time. But just as he was coming into his own as a coach, the political sands of rugby league shifted again. Happy Frank became a victim of the takeover of the ailing Warriors, with Mark Graham installed as his replacement. He moved on to Wigan where, like many coaches at the club before and since, success was not enough to ensure job security. Frank Endacott finally stepped down as boss of the Kiwis after the 2000 World Cup final, disillusioned that some of his own directors refused to support him despite his undoubted commitment, passion and success at the post.

So the nicest man this reporter has met in a decade and a half covering league exited for good in May 2001, when Wigan told him his services were no longer required. He did so with his dignity and integrity intact — both qualities which rugby league will find much more difficult to lay claim to without his involvement.

Steve Mascord
Sydney, March 2002

Introduction

I can't remember too much about the first time I (literally) ran into Frank Endacott. The programme from the 1958 inter-island rugby league match in Christchurch lists F. Endacott, of Canterbury, and J. Coffee (sic), of West Coast, among the players in the 12.30pm 'bantams' curtain-raiser for the Stuart Cup. But I do recall us getting a dusting from the big city boys before Runanga centre Reece Griffiths scored three tries when South Island beat the North in the main game.

Five years later a young cadet reporter from *The Press* had cause to admire the emerging and contrasting skills of the strapping Frank Endacott and little livewire Graeme Cooksley as the Canterbury inside backs when the New Zealand Schoolboys tournament was held in Christchurch. Cooksley became a Kiwi but Endacott did not even play senior representative football. It was not until I was compiling this book that I fully appreciated why.

By their early twenties, Frank and wife Joan were caring for eight children in an extended family. If working overtime just about every night to keep ahead of the bills wasn't enough distraction for a budding footballer, crippling hamstring injuries forced his withdrawal when he was selected for Canterbury teams.

In many ways the Endacott story closely parallels that of rugby league in New Zealand during the last decade. His Canterbury team displaced Auckland as top province in the early 1990s, his Junior Kiwis enjoyed success at home and away, he was with the Auckland Warriors from the start and guided the reserve grade team to a grand final, he coached the Kiwis in more tests than anyone else.

But Frank, being Frank, derived just as much enjoyment from coaching his son's schoolboy sides and the Canterbury women's touch team as he did when taking the Kiwis to a World Cup final, to home and away unbeaten series triumphs over Great Britain, and to one of New Zealand's greatest victories among his three wins at Australia's expense.

Above all, Frank Endacott likes working with people. And people like working with Frank. All of the modern mumbo jumbo about video analysis, statistics sheets, sports psychiatry and nutrition no doubt has its place in professional sport. But Endacott had an advantage not shared by all coaches. His players wanted to play for him, and they wanted to win for him.

'Frank had great man management skills, he could relate to anybody. He was one of the blokes, enjoying a quiet beer, when he could afford to be one of the blokes. But when it was time for business, Frank was the coach and he meant business,' said Aaron Whittaker, who played in Endacott's Canterbury, Auckland Warriors, New Zealand Residents, and Kiwi teams.

Whittaker tells the story of when Endacott convinced a young Canterbury side that it could beat an Auckland team stacked with professionals who were just home from Britain, in the 1993 national inter-provincial grand final.

'He detailed every one of their players and then came to each one of us who were marking them. He told us he wouldn't swap any of us for them, and convinced us to believe in ourselves. "They might have all the imports, the Tawera Nikaus, the Iva Ropatis, the Craig Inneses, but they are only human, they eat, they sleep, they breathe, they bleed, the same as you guys," he said. He made us into a champion team to beat their team of champions. We could have done it blindfolded, we were that well drilled.

'Frank was the complete package. He wasn't just a man who could teach the basics, or just a tactician, or just a motivator. He was all of them, and a buddy as well. At the Warriors Frank used the available technology but still had excellent one-on-one relationships with the players — he didn't bag individuals in front of the whole team and sap their confidence like John Monie. His New Zealand Residents were unbeaten and his record for the Kiwis speaks for itself.'

Endacott made an unforgettable impression on his contemporaries from an early age. A fellow pupil at Shirley Boys' High School recalls he was 'a tough bastard', and not just because he became the youngest ever first XV player. One particular school bully, later an All Black forward prospect, is going through his adult life with a bent beak after Endacott caught him bullying a smaller classmate. Something similar happened during a year's schooling in Sydney. Appreciative schoolmates voted him a prefect.

Frank has always had a soft side too, and his players inevitably come up with the description 'father figure' when talking about him. To hold a conversation with Endacott at a public function is decidedly difficult. He attracts people like a magnet, whether they are old neighbours from the state housing area where he grew up, former team-mates and opponents, past players from his various teams, or the New Zealand netball representative who was in his touch squad. All receive the same huge grin and cheerful greeting.

It was never going to be all plain sailing when Endacott took on fulltime coaching. Twice at World Cups his Kiwis eyeballed the Australians without quite toppling them, and a late try and the subsequently admitted inattention of the match officials cost him overall victory in the 1999 Tri-Nations series. But Endacott swallowed his disappointment, put on a brave face, and always fronted up at after-match news conferences. He never ducked a question, and was invariably honest in his dealings with the media.

Professional coaches who survive without being sacked are about as rare as unbeaten heavyweight boxing champions. Endacott was shown the door by the Auckland Warriors and Wigan before his contracts had expired. He enjoyed neither sufficient financial backing nor the time to build his own Warriors team. Cutting Endacott adrift was one of the first mistakes by an administration that all but steered the club into oblivion. It was an error to be repeated by autocratic Wigan chairman Maurice Lindsay, to the frustration of the club's players and supporters.

'Sure, Frank got sacked at Wigan. But Wigan has gone through seven coaches in eight years. Keeping that in mind, I don't think Frank Endacott was the problem,' said Australian international Matthew Johns after cutting his own ties with Wigan.

'Frank is not only an outstanding coach but he is one of the most outstanding blokes you could meet. Wigan is a club that is trying to sort itself out. Mate, the boys really liked Frank and the fans there really liked him as well. I was sad to see him go. I went to Wigan to play for Frank.'

Stephen Kearney, who appeared in all but three of Frank Endacott's 35 tests, made an emotional address to his retiring coach in the Old Trafford dressing room after the 2000 World Cup final. Thirty-test veteran Ruben Wiki spontaneously presented Endacott with the No. 13 jersey he had worn in the biggest game of his life.

I could have filled this book with tributes from players. But I felt it was sufficient only to chat with Aaron Whittaker, an 'Endacott original' who featured in so many of his teams, and Matthew Johns, who went from being a thorn in Endacott's side during the 1999 Tri-Nations final to an appreciative pupil at Wigan. In all the years I have been covering the Endacott teams I cannot recall any player bad-mouthing him. The tributes would have become repetitive. And this, after all, is Frank's story.

Well, not just Frank's. The Endacotts, Frank, Joan, and sons Wayne, Frank,

Gary and Shane, are far from an ordinary family. They started out packed into a three-bedroom house, sleep-out and caravan in suburban Christchurch as Frank and Joan raised Joan's family along with their own. Wayne is a down to earth character typical of the clan, Frank junior survived a life-threatening illness as a baby to thrive as an adult, Shane became a professional rugby league player in England and New Zealand, and Gary has achieved incredible feats despite being afflicted with cerebral palsy.

It has been a pleasure putting Frank Endacott's story on paper. His memory in recalling people, places, even penalty counts, was remarkably accurate. But even Frank could not remember the score from that 12.30pm encounter between the Canterbury and West Coast 'bantams' at the Addington Show Grounds on July 12, 1958. Maybe he didn't want to embarrass 'J. Coffee'.

John Coffey
Christchurch, March 2002

Chapter 1.
The hard yards

Just before starting the manuscript for this book Frank Endacott took a trip down memory lane, parking outside his childhood home at 127 Emmett Street in the Christchurch suburb of Shirley. Emmett Street had recently been in the news because of gang activity. Some residents complained of intimidation, that the gang was attempting to set up an enclave in the Emmett Street, Acheson Avenue and Riselaw Street area. Endacott's mind went back almost 50 years, to a more innocent but no less tough time in what was then a new state housing project.

I was about nine years old and walking down Emmett Street with Dad when it struck me that he seemed to know everybody. At least he talked to everyone we met. So I asked him about it.

'Son, it costs you nothing to say hello to people and give them a smile,' he said. That was probably the best advice I ever received and it has stayed with me throughout my life. Being pleasant to people doesn't drain your wallet, and that was important in those days.

Emmett Street was my first permanent address after I was born in what is now the Christchurch Women's Hospital on June 2, 1948. The hospital was then named St Helens. I guess you could say I went from St Helens to a rugby league coaching career which ended in Wigan. But the first port of call for Dad (Frank), Mum (Marie) and baby Frank was a tent at the back of my grandparents' place in Spreydon, near Barrington Park. Mum's parents, brothers and sisters lived in the house and we camped on the lawn. We went from there, when I was about two years old, to the Harewood Transit Camp, which later evolved into the United States air base near Christchurch Airport. That remained the Endacott residence until our new state house was available in Emmett Street.

I can remember the street before it was sealed. It was a red-letter day when they planted those big trees that are there now. The memories are still vivid of when MacFarlane Park was buried under tall grass and had a creek running through it. Even before they laid out the rugby league and soccer fields, the park was our backyard, our playground.

Obviously, there wasn't a lot of money around in those days. Dad was an Australian professional boxer who came over to New Zealand in 1947, met Mum, and stayed. He was a good fighter and had been middleweight champion of the Australian Navy. But boxing as a pro wasn't a lucrative occupation. We were never a wealthy family, hence the transit camp as a stepping stone between our tent and the government's state house. Dad was a big influence on my life. He was born in Cessnock, where Jarrod McCracken now owns a pub, and lived most of his young life in Mudgee, just over the mountains.

The Mudgee Mauler was discovered by a trainer at one of those boxing circuses which travelled around the country shows. Local lads were invited to step into the ring with the show's champion and if you lasted three minutes you won a prize. Dad climbed through the ropes and knocked the so-called champ cold. Dad also did some professional cycling in Australia, and was interested in most sports. But his main loves were boxing and rugby league and he was instrumental, along with some mates from the area, in forming the Shirley Rugby League Club in 1955.

Mum was very involved too, on and off the football fields. She was one of the first female coaches in New Zealand, fitting that in with a fulltime job and all her domestic duties. I can still see her riding her bike up the street into the teeth of a south-westerly wind. She worked all her life but was always there for me, my brother, Ray, and sister Julie. No one could ever say anything nasty about Mum's kids. In her mind we could do nothing wrong, though we sure did. Where we would get kicked up the backside by Dad, Mum always defended us. Whenever we were in trouble there was never any doubt who we would go to.

Maybe it was because of the financial difficulties shared by so many families in our district that they all seemed to get on so well. Most of them had moved in about the same time as us, there were plenty of kids, and the street and MacFarlane Park were our territory. Number 127 seemed to be the district house. The back door was always open for people to call in and have a cup of tea and a chat.

I can remember some unwelcome guests turning up when I was about 10, a night when I really learned what people meant when they said Dad could 'handle himself'. We had a party and there were about three guests and their wives left, with one guy playing a guitar, and the rest singing along. Three huge men turned up on the doorstep and tried to get in. Dad was pretty diplomatic about it, saying it was a private party, wishing them all the best, and asking them to go. But they just kept banging on the door and one of Dad's mates opened it, said, 'You heard the man' and gave this big bugger a push in the chest. It was all on. Dad creamed one of them. Then he ran into the biggest bloke and it was bang, bang, bang right across the street. Dad was dynamic. I'd never seen anyone fight like it in my life. They had the gatecrashers in a cab when the police turned up and asked Dad if he wanted to lay charges. When he said he didn't, one of the cops took another look at these guys sitting there covered in blood and agreed they had suffered enough punishment anyway.

Dad was in a hard crew when he got caught up in the wharfies' strike. There was a lot of funny stuff going on as the strikers struggled to keep their families fed without a wage to fall back on. I remember Mum saying they were the toughest days of her life, and that it was hard even to survive. Although Dad was working for the harbour board in Auckland when he died in 1980, you couldn't call him a watersider by occupation. He sat up one night, counted the jobs he had had, and got to 112. For a time he and Mum lived a nomadic existence, moving between Australia and New Zealand, Auckland and Christchurch.

When we settled in Emmett Street it only extended as far as number 127. Dad had a stock answer when asked where he lived. 'In Emmett Street,' he would say. 'It's tough. The further down the street you go the tougher you have to be. And we live in the last house.' I doubt if anyone disputed his claim. It's sad to look at the area now. Most of the shops in Acheson Avenue, just around the corner from where we lived, are boarded up, as if people are too frightened to open a business there. The second shop used to be the MMM Butchery, where I had my first job after school two days each week. They paid me 10 shillings for cleaning the tools and butchers' block, and sweeping the floors.

To make a few bob my brother, Ray, and I would go raspberry picking in Shirley. We made a cart out of an old pram and had our sister, Julie, wait with it on the other side of the poplar trees. As we were picking the raspberries, one tray would go to the weigh-in centre and the next tray would be quietly slipped through the fence to Julie. When the cart was full we would sell them at the bus stop outside our front gate. There was a steady supply of customers coming home from work and Endacott Enterprises was a successful little business.

Shirley had become one of the strongest schoolboy rugby league clubs in Canterbury because it was based in an expanding suburb. You had to be reasonably hard to live in Shirley, so we always had good young teams that could compete well. There was a real club spirit provided by the parents, and we had an annual exchange with the Blackball club on the West Coast.

In 1963 five Shirley players were chosen in the South Island Schoolboys team and Maurice Perreau and I went on to play for the Schoolboy Kiwis. That coincided with the first trans-Tasman match. We beat New South Wales 6–3 at the Addington Show Grounds in Christchurch. A big, fast Bay of Plenty winger named Phil Orchard scored the winning try, just as he was to do regularly at senior international level a few years later.

Dad had coached our age group team up to 13 years and then handed us over to former Kiwi winger Allen Amer. Allen was coaching us when I made the Canterbury, South Island, and Schoolboy Kiwi teams at stand-off half. The scrumhalf was Graeme Cooksley, who also went on to play test football. An old family scrapbook shows Dad was variously the Shirley club president, chairman, club captain, and coach of championship winning teams. But Mum's name was always there too. I think she was the second woman in New Zealand to officially become a rugby league coach after Joyce Phillips, who lived down the road from us. Joyce was later a top softball umpire and basketball referee, her husband, Eric, was a leading soccer referee, and their son Derek played soccer for New Zealand as a goalkeeper.

Ray played rugby league but was better at cricket. The scrapbook shows Ray took six wickets for seven runs in Ashburton's innings of 67 and then opened the batting and retired on 55 out of his Christchurch junior team's total of 117 in one match at Ashburton. Among his team-mates was Richard Hadlee, who managed one wicket for five runs and scored seven. But Ray has been a better golfer than anything else. When he was 12, he caddied for Bob Charles at Shirley, later got down as low as a one or two handicap and still plays to a six. Ray, though, never had the commitment to take any sport too seriously and just played it for relaxation. I'm sure he could have played professional golf.

Julie was more into netball but was interested in sport generally and now has a few golf trophies of her own. We were brought up on sport as a family. Most of my time at school seemed to be spent gazing out the windows at the sports fields, dreaming. I went to Shirley Primary School for a year or two and still remember it cost one penny on the bus. Then Quinns Road School opened and I was a first day pupil. From there I went to Shirley Intermediate and Shirley Boys' High School.

Not totally, though. Dad could never stay in one place for too long and when I was in third form he decided to pack up the family and move to Australia. We lasted there for a year before Mum got homesick and we came home again.

It gave me the chance to experience rugby league Australian schools style and I played against some of the New South Wales players who were to tour New Zealand the following season.

It was while I was at Dulwich Hill High School that I first lost my cool in public. There was an Italian kid named Bruno who had quite a following. He was the biggest bloke at school, and the school bully. He got his kicks terrorising the smaller Australian kids. One day at Petersham railway station, where I caught the train home to Summerhill, Bruno was tearing into one of my little Aussie schoolmates. I don't know what made me do it to this day but I went racing down the steps and punched him on the beak. At the sight of blood he turned coward and didn't want any part of it. The word got around school real quick, and a week or two later it was time to vote for the prefects. That was traditionally done by a show of hands at assembly and I had apparently made such an impression that they elected me head prefect. Dulwich Hill never had the same levels of discipline as Shirley Boys' High.

We returned to Christchurch and I went back to Shirley Boys' High in fourth form. I was playing league on Saturday mornings when I also got selected for the school rugby first XV which played on Saturday afternoons. I was still only 14 and they reckoned I was the youngest player to make it.

One morning I was summoned into the office of Charlie Gallagher, the headmaster, who was basically a good bloke. Even though he was very strict I always had a bit of time for him. But I think Charlie had been got at and the old bogey about not being allowed to play league while at secondary school was raised. He wanted me to play first XV and nothing else. It was put to me that I should give league away and he even threatened expulsion.

So I went home and spoke to Dad about it. Next day he came along to school to see Charlie Gallagher while I stood outside the headmaster's office. There were some loud words spoken, then Dad strolled out of the room and just said, 'I'll see you when you get home son' as he went past. I was called in by Charlie Gallagher, who had an unusually red face and was still adjusting his tie. 'Frank,' he said, 'I think we can overlook it this time. You can play league in the mornings and rugby in the afternoons.' The Mudgee Mauler had obviously got his message across.

As it happened, though, the first XV rugby team was in such a good competition that I put most of my time and energy into it. One game against Cashmere High School was particularly brutal. They had this big kid in their backline and he and I took each other on. If we had the ball I would run straight at him and he would try to knock my head off. If they had the ball he would zero in at me and I would do my best to put his lights out. Late in the game he got the best hit in and I woke up about three or four minutes later. That was my first lesson about stiff arm tackling. I don't remember his name but funnily enough we both turned up for a Sydenham club trial at Waltham Park about two years later. I returned the compliment and haven't seen him since.

It wasn't solely a schools rugby grade. Although there was an age restriction of under-18, club teams were also included, full of young men hardened by a year or two in the work force. I was still eligible for the under-15 Schoolboy Kiwis so had to be tough to match them. I enjoyed it thoroughly because the whole school would turn up in support. We were the youngest of all the schools and there was great pressure to be competitive with the established sides such as Christchurch Boys' High. Our captain was Calvin Cochrane, a natural leader who went on to represent Canterbury and Nelson-Bays before breaking a leg and not going any further. Just to name drop a little, his sister, Raewyn, married rugby coach Graham Henry.

I left school soon after my sixteenth birthday. Schooling wasn't my thing. The shift to Australia meant that I had never settled into the examinations system. I couldn't study properly, not with my mind always on sport. So I left and joined the printing industry, where I stayed for almost 30 years.

I met my wife, Joan, on her nineteenth birthday when I was still 16. She was out with her boyfriend and they were going to a dance when we gave them a lift. But he hadn't eaten so we stopped the car at the pie cart for him to pick up some fish and chips. While he was away Joan and I had a bit of eye contact in the rear vision mirror. I winked, she winked back, and then she agreed we should go. Instead of being left at the altar he was left at the pie cart. But there were no lasting recriminations — we all stayed friends. And Joan and I are still together 37 years later.

After 18 months with one company, I went up to Auckland with Joan and joined Morrison Inks. They transferred me back to Christchurch and I stayed with them almost through to when I became a professional rugby league coach. In 1992 Ron Parry, the general manager of Sicpa Limited, headhunted me. Ron has been a good mate since then, teaching me a lot about management and business in general, philosophies that I was able to take into the sporting arena. I was with Sicpa for two years before starting with the Auckland Warriors.

Joan and I were married a month before my eighteenth birthday, when she was 20. The family wasn't too keen on me getting married so young but I had made up my mind and was going to do it right or wrong. In just a few years we were responsible for eight children, in tragic circumstances. Joan's mother died at 45 and her father died a couple of years later. Joan was the oldest of six children, down to very young kids. By then we had three little boys of our own. With Joan and I, and my brother, Ray, as a boarder, there were 11 of us. I was 20 and Joan 22. We raised her family and our own at the same time, helping them through school and into jobs and the rest of it.

I was working until nine o'clock four nights a week on overtime and again on Saturday mornings just to keep our heads above the bills. Young blokes mature very quickly in situations like that. It was a hell of a struggle but I was also determined to keep playing football. I would slip out to training on Tuesday and Thursday nights. Another bloke covered for me at work and I covered for him whenever he had somewhere to go. But I always made it up to the company by doing extra hours. On Saturdays I would work in the mornings, go home, get changed, and rush off to our games.

It was a squeeze at home. We had a three-bedroom house in Hei Hei, where we lived for about 15 years. The kids had to double up in their beds, there was a sleep-out at the back, and a caravan on the lawn. Joan was fantastic. She had been used to preparing big meals at home. Now the meals were just so much bigger. It was obviously very rough on her, losing both her parents at a young age. When we got married I had one shilling in the bank.

All of Joan's brothers and sisters have turned out to be fine people. They all have good jobs and I have always said that is a credit to Joan. We are proud of our boys, too, Wayne, Frank, Gary and Shane. Both Frank and Gary were seriously ill as babies, one wasn't expected to live, and the other not expected to walk, but you wouldn't know it now. I have saved Gary's story for last because he really deserves a chapter of his own.

It has been said that my family commitments affected what had been a promising rugby league career, but that is only partly true. I also had the worst hamstrings in the world. We never knew how to treat them properly in those days, knew nothing about stretching or icing. One time I pulled the hamstring right off the bone and was black from the back of my knee right up to my bum. I went along to Pat Long, who was known as the best physio in the business, and he rubbed hell out of them. The accepted treatment then was exactly what you wouldn't do now. Even today I can still feel those hammies. I only have to jog and I pull them.

My best years were probably those playing in the centres for the Addington club, when I was scoring a few tries and really revelling in it. Then I slowly gravitated into the pack. Jim White, our Kiwi lock forward, was injured one week and they put me in his place. From there it seemed a natural transition to second row before I finished up at prop. I even had a couple of unsuccessful stints at hooker. At least all the moving around gave me an insight to most positions for the coaching career that was to follow.

I played my first premier game in 1967 and went right through to about 1980 after transferring to Hornby. But it was always a hassle getting over those hamstring problems and not knowing what to do about them.

They tell me I still hold the Canterbury record for the quickest sin-binning, eight seconds into a game for Hornby against Eastern Suburbs at Avon Park. Eastern had a big copper, a skyscraper of about 6ft 6in. We kicked off to start the game and their fullback, Noel Turner, ran the ball up. Our defensive line was moving up for the first tackle, Noel was well covered, and I thought he was going to pass to this tall copper. So I left the ground and unleashed a mighty hit on him. But Noel hadn't given him the ball. He was taken off in a fairly groggy state and referee Don Wilson sin-binned me. It was pretty high all right so I wasn't going to argue when Don told me where to go.

That was the heyday for club football in Christchurch. Bill Noonan, who played for New Zealand in the late 1960s, had signed for Canterbury-Bankstown in Sydney but he was the exception. There could be six or seven former, current or future Kiwis in one club game. It was good, hard football, very competitive, and big crowds went to the big games. Instead of losing players Canterbury gained internationals like Wayne Robertson, Bob Jarvis, and Murray Wright, who came down from Auckland to link up with Hornby, and Mocky Brereton, Michael O'Donnell, and Leo Brown who moved over from the West Coast.

The individual star was Rodney Walker. He was ahead of his time. They say Wally Lewis was the first to bring in the long cut-out pass but Rodney Walker was doing it years before Lewis. Rodney could miss out four or five guys and hit his mark like a champion dart player. He didn't play much for New Zealand, which was a shame, but he was a local legend and made representative players out of many of his Papanui team-mates. One day my instructions were to 'get Walker, no matter what' but I ran myself to a standstill and never got near him. He was too clever.

Then there was Angus Thompson, who played for University. Angus didn't have any degrees. In fact he was a deer culler, but the Varsity boys needed someone to stiffen their forward pack. Jeez, Angus stiffened a few opposing forwards too. In one game we went through three props trying to restrain him in the scrums. Tony Ratu, who was a really big unit, went down first, I think Russ Cotter was next, and I know damn well I was the third.

There were plenty of Kiwis around. As well as the imports they included home grown stars Eddie Kerrigan, Bruce Dickison, Graeme Cooksley, Alan Rushton, Mark Broadhurst, Barry Edkins, Jim Fisher, Angus Thompson, David Field, Lewis Hudson, Mita Mohi, Gerard Stokes, Rod Walker, and a whole host of top-line Canterbury and South Island representatives.

I played in Addington and Hornby sides that made the semi-finals but never appeared in a grand final. On two occasions they picked me to play for Canterbury against Auckland but the hamstrings put paid to that. It was frustrating, so much so I gave away any grand ambitions as a player and settled for enjoying my club career.

Chapter 2.
Coach by accident

Frank Endacott's coaching career took him to such grand venues as Stadium Australia, Old Trafford and Wembley Stadium. But it had its modest beginnings in a little wooden hut perched on a corner of a frosty, barren Jerrold Street Reserve in Addington. The dilapidated hut was never going to be one of Christchurch's protected heritage buildings and has since been replaced by a bland concrete block structure. The wooden hut, though, was a home away from home to generations of Addington club players who trained and sometimes played at Jerrold Street.

We turned up for training one night in 1972 to learn our coach, Arnie Turnbull, had taken off to Wellington on business and was not to be seen again that season. It's a rather weird feeling, sitting around the changing shed waiting for someone to give the traditional coach's call about getting out onto the field and warming up with a few laps. And not knowing who would do it. Instead, we were telling each other that we had to get through the rest of the season, so someone had to take over from Arnie. It should be mentioned here that Arnie was a real Addington stalwart who had not totally deserted the Magpies. He returned to do a lot of work for the club and when we held a reunion a few years ago he was chief organiser as always.

But the immediate need was to find a stand-in coach and get moving before we all froze to death in our little igloo. The players voted and, even though I was about the youngest there, I was given the job as player-coach. I still don't know why they chose me, but I thoroughly enjoyed the experience. There was something about coaching that clicked with me. Something similar happened in 1974. Bill Stevens, who had come down from Auckland, was coaching us at the time but was abruptly sacked by the club's board. Bill had some very good ideas about rugby league and professionalism, very advanced ideas, and he was a real tough coach.

I admired him because in my opinion he knew his stuff, but his methods were new to us and something the majority of the players couldn't accept. There was friction between Bill and the senior players, the committee reasoned they could better afford to lose one coach than the nucleus of their team, and suddenly Bill was gone. Some club officials came down to training, another vote was taken, and I had my second part-season as player-coach.

There was no Hollywood climax to either of those stories. The Addington Magpies did not soar high on grand final day or anything like that. Expectations were modest, at best. The club had not held the Canterbury championship since 1944, and was situated in an inner-city suburb where there was an increasingly smaller supply of emerging rugby league players. But we knuckled down to be as competitive as possible in what was an excellent club competition. There were no easy games, even for the top teams, because of the style of football. Even the games you won by a reasonable margin were tough because players could get away with a lot more in those days than they do now. It was always physical and sometimes brutal. There were no video replays to review any incidents. What happened on the field usually stayed on the field. I'm pleased the game has moved away from that, and don't know of any modern coaches who preach ill-discipline.

In the circumstances I inevitably learned a hell of a lot in a very short time. There was no one there teaching me; I just picked things up as I went. I have always believed coaching is about making a good environment for players to bring out the best in them. I did that as best I could. We had a good time playing our rugby league. There were no big contracts to worry about. Any pressure on us to win for ourselves and our supporters didn't amount to life or death.

That was my last senior coaching until I returned to Addington as premier coach in 1982 after finishing my playing career with Hornby a couple of years earlier. By then I was also coaching youngest son Shane's Hornby junior team, so weekends were pretty full on with football commitments.

With Joan as my team manager, I coached those Hornby schoolboys from the ages of 10 to 17 and derived extreme satisfaction from seeing them develop as footballers and young men. By the time they were 14 their ball drills were better than those of most premier sides. All that culminated with a run of 45 consecutive wins and the selection of seven players, including Shane as captain, in the New Zealand 17-years Kiwi team. Because of other coaching responsibilities I then passed them on to Owen Thomas, and their successes continued for another two seasons until the players cleared age-grade football.

Those young guys were like an extended family to Joan and me. Saturday mornings had a family feel about them and we are proud they have turned out so well in their individual lives. Those guys are all about 30 now, and we still get together whenever possible.

Addington had been well beaten by Eastern Suburbs in the 1981 grand final and captain-coach Grant Findlay was one of seven regular players who either retired or transferred. Most people predicted a rebuilding year for us, but we gained useful recruits in forwards John Tapiata, who returned from Sydenham, Lawrence Hale and Mike Smith. Centre Grant Stocker came back from Dunedin, where he had played rugby for Otago B. After a few early losses we strung together six wins before I made the news in a manner I had never imagined. *The Press* newspaper trumpeted the headline 'Addington Team Walks from Field on Coach's Call' and there would have been plenty of people prepared to bet my coaching career was destined to be very brief.

We had been playing well through our winning streak. I was emphasising to the players the need for discipline, to control their tempers, and we were all confident of going all the way to the grand final. But for some reason I could never put my finger on, everything was going wrong against Linwood. After 76 minutes we were trailing 8–15. Deservedly so too, and it was not because we were getting beaten that I took the action which got me in hot water. Our players were getting frustrated to the point they were losing their cool. Rod Mackenzie, an old front-row rival of mine, was refereeing, the penalty count had soared to 22–2 against us, and threatened to keep rising. I could see penalties being given out that just weren't on. Standing on the hill, I made the mistake of yelling out to Mackenzie when he was near the sideline, asking him why his other arm wasn't working. He turned around and just smiled at me, set the scrum, and immediately gave Linwood another penalty. I learned pretty quickly that coaches should be seen and not heard as far as referees were concerned.

With a few minutes to go I simply couldn't take it any more. I called John Tapiata, our captain, over and said, 'Mate, walk them off, I've had a gutsful of this.' The players were near boiling point and I considered that another two or three tackles might have been all that was needed for the game to erupt into an all-in brawl.

It was not sour grapes that we were being beaten. A senior third grade side would have beaten us on that penalty count. Rod Mackenzie and I had played against each other dozens of times and Rod was something of a poacher turned gamekeeper. I doubt whether anyone in the history of Canterbury rugby league had fronted the judiciary more often. He was a good footballer but could be baited and would lose it completely. Rod became a well-respected referee, and what he did that day was right out of character. I remember saying at the time that Rod's performance in a game we lost to Eastern Suburbs by the unlikely scoreline of 1–5 (a field goal against a converted try) was one of the best I had seen for years. But that day against Linwood Rod gave the worst refereeing display I had seen in 16 seasons of premier football so I did what I did even though it made me squirm about my future in coaching.

Straight after the game I told Rod what I thought of him, his whistle, and his ancestry but when we see each other now we laugh about it. I don't know whether he was being vindictive or not but something was going on and Rod has never told me what it was. I got suspended by the Canterbury Rugby League, of course, banned from the Show Grounds, and ordered not to take part in any training sessions for the month leading up to the championship play-offs.

We had one training run before the league's letter arrived officially informing the club of my suspension. *The Press* sent a photographer along and the picture they printed next morning would not have pleased the Canterbury officials. What happened after that had all the makings of a spy thriller, and has gone unpublished until now.

For the next training I put on a big coat and hat and went down to the park. There was a board member's car sitting on Jerrold Street, a fair way across the ground from where the changing shed and training lights were situated. But close enough to spot me if I went on the field with the players.

So I used the shadows to perch up a tree behind the lights where it would be just about impossible for anyone to see me. It just so happened that every now and again, between training plays, the team would jog around and pause under the tree so I could throw a few instructions down to John Tapiata. That car returned for most of our trainings during the month I was supposed to be in limbo. I kept my position up the tree, and John relayed my messages to the players.

John Tapiata worked in the railways and was a resourceful sort of bloke who could play hooker, prop and second row, and even kick a few goals. A year or two later he stunned everyone by switching to rugby union. That was until someone discovered a New Zealand Railways rugby team was being chosen to tour Australia, and league players were not eligible. John got his tour, then suddenly realised league was his true sporting love after all and returned to Addington.

Despite all the drama we shared the minor premiership with Hornby, and then beat Hornby in the major semi-final to give the club another chance at winning a first championship for 38 years.

We did just that. The scores were tied at 5–5 for 40 minutes, we made a winning break at 11–5, then clung to the eventual 11–10 lead for the last 11 minutes as Hornby missed a field goal attempt. That was a very special win for such a new-look side. The clubrooms were rocking that night and kept on rocking for more than 24 hours. I think they took more income over the bar than in the previous two years. It really had been a long time between drinks.

That Hornby side was strong enough for Kiwi test hooker Alan Rushton to be named in the reserves. Barry Edkins had also played for New Zealand, and Robin Alfeld, Ross Taylor, and Wayne Wallace were on their way there. They were coached by Brian Langton, himself a Kiwi centre and wing in the 1960s.

We didn't have any big names but that Addington team had a big all-round heart. That made the victory all the sweeter, watching them grow up against five current or future Kiwis. Hornby gained their revenge the next season, though, when they knocked us out in the semi-finals, and subsequently went on to win the 1983 and 1984 grand finals under a smart coach in Kevin Woodham.

I had a season with Canterbury B before taking over the Hornby team when Kevin stepped down. It was a logical move for me, having played for Hornby, having lived in the district for years, and was coaching Shane's schoolboys side. I also saw it as a stepping stone for my career. Anyway, my old mate John Tapiata was Addington's coach by then, no doubt putting into practice everything he had learned on that railways rugby tour. Returning to club coaching meant resigning as a Canterbury selector but that could wait.

In all three of my years at Hornby, from 1985 to 1987, we clashed with neighbouring Halswell in a series of grand finals that must have been as intense as any inter-club rivalry in New Zealand sport. This was still the era when top sportsmen turned out for their clubs, and where pride and performance meant much more than payment.

Halswell was a much younger club than Hornby and was reaping the benefits of a vast pool of schoolboy players in a fast-growing new housing area. It's more than fair to say that league was more popular than rugby in both suburbs. The on-field action was hot enough but there were some horrifying stories about the off-field rivalry among the more passionate fans. League in Canterbury had adopted the Australian grand final system well before other sports and plenty of rugby and other folk rolled along to the Show Grounds for the showdown every September.

After my relatively raw Addington outfit, I suddenly had a team stacked with quality players. But you can never take anything for granted, and Halswell was still smoldering with ambition after having lost to Hornby in the previous year's grand final. They say you have to lose one before you can win one, and Halswell was hell bent on proving that.

Phil Bancroft, the little stand-off half who went on to tour with the Kiwis, proved to be our nemesis, winning both the 1985 and 1987 grand finals with late field goals. In between, we romped away with the 1986 title.

In '85 we were locked at 16–16 in front of more than 6000 spectators when Bancroft got the ball wide out near the halfway line. He whacked it with all of his strength and timed it to perfection. The ball went straight at first, then wobbled as it got closer to the posts. Our fullback, Robin Alfeld, swears he heard the ball scrape the back of the crossbar as it dropped over.

I had no animosity after that game. I knew we had competed well. Hornby levelled up late in the second half when Barry Edkins kicked a goal and then Wayne Wallace had a try disallowed because of a double movement. Even though we lost, that was one of the great grand finals in an era when club rugby league was really on a high.

Alfeld retired after the game and our three Kiwi forwards, Ross Taylor, Wayne Wallace, and Adrian Shelford, were going on tour to Britain and France so I didn't want to risk them getting hurt in the annual Thacker Shield challenge from West Coast champion Runanga.

We had to bring in seven new guys and one of them, a young centre named Todd Metcalf, got us home with four tries. But much of the attention was directed at Brendon Tuuta, even though he was only on the field for a few minutes. When we signed Brendon for Hornby I told him if I was selecting a boxing team he would always be first in. But he must improve his discipline on the league field. Everything was going okay until the Thursday training before the Thacker Shield when I went around the players individually, came to Brendon, and told him he had to 'harass' Runanga's Kiwi scrum-half Glen Gibb. Gibby was their playmaker, everything revolved around him, and it was vital he not be allowed to dictate play if we were to become South Island champions. Brendon looked up and said he understood what I meant. Just before the kick-off on match day I asked Brendon if he remembered his job and he replied, 'Yes, harass Glen Gibb.'

The players went down the tunnel, Runanga scored almost immediately, and I was hardly in my seat up in the stand when referee Don Wilson's whistle had that note of urgency which makes coaches cringe. A scrum had broken up, Glen Gibb was lying prone on the ground, and Brendon Tuuta was trudging off for an early shower, moodily unwinding the arm bandage he always wore.

At halftime I went down to the dressing room, saw Brendon still sitting there, and began to give him a bollocking. 'Brendon, what happened out there? We're down to 12 men and that makes it bloody tough on the others,' I said. He looked up in all innocence and said he had done what I told him, to harass Glen Gibb. Suddenly it began to dawn on me. 'You harassed him,' I said. 'Do you know what harass means?' Brendon was all earnestness in replying, 'Yeah, it means eliminate.' Maybe they have different dictionaries in the Chatham Islands.

A few years later Brendon did some 'harassing' of the Kangaroos in a test match at Christchurch's Queen Elizabeth II Park and the Aussie media dubbed him the 'Baby-faced Assassin', a label which haunted him throughout a fine career in Australia and Britain as well as for the Kiwis. Brendon was the toughest player, pound for pound, that I ever coached, fit to be ranked along with guys like Quentin Pongia and Jarrod McCracken. Clever too. I remember a mid-winter trip to Hastings to play Waipukurau in a national knock-out competition. We had just returned to our hotel wearing our best gear, blazers and all, when Brendon Tuuta and Ross Taylor decided I was going in the pool as part of team bonding. I asked them to back off while I stripped off, so my clothes wouldn't get soaked before the trip home next day. I carefully put my gear on the ground and jumped in to keep them happy. Then, as I'm swimming back to the side of the pool, I looked up to see my clothes going into the water over the top of my head . . .

We did the double in 1986, beating Halswell 20–5 in the Canterbury grand final and Runanga again for the Thacker Shield. Graham Larson's three grand final tries are still a record for a forward and the win meant Hornby went ahead of Sydenham as the club with most Canterbury championships.

Larson was awesome that day. He dedicated the match to his father, who had been killed in a car smash, and played the game of his life. But he did make one mistake. After scoring his third try he jogged past Phil Bancroft, saying, 'Drop kick your way out of this one, you little bastard.'

Twelve months later Bancroft's field goal regained the Pat Smith Trophy for Halswell after we were locked at 14–14 with time running out. It was an easier kick than in '85, and Banky had already done enough damage by scoring one try, setting up another, and kicking three goals after we led 8–2 at halftime.

Unfortunately, we lost Brendon Tuuta to Halswell that year. He had spent several months back in the Chathams and was wavering between staying with Hornby or going to Marist-Western Suburbs. Our committee stuffed around for so long that Halswell nipped in with a late offer and grabbed him. That was enough to swing the balance of power between our clubs.

By then Hornby had lost Wayne Wallace to Marist-Western and Adrian Shelford to Wellington. But they were reunited with Ross Taylor in '87 to be the front-rowers in that mighty win by Tank Gordon's Kiwis over Australia at Brisbane. All three had learned their league as kids in Hornby and it was a great achievement for them and the club that they shared in such a famous victory on enemy soil.

I had lifted my own coaching sights in '86 when by chance I heard Bob Bailey was giving the Junior Kiwis a training run at Witham Park in Hornby before their match with Papua New Guinea. After watching the full two-hour session I went home and told Joan I wanted to coach the Junior Kiwis one day. I wasn't interested in the Kiwis, just the juniors. It took me six years to get there.

During the summer of '87 I received three appointments from the New Zealand Rugby League, as a selector for the Junior Kiwis and under-17s, and as coach of a Southern Provinces team selected from Otago, Southland, West Coast, and Canterbury B to play Canterbury A. Those guys from the minor leagues trained out of their skins for that game. It was their test match. Canterbury usually thrashed Otago and Southland by 80 points each, but that combined side got up to draw. You would have thought they had won the World Cup.

One of our forwards was Stuart Simcott, from the Canterbury B team. While we were in camp he was given permission to attend his Papanui club's prize giving provided he was back by 10pm. While he was away his roommate, Troy Forsyth from the Coast, and some of the others messed up his bed and left a condom filled with condensed milk.

We were having a quiet beer when Stu walked in, red faced, holding this condom, and screaming, 'Who does this belong to?' He was really angry, and wanted to get to grips with whoever had been in his bed. Forsyth piped up, 'Don't say too much. It was the coach.' Poor Stu looked at me incredulously and spluttered, 'Frank, is this yours? And in my bed?'

I took the condom from him, dipped a finger into the condensed milk, sucked it, and casually said, 'No, it's not mine Stu.'

He turned around, ran back to his room, and spewed in the toilet. Poor bugger, he had been red when he came in and he was white when he went out. I had to follow him and tell him it was all a joke.

There was another bonus in late '88 when NZRL chairman George Rainey rang to tell me I had the job coaching the President's XIII in two warm-up matches for the Kiwis before they played Australia in the World Cup final at Eden Park.

Club football, and the experience of selecting and coaching representative and combined teams, further convinced me that coaching was to be a major part of my life. In five club seasons my teams had reached four grand finals, won two, and lost the other two to Phil Bancroft's match-winning field goals. Confident there would be no lingering grudges about Addington's infamous walk-off in my debut season, and knowing that incumbent Ray Haffenden was retiring, I applied for the Canterbury A job for 1989.

Checking out Christchurch's
Cathedral Square, circa 1952.

At home with the Endacotts (from left) Dad, Julie, me, Ray, and Mum.

I'm standing at far left, middle row, in this Shirley Boys' High School first XV photo. The coach is John Mullins and Calvin Cochrane is captain.

Suspended coach: Sorting out the Addington scrum with halfback Billy Parker before the club was officially informed of my 1982 suspension.

News Media, Auckland

Ross Taylor, tough as teak.

News Media, Auckland

Brendon Tuuta, baby-faced assassin.

News Media, Auckland

Wayne Wallace, happy hooker.

News Media, Auckland

Phil Bancroft, field goal specialist.

Chapter 3.
Changing the old order

Auckland had dominated provincial rugby league for decades, challenged only by powerful West Coast teams during and soon after the Second World War. When Frank Endacott became coach in 1989 Canterbury was ranked a distant third behind Auckland and Wellington. Canterbury's only wins over Auckland had been recorded at home in 1925 and 1962 and at Carlaw Park in 1975. During Endacott's five-year term Auckland were beaten four times and held to a draw, all at the Addington Show Grounds. The winning sequence started in front of a few hundred dedicated fans in 1990 and culminated with a 1993 triumph over an Auckland side stacked with British-based professionals in front of 10,000 delirious Cantabrians.

My Canterbury debut was far from distinguished, and it was no consolation that plenty of other good coaches had lost first-up against West Coast at Greymouth's Wingham Park. For me, it was the longest bus trip home I ever made across the Southern Alps.

I can still recall certain Canterbury Rugby League board of control members having a quiet discussion in one corner of the after-match function in a

Greymouth pub. It was going through my mind that this could be a very short representative coaching career.

Maybe they took into account that we had fallen to a very good West Coast side. We probably had the youngest Canterbury side of all time. In fact, our most experienced player, winger Lance Setu, owed his selection to something out of a Boys' Own Annual. Two of our backs, Andrew Vincent and Vince McCue, failed fitness tests on the morning before the game. By coincidence, Lance was coaching an Addington schoolboys team on the other playing field at Spreydon Domain so I didn't have to look too far for a replacement.

That first year, 1989, was always going to be one of rebuilding. The Coasters had tough nuts like Boyd Kilkelly and Bernie Green in the centres and forwards with the hardness of Brent Stuart and the Forsyth brothers. Whetu Taewa was 18 and playing his first game for Canterbury against his old province — he was hardly on the field when someone yelled 'traitor' at him from the grandstand — and Justin Wallace, Brett Rodger and Carl Hall were all 19.

The New Zealand Rugby League had not been much help in sending Brendon Tuuta, Mark Nixon, and Esene Faimalo to Sydney under the 'rookie' scheme of attaching promising players to professional clubs. Kiwi prop Ross Taylor was forced into retirement by a knee injury and Wayne Wallace copped a suspension, which kept him out through most of the representative season.

It was widely mentioned at the time that Coasters just loved knocking over first division teams on their home patch. Auckland had lost their last three games at Wingham Park before finding the perfect solution of how to stop that sequence — they turned down every invitation sent to them after that! Canterbury actually appreciated having such a strong measuring stick as West Coast only a few hours away.

It's a real shame that the economic situation has led to the decline of rugby league, and other sports, on the West Coast in recent years. The Coast's most valuable export has always been its youth. Unfortunately, many promising footballers now go to Australia and get lost in the crush of hopefuls trying to break into the big league.

I was fortunate that Whetu Taewa, Quentin Pongia and Brent Stuart chose Christchurch as the next stepping stone towards their professional careers. Whetu was both a child prodigy and a survivor, playing for West Coast at 17 in 1988 and still scoring tries for Hull Kingston Rovers in England 14 years later; Quentin was an automatic choice in all my Canterbury and Kiwi teams; and Stewie was the no-nonsense sort of prop you could always rely upon.

Fortunately for my peace of mind, we regrouped after that initial setback to put 50 points on Bay of Plenty in our opening national championship match. But there were the two customary hefty losses to Auckland, and Wellington still had the better of us at home and away. We were third again, but the signs were promising. Fifteen players had made their debuts and foundations were being laid. In 1988, at Massey University, I had watched the national 19-years final between Auckland and Canterbury. It was one of the best games I had seen. Quentin Pongia and Jason Lowrie engaged in a titanic front-row battle, and the young Canterbury players showed enough for me to know we would soon have a senior team to be feared.

Those youngsters became the nucleus of the sides that beat Auckland in 1990 and 1991, drew in 1992, and creamed them by 40–12 and 36–12 in 1993. By then the Aucks weren't too keen to pick up their Air New Zealand tickets. As soon as they landed in Christchurch the baggage handlers and other airport workers were not slow to remind them of their ever-worsening record at the Show Grounds.

But the build-up to that first game in 1990 didn't go to plan, not by any means. Canterbury suffered a record 2–42 hiding from Wellington in a pathetic display at the Hutt Recreation Ground. We had only five days to put that behind us and prepare for Auckland. Some strong words were spoken at training about not wanting our own supporters knocking us, and I made several team adjustments that would have me looking like a hero, or a zero. Fortunately, they worked, and our 25–22 win must have been the greatest turnaround in provincial rugby league history.

Logan Edwards scored the clinching try down the left-hand flank from one of our short-side plays, slicing between Tony Tuimavave and winger Warren Mann. Logan cut Auckland to ribbons that day as well as making 30 tackles. It was his first game back at lock forward after completing a club season in England.

Another who had a mighty game was former Kiwi hooker Wayne Wallace. Waldo was getting near the end of his career and was thrilled to have finally beaten Auckland. Our props, Ron Simanu and Ricky Cowan, were great too.

There was still plenty to be done, though. Wellington and Auckland both beat us in the return games, but we at least had the satisfaction of scoring 66 points against the same West Coast side that had beaten us in Greymouth the previous year. Unfortunately, we lost the Rugby League Cup to Wellington after Auckland had sportingly brought it south with them.

But the young guys were developing a big-match mentality, as they showed when they downed Great Britain 18–10. The Brits were actually flattered to finish so close because their second try came after the fulltime hooter.

The result had the statisticians busy too. Canterbury's only previous win over a touring side had been against France in 1955, so there was good cause for us to party for several days. Gary Leck, a workaholic second-rower, was outstanding. Aaron Whittaker had been one of the new boys on the bench against Auckland and against the Lions he scored one try and very nearly laid on another.

We had the measure of Auckland and Wellington in Christchurch in '91 but a two-point loss at Wellington cost us a share of the championship which was again won outright by Auckland. Wayne Wallace had retired after more than 50 appearances for Canterbury and I switched a young back-rower, Mike Culley, to hooker. He wasn't too happy when he first heard the news but adjusted well, was a crack goalkicker and should have gone on the 1993 Kiwis tour to Britain and France.

That was a pretty good pack we fielded in the 33–24 win over Auckland. Logan Edwards was the new captain and he, Quentin Pongia, Simon Angell, Esene Faimalo and Brent Stuart were all to become Kiwis, while Mike Culley should have been. Aaron Whittaker and Mark Nixon formed a slick combination in the halves, and the other backs were Whetu Taewa, Brett Rodger, Andrew Vincent, Mike Dorreen and Carl Hall. Only Culley didn't go on to play for Australian or British clubs.

There were 12 Kiwis in the Auckland team, including Phil Bancroft, who had moved up there and was booed every time he touched the ball on his homecoming — even by the Halswell supporters he had won two grand finals for. Faimalo was a real powerhouse that day, and Edwards, Whittaker and Nixon dominated around the scrum-base. Tawera Nikau stood out for Auckland but he couldn't do everything. That was Owen Wright's first look at the Show Grounds as Auckland coach, having taken over from Graham Mattson. It was nice of Auckland's officials to tempt fate a second time by bringing the Rugby League Cup with them.

People in high places were beginning to notice something positive was happening in Christchurch. The Kiwi Colts side I coached to beat France by 20 points at Rotorua had an almost all-Canterbury backline with Mark Nixon as captain. The French never recovered from that, got belted in the tests, and also by Howie Tamati's President's XIII which boasted most of the Canterbury forwards and a few backs for good measure.

At the end of '91 Auckland and Canterbury took part in a $100,000 quadrangular tournament against Aussie sides North Sydney and Western Suburbs. That old Carlaw Park hoodoo struck again as we lost to Auckland by one point but we were mighty proud of our 18-all draw with Wests. To us that was as good as a win, and even better for some of our players.

The weekend clashed with the Lion Red Cup club quarter-finals and our big contingent of Halswell and Hornby players returned to Christchurch after the Auckland game. We fielded an incredible eight new guys against Wests. Damien Mackie, Tane Sutton, Jason Duff and Kenny O'Brien were in the starting 13, and Maea David, Dennis Taylor, Jason Diggs and Greg Muir came off the bench. For some it was their only representative match. For Greg Muir, who was from second division club Kaiapoi, it was his debut in senior football.

Coaching had its glamorous side in '90 and '91, when I was also in charge of the Canterbury women's open touch team. They should have been models, not football players. Most of them were wives, girlfriends or sisters of the players I was coaching at the time, such as Lance Setu's sisters Mary, Maureen and Serena, and Mike Culley's wife, Ricky. Margaret Bray (now Foster), the New Zealand netballer and Canterbury Flames coach, was also there.

We went to two national tournaments, and I don't think I ever coached a more enthusiastic group. They were very gifted, with skills and speed, and fit enough to demand more work even after a two-hour training session.

I mentioned they should have been models. A certain bus driver thought so too. The girls wore bright pink uniforms and were doing their stretches against the trees one day when the New Brighton bus trundled along the road. The poor old driver was so distracted he steered it straight into a power pole.

I tossed my hat into the ring for the Kiwis coaching job but missed out to Howie Tamati. It was disappointing but I felt I had some unfinished business. I wanted to help develop as many of the young Canterbury blokes for the 1993 tour to Britain and France. With Howie moving into the top job, he left a vacancy with the Junior Kiwis that I was very happy to fill.

Canterbury suffered some serious blows before the '92 season. Logan Edwards broke an arm in his last game for English club Oldham and again in his first club game in Christchurch. Esene Faimalo was now fulltime at Widnes, Carl Hall stayed in Doncaster, and Aaron Whittaker went off to play for Illawarra. Consistent centre Brett Rodger was my first choice to succeed Logan as captain but when he also got injured that honour went to Mark Nixon. Phil Bergman replaced Aaron and became one of the great characters of the team, and from a personal viewpoint I was both a contented coach and proud father when my son, Shane, scored three tries on debut against Bay of Plenty.

When Wellington took away the Rugby League Cup most pundits expected Auckland to be too strong for us as well. Yet despite their inexperience guys like Maea David, Albert Atkinson, Phil Bergman and Shane Endacott fronted up in a dour game that was 4-all at halftime and 8-all at fulltime. I was happier than Owen Wright with the result. We went on to regain the Cup from Wellington after trailing 2–18 at the Basin Reserve, kept our second ranking, and gave the

'92 Lions tourists a good workout. But we knew we had the talent to be top province and were determined to do that in 1993.

I made it clear when the Canterbury board reappointed me that it was to be my last season. Five years is enough for any coach at provincial level, and this was just about the biggest possible season imaginable with both the Kiwis and Junior Kiwis to tour Britain and France. Our biggest loss was Quentin Pongia, who had gone to Canberra, while another tough prop, Moko Rangiaho, retired. But Aaron Whittaker and Marty Crequer arrived home from Australia and Logan Edwards and Brett Rodger were fit again. It looked promising.

We won every game except the one at — you guessed it — Carlaw Park, where we dipped out 6–9 in the wet. But the NZRL had introduced a first division final and there was no doubt where it had to be played after our 40–12 home win over Auckland. The crowds had steadily risen to about 5000 for that match and the fans went crazy as winger Mike Dorreen kept about two metres ahead of Richie Barnett in a 70-metre foot race for one of his tries. It was Auckland's heaviest loss to another province.

Mark Nixon had been retained as captain despite Logan Edwards' return. That was probably a good thing because I had reason to drop Logan to the bench for the next game against Bay of Plenty. Logan turned up for a Saturday morning training run late and smelling of beer. When I told Logan he was going to be fined and dropped he was contrite, but I still ordered him to explain his actions to the whole team. Logan sat down on a big ice container in the dressing room, told the players how sorry he was, and that it wouldn't happen again. He explained he was late because he'd managed only a few hours' sleep 'after night-clubbing with one of the coach's sons'. Logan was a good mate of my son Frank. When he said that, I was the one looking for somewhere to hide.

A week before the final, word leaked out that Auckland coach Owen Wright was beefing up his team with professionals returning from England. He named Tawera Nikau as captain, plus Iva Ropati, Dean Clark, Tea Ropati, Se'e Solomona, Duane Mann and Craig Innes, the former All Black who was then with Leeds. Apart from Innes, they were all Kiwis. Auckland also had Mark Elia and Vila Matautia starting, and Hitro Okesene and Joe Vagana on the bench. Only Matautia didn't play for New Zealand but he later spent many seasons with St Helens.

The Canterbury Rugby League hardly needed to promote that game to the public. Owen Wright did it for them. Our only 'outsider' was Brendon Tuuta, who was home from Featherstone Rovers, but we reckoned he was all we needed. We lost Phil Bergman with a hamstring problem and Blair Harding was given his first start in a Canterbury jersey. Along with the jersey went the job of marking Innes.

Asked to comment on the Auckland selection, I said I wasn't sure whether we were playing Auckland, Great Britain or New Zealand. But it was still a case of 13 blokes in blue and white up against 13 from Canterbury.

Our players had plenty to prove as individuals. Solomona had displaced Brent Stuart in the Kiwi front row and Tuuta wasn't happy about being Nikau's understudy in the Kiwis. Stewie told me he couldn't wait to get to grips with big Solomona, and no one could print what Brendon said he was going to do to Nikau.

We were playing the final on a Sunday and the Saturday morning training was the best I ever experienced, anywhere, with any team. It was so good I had to pull the reins in halfway through. When I got home I told Joan, 'We'll beat Auckland tomorrow, and we'll beat them good.'

The whole of Canterbury got behind the game. This time the Air New Zealand hostesses were even telling the Aucklanders what they were in for, and I believe the pilot made an announcement over the intercom. When they got to the Show Grounds they found 10,000 one-eyed Cantabrians baying for their blood. This was my last game at a venue some Aucklanders were calling the Killing Fields. Since 1990 we had lost only three and drawn one of 17 home matches against all comers. We weren't going to drop this one against what everyone regarded as a bunch of mercenaries.

Most of the Canterbury representative rugby players and their management were there, and a lot of Lancaster Park regulars followed them to unfamiliar territory. I heard of one fellow who arrived at the turnstiles with a red and black pompom on his hat, a red and black flag, red and black eye patch, red and black jacket, red shirt, black pants, red socks and black shoes. 'How much to get in today?' he asked the gatekeeper. When he was told $10 he said, 'Well here's five, I'm only here to see one team.'

The crowd helped, but our players were on fire. We scored seven tries to two in that 36–12 win. Logan Edwards set up two tries in the opening five minutes, one to Marty Crequer and the other to Mike Dorreen. Then Brendon Tuuta ran over some defenders and Simon Angell scored. It was 16–0 at halftime and only got better. New boy Blair Harding not only looked after Innes but grabbed the last two tries and almost had a third. It was a dream finish for me, and Canterbury deservedly had a record eight resident players included in the Kiwi touring team.

Of all the players I coached, Logan Edwards was the most naturally talented. He just lacked the physical size and the absolute, total commitment needed to make it at the Warriors. Logan had commitment all right, but to become a great player more than that was needed. His skills and intuition could turn a game with one flash of brilliance, then ram home that advantage. Socially, he was a freak. Logan could go out all night yet still blitz everyone at training next morning. He played rugby league as a sport and not as a business. Logan once had a share in a horse called Pistol Knight (say it slowly) but was the world's worst punter. I remember him putting $20 to win on No. 13, his jersey number, in a pub one night and watching it run dead last. Two minutes later he spotted horses lining up again, rushed to the bookie and put another $20 to win on No. 13. Then we told him it was the replay of the previous race.

Logan was a legend in Christchurch in the 1990s. One wet day at the Show Grounds some Canterbury officials stayed too long in the boardroom after nipping in for a quick drink at halftime. They belatedly realised they had to pick the Player of the Match in a club game which was just finishing. They quickly consulted a programme, spotted Logan's name, decided he was the best player in either side, and one of them raced out to tell the ground announcer to give him the award. Unfortunately for them, Logan hadn't played that day.

Logan and Mark Nixon were great mates, and surprisingly still are despite one little incident when they were roommates in Auckland. Logan knew Mark had put a bottle of Lemon and Paeroa in the fridge for the next morning. While Logan pretended to be asleep, Mark got up, took the cap off, and had a big swig. Next moment the poor bugger is spitting it out in the sink and gasping, 'What the hell's that? It's not L and P!' Then a voice filtered through from the bedroom, 'Oh yes it is — it's Logan's Piss.'

Mark Nixon was a really good footballer who inherited the captaincy because he could handle responsibility on the field. His forte was support running, and like Shaun Edwards at Wigan he always turned up on the right spot at the right time. Mark loved winning and wearing the Canterbury jersey and it's great to see dedicated players like him and Brent Stuart now involved in coaching.

While Canterbury put a lot of emphasis in finally wresting that first division championship away from Auckland, we never had anything but the utmost respect for Wellington. The game in the capital city was never stronger, with Wainuiomata and Randwick playing in four consecutive national club finals between them, and the Lomax brothers muscling Wainuiomata to two victories.

In 1988 Wellington beat Auckland for the first time in 75 years. Howie Tamati had been coaching them for three seasons, and he had plenty of powerful forwards and strong, fast backs at his disposal. Forwards John Lomax, Mike Kuiti, Robert Piva, Mark Woods, Emosi Koloto and hooker Barry Harvey all played for the Kiwis and Daroa Ben Moide for Papua New Guinea. Fullback Morvin Edwards was the backline star and David Ewe, Victor Aramoana, Jason Gilbert and Charlie McAlister were bigger than most forwards.

Wellington scored double wins against us in 1989 and 1990, but it was that record 40-point hiding which hurt the most. Harvey scored three tries that day and their already monstrous pack had been reinforced by Upper Hutt's signing of Esene Faimalo from Canterbury.

I must mention our 18–20 loss at Wellington in 1989, a scoreline which didn't look too good after we led 16–4. But the dressing room looked like a war zone at halftime. Prop Stuart Simcott had been outstanding but was lying on the floor with a head injury and fullback Carl Hall had done a hammie. Jason Williams was hobbling with a crook knee and Glen Moore was nursing a broken cheek bone. But Jason and Glen went back out there when they realised the only other option was to leave the team two men short. Glen had no memory of that second half even though he kicked a goal. We defended courageously but George Lajpold put over the winning penalty for Wellington just before the finish.

Our two provinces kept exchanging the Rugby League Cup for a while and it wasn't until 1993 that Canterbury could truly claim to have shaken Wellington off. That year we proved pace could beat power when we ran in plenty of tries in convincing wins at home and away.

Although Bay of Plenty seldom seriously threatened the big three, they were a welcome inclusion in what was a competitive and enjoyable provincial competition. Coach Tony (Tank) Gordon never had the resources or the player depth of his big city rivals but the district produced such fine footballers as Gary Mercer, Russell Stewart, Paul Nahu and Alex Chan. It was unfortunate they had to go overseas to prove their worth.

Throughout my term as Canterbury coach I had numerous reasons to be thankful for the support of Neville Diggs, the team manager. Neville was a former Canterbury and South Island front-rower, a conscientious worker who contributed so much to the team's success. Without someone like Neville the task would have been just that much tougher.

The face of rugby league in New Zealand changed dramatically after that 1993 showdown between Canterbury and Auckland, and it is almost impossible to imagine anyone being selected out of domestic football for future Kiwi teams. The best players are now scouted by the professional clubs at a younger age, and New Zealand has a much bigger pool of professional players to draw from.

Head coach John Monie and other Warriors staff were at the Show Grounds for that '93 final. Soon afterwards they signed Logan Edwards, Simon Angell and Whetu Taewa, and it's fair to say the result didn't hurt my chances of being invited to coach the Warriors' reserve grade team.

Chapter 4.
Winning at Wembley

In 1986 Hornby club coach Frank Endacott had watched Bob Bailey put a Junior Kiwis side which included Kevin Iro, Tawera Nikau, and Tony Kemp through its paces before playing Papua New Guinea's Junior Kumuls in Christchurch. Six years after vowing to one day coach New Zealand's best young players, Endacott found himself holding the Junior Kiwis clipboard, and facing the most formidable opponent of all.

When the Australian Schoolboys came to New Zealand in 1992 they brought with them an amazing heritage of success, and an enviable strike rate for producing full Kangaroos and first grade footballers. In the previous 20 years the Australian youth teams had won 57 of their 58 games during tours to Britain and New Zealand and in home internationals. The sole blemish was a loss to Auckland after the 1982 test series, but the Australians remained unbeaten against the Junior Kiwis and Young Lions.

We brought gifted stand-off half Gene Ngamu, a graduate of the New Zealand elite system, over from the Manly juniors and reckoned we had a fairly competitive side captained by Willie Poching. Our centre pairing of Tana Umaga and Ruben Wiki looked capable of casting doubts in the minds of even the most confident opponents. A raw-boned young guy named Joe Vagana partnered Poching in the second row, and it's interesting to reflect now that reserve back

Alex Chan, from Bay of Plenty, played prop for Parramatta in the 2001 NRL grand final. Several of the other guys went on to professional careers overseas. Poching, who is still playing in Britain, had captained Auckland to win the national 19-years tournament, and with Umaga was selected to train for two weeks with the Brisbane Broncos under a scholarship scheme. Auckland prop Brady Malam, who later played for me at Wigan, Umaga and Chan had already played senior representative football in the first division championship for their respective provinces.

Australia beat us 26–24 in the first test at Rotorua after leading 20–4 at halftime. The Junior Kiwis were clearly overawed. I gave them a good, old-fashioned halftime 'talk' and they came back to eventually outscore the Australians five tries to four. They showed enough in that 40 minutes to convince me, and themselves, we could win the second test at Carlaw Park and finally put a dent in that Australian boast about being unbeaten.

It wasn't going to be easy though. Nathan Barnes had already played fullback for Penrith in the Winfield Cup and most of the other visiting players were under contract to professional clubs. Barnes was used in the centres against us, with Robbie Ross at fullback. Steve Menzies was then a winger who has since gone on to become the most prolific try-scoring forward in Australian first grade football. Mark Mom, the scrum-half, represented Papua New Guinea at senior level, the hooker was none other than Robbie Mears of Warriors fame, and Matt Sears, John Driscoll, Syd Domic and Nick Graham all made their names in the big league. Captain Garen Casey found his niche in the English Super League.

They had some great emerging players but the Junior Kiwis took them to the cleaners by 36–14 at Carlaw Park. Gene Ngamu scored two of our seven tries and there was only one team in it after we led 12–8 at halftime.

Australian manager Bob Cochrane said afterwards his squad was up to the high standard set by its predecessors but this Junior Kiwis team lifted itself above anything else they had encountered. Cochrane recommended the Auckland Warriors sign up the whole lot on the spot. From my viewpoint, I felt we had not only bettered the Australians in skills but also had them for pace.

I have no doubt that Tana Umaga would have made it in rugby league, as he has in rugby union. He was immensely talented as a lad. A quiet bloke, he would walk around with his head down all the time. In fact, at the last training session before the second test I ripped him up because I didn't think he was showing enough enthusiasm. He hadn't told me, but it transpired he was full of the flu.

Tana would have played for the Kiwis if he hadn't changed codes. His combination with Ruben Wiki was devastating. Tana was a firm defender but he was good with the ball too. Ruben was our best defensive player, and they both benefited from the good ball they received from Gene Ngamu. Willie Poching led by example that day, and Joe Vagana was the youngest and biggest bloke on the field.

Five of the '92 players, Alex Chan, Canterbury half Tane Manihera and Aucklanders Peter Lima, David Fatialofa and Joe Vagana, backed up for the tour to Britain and France in my second season with the Junior Kiwis. This was the second time the New Zealand Rugby League had mounted such an ambitious venture, but whereas Bob Bailey's 1987 side played against amateur opposition we were to be hosted and opposed by the professional clubs.

The two-month tour was a tremendous experience. We won 11 of our 12 games, and the obvious highlight was beating Great Britain Academy at Wembley Stadium in London. Our match was curtain-raiser to the first test between Great Britain and Howie Tamati's Kiwis. The senior teams naturally got the dressing rooms and we were assigned a portacom out the front of the stadium. A lot of support seemed to be coming from a group of women, and when they came down at halftime to wish us the best it turned out to be Debbie Hockley and the New Zealand women's cricket team.

Just about all of those British academy players went on to pick up full professional contracts. Andy Farrell was captaining Wigan and Great Britain when he was 21 and Iestyn Harris captained Wales at the 2000 World Cup before being signed by the Welsh Rugby Union.

That game was the first time I saw Graham Holroyd, who was then playing for Leeds. Eight years later he was to kick the vital field goal for Salford in what turned out to be my last game as Wigan coach, bugger him.

The Wigan academy was the strongest in Britain even in those days and had not been beaten for three years until the Junior Kiwis turned up at Central Park. Despite Wigan having future first grade stars such as Kris Radlinski and Simon Haughton, we whipped them 51–4 in what was the quality display of the whole tour.

Our only loss was in the second British test, when we were outsmarted by our lack of geographical nous in approving the itinerary. We were sent up to Whitehaven to play Cumbria, spent the next day travelling, and didn't get much preparation in before the test back at Central Park. The young Poms really played well that night and once they had the initiative we couldn't wrest it off them.

That made us all the more determined not to lose in France, but didn't prepare us for what we walked into during a pre-test game at Tonnes. This was an under-19 tour and the opposition teams were supposed to be of the same age. But when we got there we found out the French Selection had been chosen from the military services and included some obviously ageing 'teenagers'.

It was 12–0 to the home side until Henry Paul scored under the crossbar and converted it just before halftime. Our players came off and complained their crown jewels were being grabbed, and about gouging, ear biting and punching. The referee was doing nothing. The players wanted to retaliate but we preached discipline and I said if they kept their cool they would run away with the game. We put the next five tries on to remove any doubts about the outcome.

With six minutes to go, and us leading by 30-odd points, someone was injured and I thought if we were going to stay unbeaten in France we had to show we would not tolerate that sort of rubbish in the test match. So I sent Alan Glasgow, our trainer, to tell the lads to give the ball to the Frenchmen and belt the shit out of them. When he delivered the message the whole 13 players turned to me in the stand and flashed the biggest smiles you could imagine. They had worn it for 74 minutes and were going to enjoy the last six.

At the restart of play Henry Paul put up a bomb, a French winger caught the ball at 100 miles an hour, and ran straight into prop Billy Weepu. Billy was even bigger than Joe Vagana, and he flattened him. While he lay on the deck the other 25 players engaged in an all-in brawl. The other French winger raced across the field and laid the boot into one of our guys, and what happened next was a real French farce. Two of our players chased him the length of the field. Boy, could he run, and jump. He hurdled the metre-high fence which circled the ground, disappeared out the arched gates and onto the main road. We never saw him again.

Eventually the officials restored order and the French Selection was given a penalty. But our blokes had done a real job on them. When the French hooker took the tap kick, no one wanted to take the pass and run into the defensive line. The hooker tried again. Same thing. There was more dialogue between the local players and the referee, and I asked the liaison officer what was going on. He said the locals had 'put the white flag up' and didn't want to play anymore. The game was called off. Nor was there any chance of us meeting up again with the disappearing winger at the mayor's civic reception because they also cancelled that. We didn't have any problems winning the sole French test at Carcassonne three days later. And there wasn't a stray boot or swinging arm seen all day.

While we were in France Howie Tamati rang from England to tell us the Kiwis had suffered a few injuries and were looking for a player to stay on and complete the senior tour. He made a couple of suggestions but I said there was only one player he should grab, and that was Henry Paul. Henry was our fullback and captain and was playing terrific football. Also, he was held in such high esteem by the players that when Laurie Stubbing, the Kiwi manager, came to pick him up at Gatwick Airport the entire Junior Kiwis team broke into a song and haka. I'm not kidding when I say the whole airport stopped and watched. There were tears everywhere, something I'll never forget. That tour was the making of Henry Paul. The rest, as they say, is history.

Tevita Vaikona was another tourist who became a big star in Britain, as a high scoring winger who built up a big following at Hull and more recently in the champion Bradford Bulls side. Tevita arrived in Christchurch from Tonga to study at Lincoln University and had never even seen a rugby league game until he went along to training with a few mates. In one season he emerged from obscurity to be in the Junior Kiwis and he has since played for Tonga in two World Cups.

Most of the players in that '93 Junior Kiwis team became professionals in Australia or England, and Henry Paul and Joe Vagana went on to long international careers. But even those who stayed home have done well. Maurice Emslie captained the Canterbury Bulls to win the first Bartercard Cup grand final, Jonathan Hughes, Jermaine MacDonald and Chris Faifoa have all been top players in their respective provinces, and Jason Hita represented Northland at rugby union.

The Junior Kiwis are a very satisfying age group to coach and, with such able managers as Bevan Olsen and John Devonshire, it was a completely stress-free tour.

But there was a dramatic career change waiting back home. I was to join the Auckland Warriors in 1994, their year of preparation before entering the Winfield Cup, and early in the new year the New Zealand Rugby League appointed me to coach the Kiwis. The NZRL and Warriors dovetailed the two jobs to make it fulltime, which also included being the national coaching director. That meant a move to Auckland, leaving family and friends behind in Christchurch. But the challenge was immense and with the Kiwis and Warriors it seemed I had the best of both worlds.

Chapter 5.
Best of both worlds

If the Kiwis had always represented the pinnacle in rugby league excellence for New Zealand players and coaches, the new Auckland Warriors franchise offered an unprecedented opportunity to pursue a professional career without having to live overseas. The top coaching job available was assistant to Australian John Monie, who had won a premiership with Parramatta and a truckload of trophies at Wigan. By late January 1994 Frank Endacott was both Monie's right-hand man and successor to Howie Tamati in charge of the national team.

Ian Robson, the Warriors' chief executive, knew it would put plenty of northern noses out of joint to appoint someone from Canterbury as coach of an 'Auckland' team but he reckoned our provincial record, culminating with that 1993 final, was too good to ignore. However, I wasn't due to start at Ericsson Stadium until mid-year. The Kiwis were to be first on my agenda.

I was in Greymouth with Canterbury trainer Bruce Everest putting the West Coast squad through a pre-season session when news came through that I was also to coach the Kiwis. Pat Taylor, a stalwart of the game on the Coast, heard it on the radio and any thoughts Bruce and I had of returning to Christchurch that afternoon were quickly forgotten. The Coasters persuaded us to pop over to the

Australasian Hotel for a 'brief' celebratory drink that lasted until 5am. Bruce and I even had whitebait delivered to our room for breakfast.

Trevor Maxwell, the judge who was then New Zealand Rugby League president, said he was looking for stability. Although my initial term was for two years, he was hoping it would extend beyond the 1995 World Cup. Since Ces Mountford (1979–82) and Graham Lowe (1983–86) there had been a rapid turnover of coaches. Tony Gordon lasted three years but Bob Bailey and Howie Tamati were gone after two each. Some people, including other coaches, were surprised one man was given both jobs. But Trevor Maxwell was adamant my association with the Warriors, and especially working with John Monie, could only benefit the Kiwis. The NZRL was also employing me as national coaching director, assisting with elite camps and age-group tournaments. A planned mid-season test match against France never materialised, so the 1994 international programme comprised a short tour of Papua New Guinea with a warm-up game in Cairns on the way.

The Kiwis had slipped well behind Australia and Great Britain during 1993. Howie Tamati was unlucky not to chalk up a win over the Kangaroos when Laurie Daley kicked a desperate late field goal to rescue a 14-all draw at Auckland. But Australia got stronger as the series went on and won comfortably at Palmerston North, on the infamous night when they ran out of footballs because the spectators were pinching those that were kicked over the sidelines, and again at Brisbane.

The Lions had drawn a tight two-test series in New Zealand in 1992 and Howie was obviously under pressure when he set off on the 1993 tour to Britain and France. Just about everything that could go wrong, results-wise, went wrong. The Kiwis lost 0–17 at Wembley and the other tests were almost identical with losing margins of 17 and 19. By then Howie had dropped captain Gary Freeman and vice-captain Duane Mann from the third test line-up. Although they beat France it was too late to save the tour, or Howie's job.

The Christchurch media saw my appointment as a good omen. The local newspaper pointed out that only two Canterbury coaches had been in charge of the Kiwis in the previous 40 years, with very favourable results. Jim Amos won back-to-back test series against Australia in the 1950s, and Lory Blanchard coached the 1971 Grand Slam Kiwis to a big win over Australia at Carlaw Park and test series triumphs in both England and France.

Bob Fulton, the Manly and Kangaroos coach, was in Wellington at the time and agreed having the dual Kiwis and Warriors positions made sense. He expressed sympathy for Howie, stressing the need to get the right structures in place. Fulton took a staff of eight when he travelled with the Kangaroos, a luxury his Kiwi counterparts had never known.

The Papua New Guinea tour was set for season's end. First, I took a New Zealand Residents team to Australia. We won all four of our games over there, then beat Western Samoa by 60 points at Carlaw Park. The Residents proved more than equal to their Australian counterparts, with Australian Residents and Sydney Metropolitan Cup teams among the victims. Of the 22 players only halfback Aaron Tucker, a good little player, did not take up a professional contract.

Duane Mann and Whetu Taewa set up manager Sel Shanks with their notorious piano joke at Brisbane. Duane suggested to Sel he ask Whetu how his brother's piano lessons were going, and Sel innocently did that when we were all sitting around the team room. Whetu looked at Sel, turned white (true, he was good at this one), and started crying. He blubbered, 'Sel, how could you say something like that? I thought you were a good bloke' and rushed out of the room. Sel was taken aback and didn't realise everyone was trying not to laugh. Then someone told him Whetu's brother had been in a work accident and had lost the use of his hands. Now it's Sel racing outside, trying to console Whetu, who is still keeping up his Oscar-winning performance. Sel was absolutely distraught when he came back and announced he was chucking in the job and going back to New Zealand. Then someone started laughing and we all broke up. But Sel took it pretty hard. Maybe we had gone too far. I had a cup of tea with him and we went into town. Sel regained his composure, and his sense of humour, and bought a couple of toy pianos, which he presented to Duane and Whetu at the team meeting that night. That eased what inadvertently had become a tense situation and Sel not only stayed but went on to become one of my managers with the Kiwis.

Two little clouds, which in later years became major storms, took some of the shine off my first Kiwi selection. The team had hardly been announced before British chief executive Maurice Lindsay was writing to the International Board complaining we had selected British-based players Kevin Iro (Leeds), Tawera Nikau (Castleford), Brendon Tuuta (Featherstone), and Aaron Whittaker (Wakefield). We had already ignored Frano Botica because his Wigan club put him under pressure not to tour. I did some checking and found only Leeds had objected. Nikau told me there was no problem at Castleford, Featherstone generously let Tuuta go against the wishes of coach Steve Martin, and Whittaker was so keen he would have swum to Port Moresby no matter what Wakefield thought. The International Board backed New Zealand and Britain reluctantly released them, though a hamstring injury subsequently forced Iro's withdrawal.

It also came to my attention that Graham Lowe, who was to coach Western

Samoa at the 1995 World Cup, had approached Ruben Wiki in the Canberra dressing room only minutes after they had won the Winfield Cup grand final. Lowe made it known he also had Hitro Okesene and Tony Tatupu, two other current Kiwis, in his sights. When Ruben, who was already embroiled in a contractual dispute between Canberra and the Warriors, had time to think about it he pledged his loyalty to New Zealand. Lowe later called me about it and I told him I would fight him all the way. I didn't like him using his media contacts to play his games.

I was really impressed with Duane Mann's captaincy on the Residents tour and promoted him to lead the Kiwis to Papua New Guinea. Duane had been a model professional at Warrington, appearing in more than 100 consecutive games before returning home to captain North Harbour in the Lion Red Cup. He was one of four domestic players in the touring team, along with Tony Tatupu from North Harbour and Counties-Manukau's Hitro Okesene and Whetu Taewa.

When Kevin Iro was hurt at Leeds and Quentin Pongia broke his elbow at Cairns we called up Mike Dorreen and Brent Stuart as reinforcements. Mike was then Hawke's Bay captain in the Lion Red Cup but had been an outstanding finisher on the wing for my Canterbury teams. He went on to play professionally and got his revenge on the Warriors for letting him go by helping Balmain beat them at Lancaster Park. And who better to compensate for the loss of Quentin's traditional West Coast work ethic than Stewie, another Coaster?

The Papua New Guinea Kumuls are never easy to overcome at home. They have upset a few touring teams, including Graham Lowe's 1986 Kiwis, and they hold the Kangaroos and the Australian competition in awe. Adrian Lam and Marcus Bai are national heroes and the government declared a public holiday when the Kumuls reached the 2000 World Cup quarter-finals. I don't know of any other sports fans in the world who walk barefooted for three days, or more, to get to matches. When they can't gain entry to the grounds the trouble starts, and the tear gas is brought into play. Touring there is a unique experience, not to be missed if at all possible.

A week before our arrival a volcano erupted in Rabaul, so our opening game was transferred to Port Moresby. We got over that but the first test in Goroka, up in the highlands, was a real struggle. At halftime we led 2–0 and I had never seen a team so fatigued. Even Gary Freeman couldn't find the energy to talk and I knew then we were going to struggle. Luckily, some cloud cover came over, a shower cooled things down, and we had a heartening win. Gene Ngamu starred, backing up smartly for two tries, and John Lomax was a stand-out performer in the pack.

One of our managers, Ray Haffenden, paid a local bloke to arrange a trip to visit the Mud People in the jungle on our day off. The Mud People are a tribe of smaller than average New Guineans who had fought their wars over the years wearing big masks to scare their enemies. We went up a mountain road in two vans, turned into a jungle road, and stopped when this fierce looking figure waved us down. He started arguing with our driver and it was getting really ugly. All of a sudden tribesmen appeared out of the bush on both sides of the vans. They were brandishing machetes and giving every impression they wouldn't be reluctant to use them. I can honestly say it's the most frightened I have been in all my life. These guys weren't joking. I was sitting next to an unusually silent Peter Leitch, the Mad Butcher, and the two guys nearest us, Hitro Okesene and John Lomax, were turning pale. I had visions of them climbing into the vans and lopping our heads off. Then a car screamed up behind us, and the bloke who Ray Haffenden had paid jumped out and started pressing money into the hands of some of these tribesmen. The machetes were put away and the smiles came out. They took us further into the jungle, to their camp, and showed us their tribal dances.

Even these guys had some knowledge of Australian rugby league because they decided I was Marty Bella, the big, bald Australian front-rower. I was that bloody petrified from what had happened around the vans that I didn't argue. I just signed about 50 Marty Bella autographs. If you ever have a hankering to drop in on the Mud People, don't go uninvited.

They don't take prisoners over there. One night at the Port Moresby Golf Club a security guard showed Daryl Halligan and I how far and accurately he could fire an arrow down the first fairway. He also casually mentioned he had killed a few trespassers. They don't need machine guns, a bow and arrow was lethal enough.

Daryl did get his hands on a machine gun though. When we had a reception at the New Zealand High Commissioner's residence the local police guards got drunk while waiting outside. Some of the players saw them and obtained permission from the managers to travel back in the guards' jeep. The rest of us were on our way back to Port Moresby to watch the New Zealand women's soccer team play a World Cup qualifier when this police jeep overtakes us. Terry Hermansson is driving, Daryl Halligan and Hitro Okesene are leaning out the windows brandishing sub-machine guns, and the two guards are lying in the back waving their berets at us. Terry, Daryl and Hitro gave us an escort right into the soccer ground.

There is a serious side to life in Papua New Guinea as Ray Haffenden and I found out one day. We were walking down the main street in Goroka when an Australian guard invited us into the local prison compound. It must have been 35 degrees and 100 per cent humidity, and there were big wire cages with the only shade offered by something that looked like a car case. Inside the wire was a kid, about 13 years old, and we asked what he was there for. The guard just said, 'Funny you should ask that, we were just talking about him this morning.' It transpired the kid had been there three weeks and no one seemed to know why.

The bus trip from Goroka to Lae had its moments too. We were told if you ran over a pig to keep going because they are sacred and the old story about an eye for an eye also applied to pigs. Suddenly a pig dashed out of the bush and started weaving down the road ahead of us. Every time it zigged we zagged, trying to avoid bowling it over. Fortunately the pig sidestepped into the jungle before we hit it or our driver lost control completely. One thing's for sure, the driver wasn't going to stop if the pig had become road kill.

Tear gas stories emerge from every tour and ours was no exception because they never seem to appoint police commanders who can tell which way the wind is blowing. They have their men aim at the packed crowd, or the people outside trying to get in, but the gas always seems to blow back over the field. It happened in Port Moresby, but we had the support staff ready with wet towels. All the players can do is lie flat on the deck until the towels arrive and then cover their heads.

The crowds, and the hero worship, are amazing wherever you go. At Goroka we couldn't get anywhere near the ground for the first test because there were literally thousands and thousands of brown faces pressing forward against the bus. Then the Mad Butcher says, 'I'll sort this out.' He grabs a tag off one of the Lion Red bags, bright red with yellow trim, gets out in front of the bus and yells, 'Chief of security for the New Zealand rugby league team.' They might not have known what he was saying but took one look at this Lion Red tag and parted like Moses at the Red Sea right up to the main entrance. The Butcher was in his element, even showing the tag at the gate and telling them who to let in and who not to let in. We had a great bunch of supporters on that tour, all three of them, the Butcher plus Auckland publicans Sel and Ivy Bennett.

Poor old Ray Haffenden got conned when he arranged the team photograph in Port Moresby. Two characters turned up with a dodgy looking camera. We all got into our gear and flashed our best smiles. They demanded the money up front, Ray paid it over, and we never saw them again. Ray then had to find a real photographer and do it all over.

The second test at Port Moresby was won more comfortably. Brendon Tuuta and Tawera Nikau were outstanding and Terry Hermansson made a strong test debut after Jason Lowrie was ruled out with a hamstring problem. Matthew Ridge was troubled by blisters on his feet throughout the tour but showed plenty of guts in fronting up. Daryl Halligan took the kicks and he put over six in the first test and seven, as well as scoring a try, in the second.

That tour was the first involving New Zealand when the visiting side brought their own referee, something that was to backfire on us when the French came over in 1995. Jim Stokes, from Christchurch, was our referee in Papua New Guinea and copped plenty from the crowd at the second test. Cans and bottles were thrown at him at halftime and fulltime, and some hit their target but Jim wasn't hurt.

I had no hint then that Duane Mann would have such a short term as New Zealand captain, something that distressed me at the time and still aches a bit when I think of it. Of course, I didn't know I would continue coaching the Kiwis for seven years, but if I had a crystal ball back in 1994 there is no way I would have expected to name eight different test captains. When I left home for my first selection meeting of 1995 Duane Mann was both hooker and captain in my team for the French series and I thought he would remain for the Australian tests and on to the World Cup. But when I left the New Zealand Rugby League offices, then at Newmarket in Auckland, Duane wasn't even in the squad. I felt sick for three days after that.

Ray Haffenden was convener and Hugh McGahan the other selector. In all fairness, I can understand why Hugh plumped so hard for Syd Eru as hooker because he was the up-and-comer at the Warriors and Duane was getting near the end of his career. It was just a matter of timing when one took over from the other in the Kiwis too. But I had no doubts that Duane had enough left in the tank for one more year.

If he had been captain, and with his personality, we would not have experienced the discipline problems which blighted our tests against France. In Papua New Guinea Duane had played well and captained wisely. To this day I feel I let him down. As convener, Ray first delivered the bad news, but I rang Duane later because I owed it to him. He took it like the man he is but I know deep down he must have been hurting. In hindsight, I wish we had taken Duane to the World Cup. Instead, he captained Tonga and almost led them to victory over us at Warrington in our first game. Then Syd, after playing against Tonga, was suspended from the rest of the tournament for testing positive to pseudo-ephedrine. Syd wasn't a druggie. An infection had put him in Middlemore Hospital and after his release he was careless in buying pain-relieving tablets over the counter from an Auckland chemist without establishing exactly what was in them. We were left without a specialist hooker, and that was costly.

The NZRL had decided to appoint an Australian-based selector because of the number of Kiwis in the Winfield Cup. When Hugh McGahan left to join

Leeds after the French and Australian tests he was replaced by Mark Graham to pick the World Cup team. But because of the Duane Mann saga I subsequently went to the New Zealand board and asked to be sole selector. If I was going to be chopped I wanted it to be for something I had done and not someone else. From '96 I was sole selector, and that's when we started getting really good results.

The captaincy turnover was rapid but there were good reasons. John Lomax had three tests and then got hurt, Gary Freeman filled in for the remainder of the Australian series, and Matthew Ridge called the shots from the 1995 World Cup until his retirement three years later. Matthew missed one test in 1997 so Stephen Kearney was the stop-gap. Quentin Pongia led the team in the last four tests of 1998 before he was injured. Jarrod McCracken became another casualty after just one test, then Richie Barnett took over from the 1999 Tri-Nations until I finished up after the 2000 World Cup. It didn't stop then either. Richie's hamstrings sidelined him in 2001 and new coach Gary Freeman (with Jarrod McCracken as one of his selectors) appointed Nathan Cayless captain.

Circumstances dictated that eight players had captain after their names in my 35 tests, with Ridgey and Richie leading them out in 11 tests each. Lomax was regarded as a surprise choice and I suppose he was. Hugh McGahan argued very strongly on his behalf. Maybe Lomax wasn't suited to the various off-field tasks that went with the job but he had a difficult time because of the widening split between Super League and the Australian Rugby League. It was the same when Gary Freeman took over, and they can't be blamed for something that was out of their control.

The captaincy clearly needed addressing before the World Cup and I decided on Ridgey. He wasn't everybody's cup of tea but he did the right thing by me all along. Ridgey got a grip on things, people started listening to him, and he was good value. I remember saying at the time that it was the best decision I had made. Stephen Kearney had been New Zealand's youngest test skipper for Howie Tamati in 1993 but he was always considered to be a better forward without having the burden of captaincy.

Quentin Pongia had only one week to adjust to his new responsibilities after Ridgey's injury and abrupt retirement between the second and third Aussie tests in '98. Quentin wasn't an after-dinner speaker but he was a leader on the field and had the respect of his team-mates. He will always have the distinction of being the first Kiwi captain to go through a series in Britain unbeaten. Quentin played the entire first and second tests and complained when I brought him off the field in the third. Not many prop forwards can do that these days.

Jarrod McCracken would have made a good captain on the evidence of that gutsy 1999 Anzac test performance. But later that year he was gone too, and Richie Barnett did a fantastic job for the rest of my time. If there was a bloke who should have been marketed by the NZRL as the face of rugby league it was Richie. He was outstanding on and off the field, honest and popular with the media.

Obviously, we would never have had so many captains if it wasn't for injuries. There were times when we had three or four players who had the captained the side on the field together but there was never any suggestion of in-team power struggles. They just put their heads up and followed the bloke who was leading them out. Looking back, I reckon my first and last captains, Duane Mann and Richie Barnett, were the best.

I wasn't surprised when Gary Freeman went for Nathan Cayless to start off his coaching era. Nathan showed he was leadership material when moving through the grades at Parramatta, and Brian Smith had the confidence to make him the club's youngest ever first grade captain.

Meanwhile, throughout 1994 the Warriors were building towards their debut in the following year's Australian competition. Everything was going so smoothly, players were flying in to Auckland from overseas and other parts of the country, and the excitement was mounting for something that New Zealanders had wanted for so many years — a team of their own to support in what was then still called the Winfield Cup. On our side of the Tasman, at least, there was no sign of the approaching hurricane which was to hit rugby league in '95 and throw the whole game into turmoil.

Chapter 6.
Season of discontent

The Super League war clouds that had been gathering in Australia blew across the Tasman early in 1995. The season had opened so promisingly with an incredible Auckland Warriors debut night against the Brisbane Broncos at Ericsson Stadium and was scheduled to end with the biggest-ever World Cup tournament in Britain to mark the sport's centenary.

Everything was going so well for the Warriors' first year in the Australian competition. Although the first graders had been narrowly beaten on opening night they were thoroughly competitive against the big guns from Brisbane. Not for the first, or last, time little Alfie Langer made the difference when the match hung in the balance. My reserve grade team had won handsomely over their Broncos rivals, and the capacity crowd signalled a prosperous future for the club and rugby league in New Zealand.

But it soon went from one extreme to the other as the war raged on and people took one side or the other in the Super League shambles. The Warriors joined the Super League camp amid accusations of treachery after the Australian Rugby League had fostered them. People lost interest in the game because of the tension between the two factions.

It was the same with the players. Where they would previously have sat around a table and talked sport, after Super League began paying them the discussions turned to boats and cars, and the real estate they were going to buy.

It went from rugby league to more material things, everything was hinging on money and, in a lot of cases, pure greed.

I have said since the first day that I don't blame the players taking what was offered them because it set them and their families up for life. Anyone from the outside who says differently should reflect on what they would do if a competitor offered them the same job for twice or three times the going rate. Sometimes it was more, much more. There is the well-publicised story about Warriors and Great Britain forward Denis Betts holding a hotel telephone in one ear and his cell phone in the other as the two sides auctioned for his services. The bidding was going up in lots of $50,000 or $100,000. Why should he tell them to stop?

Yet despite all of the turmoil, 1995 was still the best year the Warriors have experienced in first grade. We have heard that the 2001 Warriors did better by becoming the first to make the play-offs, and that was a mighty effort by Daniel Anderson and his players after the disrupted preparation they experienced. But at eighth in a 14-team competition they were still in the bottom half of the table. In '95 we finished tenth out of 20, the only time the club has been above halfway, and missed out on the finals only because we lost the competition points from a 46–12 victory over Western Suburbs because the replacement rules were breached.

That was the biggest balls-up since Dunkirk, and the whole story has probably never been told. Someone was sent to the blood bin and Joe Vagana went on to the field. There was no need to put Joe, or anyone else for that matter, on with only three minutes to go and the Warriors completely in charge. It was a spur of the moment decision and, as every head coach knows, there is only one person ultimately responsible. John Monie put his hand up and accepted the blame, but it wasn't entirely his fault. The replacement rules seemed to change every year and John sent Laurie Stubbing down to the match official for clarification. The official said Joe could take the field. Then on the Monday when it was revealed Joe was not eligible to play the official promptly denied he had given permission.

There is no point now in thrashing Ian Robson for the Warriors' financial blow-outs. All of that has been well documented by people who were much closer to the action than the reserve grade coach. Sure, I saw a lot of extravagant spending going on, Ian was a champion at that. But much of what he invested in is still there today.

The gymnasium is a prime example. There's a few dollars worth of gear in there, believe me. Ian was an excellent marketing person, to the extent he sold the club and the game so lavishly that it put pressure on the players when it came time for them to do their thing. Ian Robson and Liz Dawson did such a superb job presenting the club to the public that everyone expected immediate results.

When the reserves toppled Brisbane 36–14 and the first graders just went down 22–25 on that unforgettable opening night at Ericsson Stadium it wasn't surprising that the person in the street — and especially the 31,000 at the football — expected that to be just the starting-off point for a glorious march to the grand final. In all the euphoria people forgot that even a class act like the Broncos had taken a full five years to fire. I was talking to Wayne Bennett, who is now in his fifteenth season as the only head coach the Broncos have ever had, after I had left the Warriors, and he reckoned all we needed to emulate them was stability. The rest was there.

But, of course, the staff and players were to be consistently turned over, and it was musical chairs around the board table. Daniel Anderson became coach at the end of the club's sixth season, but was already the fourth head coach after John Monie, myself, and Mark Graham. At the same time Mick Watson became the fourth chief executive after Ian Robson, Bill MacGowan and Trevor McKewen. Hopefully the lessons have now been learned.

The flak is still being fired in some quarters about John Monie bringing British forwards Andy Platt and Denis Betts with him from Wigan. But I'll defend Andy. I can remember seeing him slumped in the dressing room at halftime absolutely beaten up and bleeding, to the point most players wouldn't have gone back out there. But Andy had the courage to do it and try his best on every occasion. His best days were behind him and he was playing on a crook knee, but he was never a quitter. He was also a great help as a mentor to the young forwards at the club.

Denis Betts, on the other hand, never came up with the results to match what he was being paid, which was reputed to be $700,000 a season once Super League kicked in. The best football he played in New Zealand was for Great Britain in the 1996 test matches against the Kiwis. Denis grew another leg when he pulled on that Lions jersey and lived up to the reputation he had earned as the most devastating forward in Britain. Pity he couldn't do the same for the Warriors.

We had some great wins with the reserves after that first-up defeat of Brisbane, with scorelines like 48–0 over Manly, 50–22 against Parramatta, 44–16 over St George, and 42–18 against the Bulldogs. They were mostly young New Zealand guys, keen as anything, and it was unfortunate some were let go before they realised their potential. Stacey Jones and Syd Eru were just two who started out with us, but it wasn't long before they were promoted to first grade and before the year was out both were in the Kiwis.

That was how the system was supposed to work.

In the end the reserves snuck into the play-offs in eighth position, and lost 8–14 to fifth-placed Penrith in the club's first finals match. We were proud to have achieved that much and it proved to be the stepping stone on the way to consecutive grand finals in the next two seasons.

But, overall, '95 was probably the year I least enjoyed being a coach, all because of Super League and its war with the ARL. The two-test home series against France was most affected. It has been well publicised that simmering tensions boiled over when Matthew Ridge and Jarrod McCracken had their spat in a Palmerston North nightclub.

Matthew was with Manly, an ARL club, but had become a strong Super League advocate. Jarrod was trying to get out of the Super League contract he signed at the Bulldogs and had sided with the ARL. They were both strong-willed and were very much in the front-line of the war. You could feel the tension spread through the whole squad. Minds weren't on the job because contracts were uppermost in their thoughts.

The lack of discipline flared in the French series, ignited by the utterly stupid International Board decision that touring teams should bring their own referees instead of continuing the policy of appointing neutral officials. France was supposed to provide New Zealand with a panel to pick from but ignored that and dispatched Marcel Chanfreau. He was ranked only third in a country not noted for producing great rugby league referees, spoke no English, and was about to make his test debut at our expense.

Chanfreau rattled our players in the first test when he allowed the Frenchmen to blatantly ignore the off-side rule, scrag the Kiwis in the play-the-balls, and generally slow down a match we were trying to play at pace. With captain John Lomax speaking no French, communication was impossible. After our hard-earned 22–6 win I complained bitterly to the NZRL, but there was nothing that could be done.

In the second test Chanfreau was even worse and the Kiwis' frustrations spilled over in a shambles of a match. We were probably lucky to escape with a 16-all draw and series victory after the referee awarded France a ridiculous penalty try. Matthew Ridge tackled centre Frederic Banquet after he had kicked ahead from near halfway. The ball rolled innocuously into touch short of our goal-line with no one near it. But Chanfreau suddenly hared off to the posts and triumphantly signalled his penalty try. He also dreamed up a forward pass when Gary Freeman was off to score the winning try in what was his last test on home soil.

Chanfreau left the field with a police escort and with 11,000 spectators baying for his blood. I remember walking down towards the players' tunnel and finding

Graham Carden, who was then New Zealand Rugby League president, standing there. Graham could see I was in a foul mood and told me not to do anything silly. But I ignored him and charged straight into the referees' room. Chanfreau was there, patting himself on the back for a splendidly patriotic performance, along with Kevin Bailey, the NZRL referees' chief, and the two touch judges. I shut the door and gave Chanfreau a real serve. He couldn't get away from me because I was standing on his toe. I didn't care whether he understood English or not, he sure knew where I was coming from. Not that it did any good, apart from giving me the chance to let off steam before I exploded.

We had won the series but should have beaten France far more comfortably in both tests. The French might not have been the greatest footballers in the world but they deserved credit for their tenacity and taking their chances. Our players did not have their minds on the job. Sean Hoppe and Gene Ngamu had been the best players in the first test, but at Palmerston North players tended to stand out only when they trooped off to the sin-bin. Stephen Kearney, Brendon Tuuta and Gary Freeman were sent to the 'cooler' along with one of the Frenchmen. It really is hard to remember the game plan when you're tossing up between buying a new car or a speedboat.

The New Zealand Rugby League, as well as the Auckland Warriors, had signed with Super League so everyone was involved, like it or not. Graham Carden received a call from Sydney, disappeared overnight, and the deal was all done in 48 hours. So quick in fact that Bernie Wood, deputy chairman at the time, was one of two board members who did not know anything about it. Many believe New Zealand was sold short in getting only two million dollars and a lot of ultimately hollow promises. Some of the players' contracts were worth more.

I must admit I thought the concept of Super League was fantastic for the game when I first heard about it. Not so much because of all the benefits being offered to the first grade players but because of what they said they would do for the 17- and 19-year-olds. Australasian competitions were planned. That was by far the best scenario for both the Warriors and the New Zealand domestic game. We know now they pulled the plug on the 17-year-olds even before they got under way, and the 19s lasted only one season, 1997.

So many of those things they promised never eventuated. It's obvious now that the Super League saga was the very worst thing that could have happened to a sport that was thriving in Australia and about to really take off in New Zealand. The Super League people turned on their word. They sucked a lot of people in, including me because I could see the opportunity for young New Zealanders to go out there, compete with the best in the world, and make a good living out of it. I want to make it clear I was never a member of Super

League and never received a Super League cheque. There were plenty of others getting backhanders, and I can feel quite good now that I was not one of them.

Graham Carden, who had succeeded Trevor Maxwell as the NZRL boss, was an interesting character. I got on well with Graham from the day I arrived in the NZRL office. But as Super League went on we saw less and less of Graham. He was too busy on the road, flitting around the Pacific islands more than he was in Auckland. It got to the point where he actually wanted me to withdraw from the Warriors and put all my time into the NZRL. Graham said it had to be one or the other, and I replied, 'It's got to be the other. See you later.'

Despite the best efforts of the Kiwi team's management, the rift caused by Super League followed us to Australia, where we were beaten in all three tests. Hardly had we landed in Brisbane than Australian Rugby League chairman Ken Arthurson slapped a political label on the series. Ken said he was desperate for Australia to win because it was an ARL-loyal side taking on a team of Super Leaguers from across the ditch. Ken is a man I have always respected but he got my dander up. Maybe New Zealand was waving the Super League banner but I have always been for rugby league first and foremost and took his remarks personally.

The Aussies at last had the chance to live up to their boast that they could field two or three teams strong enough to take on any other nation. Now they could do it by picking players solely from the ARL State of Origin series and ignoring those who had gone to Super League.

We couldn't do that, and our players were dropping out for other reasons. Kevin Iro was laid up in England after a knee operation and Ruben Wiki was recovering from a broken hand. Then, in the first test, captain John Lomax lasted only seven minutes before his knee blew up, Richie Blackmore did an ankle, and Logan Edwards hurt his back. Stephen Kearney tore a hamstring at training before the second test and we were running a trans-Tasman shuttle service to bring in Tony Tatupu and Tony Tuimavave. Former All Black John Timu became a double rugby international and the second test also marked the return of Tony Iro after a five-year break. Tony, who was then with Sydney City, had made a smooth transition from the wing to the forwards.

It wasn't a bad effort to hold Australia to 10-all until the fifty-second minute of that second test. Then Tony Iro was sin-binned by New Zealand referee Phil Houston for a trifling offence and Brad Fittler didn't need a second invitation. Fittler kicked a long-range field goal and then set up a Steve Menzies try from a grubber kick as Australia went on to win 20–10. But it was still 14–10 with 38 seconds left and if a pass from Timu had found Sean Hoppe a few minutes earlier then Matthew Ridge would have been lining up a match-winning conversion. All Houston got for his trouble was a mouthful of criticism from Australian coach

Bob Fulton in the players' tunnel and again at the media conference.

Kearney limped back into camp for the third test but Bob Fulton announced his side would only get better, and they did. We were 10-all again with 22 minutes left but Fittler ran the show after that and they rattled on another 36 points. It didn't help that Ridge was knocked out making a first-half tackle and took no further part.

The on-going Tawera Nikau saga surfaced in '95, after which his name was to almost permanently feature on the list of unavailable players. Before my time, Nikau had withdrawn from the first test match against the 1992 Lions, yet turned out for Otahuhu against Mangere East in an Auckland club game the day before the test was played at Palmerston North. He had asked Kiwi coach Howie Tamati to replace him because of concern for the health of his young son in Huntly. But after watching from the Carlaw Park terraces as the Lions tied the series in the second test a week later Nikau went off to continue his career with Castleford in England and promised to be available for future Kiwi teams. One of his team-mates at Castleford was Kiwi centre Richie Blackmore.

Nikau then toured Papua New Guinea with my first Kiwi team in 1994, when Blackmore wasn't available. But with Blackmore back in New Zealand and playing for the Warriors in '95, Nikau made himself unavailable for personal reasons. The story gradually emerged that a family feud had developed from a falling-out between the players' wives while they were at Castleford. Blackmore always said he would play in any team that included Nikau, but the Nikaus, Tawera and Letitia, were staunch in their stand. I recall talking to Letitia in the NZRL office in 1995. It was an honest, frank discussion and she understood I couldn't have players picking and choosing their matches.

Tawera Nikau did play for us once again, in the 1997 Anzac test when Richie Blackmore was at Leeds, and the controversy soon flared again. When I picked them together for the return match at North Harbour in September Nikau pulled out amid a public disagreement about a meeting we had prior to the Anzac match. I had gone to the Cronulla dressing room to talk to Nikau, told him I wanted him to play for the Kiwis on the basis his availability had to be unconditional, and we shook hands on it. Nikau denied that was the agreement when he withdrew from the September test but my memory is crystal clear. As it happened, Nikau missed out on a great win over Australia and Blackmore was one of the stars of the game.

I never seriously considered Nikau again after that, even though there was media speculation of a Nikau comeback every time Richie Blackmore was out of the frame. But there was never any bad blood between me and the Nikaus. When I was at Wigan I went over to Halifax for a birthday barbecue for Martin

Moana's son and spoke to Letitia for more than an hour. She was great company and it was a tragedy she died so young.

Because he was so seldom available, Tawera Nikau's international career record does not reflect how good a lock forward he really was. He played some wonderful club football in England and for Cronulla and Melbourne. No one did more for the Storm on the day they won their grand final. The records show he played 18 tests between 1990 and 1994 but only one more after that. Tawera Nikau could have gone down as one of New Zealand's greatest players instead of just a very good one.

In only a few months what had been heralded as one of the most significant seasons in New Zealand rugby league history had degenerated into something of a shambles. The Warriors had at least maintained their popularity throughout the Winfield Cup season. There were 29,500 spectators at the last home game against Cronulla and they were still a chance of making the top eight when they went to Brisbane for a tough last-round encounter with the Broncos.

Even after the Warriors were hammered 42–6, with Steve Renouf scoring four tries, they could have snuck into eighth spot while North Sydney struggled against Gold Coast. But a late try saved the Bears and propelled them into the play-offs. Sydney City had gone into the last round with a 67-point worse differential than the Warriors, then mauled the Sydney Tigers to push the Warriors down to tenth on a countback.

The early unrealistic hype meant the Warriors fell below the unfair expectations placed on them. I had a taste of play-off football with the Warriors' reserves but the Kiwis had failed to put France away and the Australians had given their World Cup preparations a big boost at our expense.

There seemed to be more court cases than football matches going on in Australia but I was hoping common sense would prevail in the Kiwi camp. Strangely enough, the troops, both Super League and ARL, regrouped under new captain Matthew Ridge in England to present a united front — even if it was in threatened strike action against the Super League-aligned NZRL. Life as Kiwi coach was nothing if not diverse. It was not always easy living up to Dad's long-ago advice to have a cheerful smile and greeting for everyone you meet.

Chapter 7.
So close . . .

With France leading the way, international rugby league authorities took a leaf out of soccer's book and staged their first World Cup tournament in 1954. Australia, Great Britain and New Zealand teams travelled to France for the tournament, won by the British. Since then another nine cup and championship competitions had been held in a variety of formats. When New Zealand lost to Australia in the 1988 World Cup showdown at Eden Park the finalists were found by calculating the results of the last tests in every series involving the five major countries. Australia had reigned supreme from 1975 as teams from 10 countries assembled in Britain for the Centenary World Cup.

Australia was hot favourite to win again in 1995, despite the internal war raging within the game. The clean sweep of the home series against New Zealand undoubtedly boosted the Kangaroos' confidence and, if anything, the siege mentality which barred Super League players could have been seen as a strength in firming their determination to retain the World Cup.

The Kiwis were still a distant third in the rankings after our moderate results over the previous few months. Great Britain had beaten the Kangaroos in the

The immensely talented Logan Edwards taking on Lions Shaun Irwin (No. 3), Gary Price, and Ian Lucas during Canterbury's 1990 victory.

Canterbury and Kiwis stand-off half Mark Nixon had a knack of being in the right place at the right time.

Brent Stuart was renowned for his consistency in the front-row, all the way from the West Coast to the Kiwis.

News Media, Auckland

Quentin Pongia, the cornerstone of my Canterbury and Kiwis packs.

News Media, Auckland

News Media, Auckland

Briefly a Warrior, Whetu Taewa found his niche with Sheffield Eagles and Hull Kingston Rovers in England.

The Wembley walk. With Junior Kiwis Henry Paul, Gus Malietoa-Brown, Tane Manihera and Alex Chan.

Big Joe Vagana admires Junior Kiwis hooker Nick Bierne's passing style in the Wembley win over Great Britain Academy.

Co-manager John Devonshire and I flank a happy bunch of Junior Kiwis who will never forget their winning Wembley experience.

I still have nightmares about French referee Marcel Chanfreau, seen here in familiar pose as Stephen Kearney and John Lomax look on with disbelief.

The enforcers. The 1995 World Cup team enjoying a leisure break at the Wigan laser shoot.

A tense meeting with ARL heavies Ken Arthurson, John Quayle and Johnny Raper as the Super League war flares in 1995.

first test of their 1994 home series before losing the other two. Despite being split into separate England and Wales teams for the World Cup, the English were rightly seeded second.

I had raised a few eyebrows by including Brisbane Broncos forward Brad Thorn in my preliminary 40-man squad. The Otago-born Thorn withdrew and pledged his allegiance to Queensland and Australia, but naming him was the tip of an iceberg as we identified more and more players who were eligible for the Kiwis and Junior Kiwis by being New Zealand-born or Australian-born sons of expatriate New Zealanders. Thorn went on to play trans-Tasman tests against us, with mixed success. He was sledged mercilessly, especially by Matthew Ridge, after announcing his All Black ambitions in '97, but came back to haunt us later. When Thorn finally did capitalise on his New Zealand heritage in 2001 it was in rugby union. He only needed one season to get that All Black jersey and then shocked everyone by turning it down and going home.

We went to the World Cup without two outstanding back-rowers because of Tawera Nikau's unavailability and Jarrod McCracken's legal battles with Super League. He was embroiled in court cases and was not considered for selection.

After five years Mark Horo earned a recall at the age of 32, and played so enthusiastically that he went from interchange bench to the starting line-up in one step and kept his place for the semi-final against Australia. Tony Kemp was included to increase our options at stand-off half and lock forward, while 19-year-old scrum-half Stacey Jones and winger Richie Barnett were the new caps.

I was given strong support by the appointments of Gary Kemble and Shaun McRae to the coaching staff. Gary was a former test fullback who had an illustrious professional career with Hull in the early 1980s before advancing through the New Zealand coaching system. Shaun was a trainer at Canberra and one of Bob Fulton's Kangaroos assistants until getting on the wrong side of the Super League fence.

It was probably inevitable after what had occurred during the splintered domestic season, but the well-intentioned staging of a pre-tour game against the Gerard Stokes-coached New Zealand Residents at Ericsson Stadium proved to be of little value. Attitudes within the team clearly had not improved markedly. The Kiwis won by about 20 points but that did not really matter, and the Residents deserved praise for making us work really hard. The difference was they went out as a disciplined unit wanting to win, and we went out with half a team still unbalanced because of the chips on their shoulders. About the only bright spot was Jason Williams scoring two tries from fullback after we decided to rest Matthew Ridge's damaged ribs.

Two incidents underlined the contrasting moods of the two sides that night.

BEING FRANK

Some say John Lomax was still smarting after losing the captaincy to Ridge, then starting the warm-up match on the bench. Whatever was on his mind, he went on as a halftime replacement and 10 minutes later was given his marching orders for a high tackle on Auckland forward Mark Faumuina.

As Lomax walked from the field some of the spectators heckled him, and he made a gesture with his fingers. Next morning's newspaper published a photograph of it. So I had the photo put on acetate and used it as an overhead presentation at the first team meeting in England. It was the basis of me having a real crack at their ill discipline. That gesture by Lomax showed just how much attitudes had to change in a very short time. Lomax had also been suspended from our opening match against Tonga by the New Zealand Rugby League's judiciary, which reduced our front-row options in the preliminary rounds.

Just as alarming to me was what Gary Freeman did when he got over the Residents' goal-line. Instead of putting the ball down straight away for a try he turned around and sledged some Residents players who had been having a verbal battle with him. While Freeman was debating the issues, Residents stand-off half Aaron Whittaker came in from his blind side and almost knocked the ball out of his hands.

Freeman got the try but he was bloody lucky and we clearly couldn't afford a continuation of the behaviour in England. It showed an absolute lack of respect for the opposition, and that Freeman's attitude wasn't right, so that was when I pencilled in Stacey Jones for the first World Cup match.

I copped a bit of criticism for taking Gary Freeman on that trip. Jones was always going to be introduced at some stage on the tour because he had been a revelation in the Winfield Cup. But I wanted to take Freeman too and until his actions against the Residents he would have played in the first game.

Although the Kiwis went within the width of a goalpost of eliminating Australia and, in all likelihood, going on to bring home the World Cup, the players never did completely shake that Super League monkey off their backs. We had players talking about boycotts over a pay dispute with Graham Carden, who was wearing two hats as New Zealand Rugby League president and one of Super League's chiefs. The dispute stemmed from an announcement some time earlier that Super League players were to receive $10,000 for international appearances. But the NZRL did not have the resources to pay that sort of money. It should have been sorted out by Carden well before the team left for England but wasn't. The money matters flared up after we had beaten Tonga and Papua New Guinea in our preliminary games and when we were deep into preparation for the semi-final against Australia.

At one stage it seemed to me to be 60–40 that we would be packing up and going home, it was that serious. Instead of going to training, the players walked down to the nearby Haydock racecourse for a meeting while back at the hotel I was telling managers Ray Haffenden and Bevan Olsen that I had real doubts about whether we would be playing. When the players returned they made it very clear their argument was entirely with Graham Carden, not the team management, and that they were more than prepared to take on the Kangaroos. According to Matthew Ridge, the whole issue would bring us all closer together. He was right, even if training was held later than usual that day.

One mistake I did make was taking too many older players to England. Before we went it was explained, and publicly announced, that with only two pool matches before the semi-final it was very likely some of the 24 players would not get a game.

As it transpired, Daryl Halligan, John Timu, Brent Stuart and Brendon Tuuta missed out and they were disappointed. There would have been something wrong with them if they hadn't been brassed off. But they were the next best players in their positions and we needed them to be on hand if we suffered injuries.

Our close call in the Tongan match forced me to ignore any temptation to give the rest a game against Papua New Guinea. I knew we had the right guys starting but they were in need of another game together. I wish now I had included some youngsters for the experience. The lesson was learned and I took Lesley Vainikolo and Ali Lauiti'iti on the 1998 British tour.

Boy, did we get a fright in our first game against Duane Mann and his mates at Warrington. On paper we should have beaten them comfortably but it developed into something of a 'home' game for the Tongans. Duane had gone from being Kiwis captain to Tongan captain and had played more than 100 times for Warrington, so was a crowd favourite with their fans even without the underdog factor. The packed house was totally behind the Tongans, the only exceptions being our little group up in the grandstand. We played poorly and they displayed a passion that all but caused the biggest upset of the World Cup tournament.

With seven and a half minutes to go — I knew that because the timekeeper was sitting just along from me and assistant coach Gary Kemble — we needed 13 points to win. Three scoring moves with the clock running down. I could feel Graham Carden's eyes drilling into the back of my neck. After all, my two-year contract expired after the trip.

Fortunately, there was an injury break, which gave us time to get a message out to Matthew Ridge, who was captaining his country for the first time. I wanted the players to stop attempting to score miracle tries from their own goal-line and get good field position.

Gary Freeman took the message out, there was a nodding of heads, and Freeman came through on the radio to tell us, 'Matthew says not to worry, it's all under control.' Gary Kemble and I looked at each other and burst out laughing. We were lucky not to be caught by the television cameras. It was only when I read Ridgey's book that I learned he couldn't hear my instructions because of the crowd noise, and said the first thing that had entered his head.

Seven and a half minutes later we had won by a point, 25–24. Whether it was by accident or design, they had done what I wanted and played out the rest of the game deep in Tongan territory. Hitro Okesene had just gone on and scored in the left corner with about his second touch of the ball and then Richie Blackmore crashed over on the right flank. Ridgey converted both from wide angles to tie the scores.

There was a bit of a stink later that the referee gave the Tongans only four plays when they had possession between those two tries. But it wasn't the referee, it was one of the Kiwis who made the 'last tackle' call which caused Tonga to put in a poor kick. Whoever it was deserved a medal.

A draw seemed inevitable and wasn't going to look too good on our result sheet. But the team then put in their best set of the game, taking the ball up strongly five times for Ridgey to chip over the winning field goal with his left foot. He didn't have much choice because George Mann had rushed up from an off-side position on Matthew's right, forcing him to stop, step, and reset himself for the kick. Thank heavens we never had to find out whether the referee would have been courageous enough to penalise Mann for being off-side. In that cauldron of Tongan crowd fervour he might have feared a lynching.

It was after that reprieve that we lost Syd Eru, when his positive test for pseudo-ephedrine came back from the fateful painkillers he had taken before joining us in camp at Auckland. It was a tricky situation having to find a stand-in hooker or, rather, dummy-half.

I gave Gary Freeman first go in the next game against Papua New Guinea. He packed at lock forward in the scrums with Mark Horo hooking. Freeman played well in our 22–6 win but his discipline was rubbish. I just couldn't afford to take him into the Australian game in that mood and have him give away five or six penalties. So I slotted Henry Paul in there for the semi-final and he was an absolute success. Even Henry didn't know when he was going to take off from dummy-half, so it's no wonder the Aussies were baffled.

It was quite a week leading up to the semi-final. Even before the boycott threat we had the spectre of Gary Freeman being filmed by television crews sitting on the team bus when the other players trained at the Liverpool-St

Helens rugby union club's ground. A few hours earlier I had left him out of the side to play Australia. Because Freeman had been such a great player I felt I owed it to him to have a word before I publicly named the semi-final team. I asked his roommate if he would give Gary and me a few minutes. Gary was sitting on the end of his bed, cross-legged, just like a little boy. I always had a lot of time for Gary but his reaction was unbelievable. I told him I was going to name the team in 20 minutes and he would not be in it. He threw a real tantrum and gave me all the reasons why he thought he should be included. I told him it wasn't because I didn't believe he was good enough as a player but that I was worried about his discipline. Gary told me he would not be going to training and I said that was fine, but I thought he would be wiser to train with the lads, keep his head up, and retain his credibility. He then agreed to come with us but said he would not be getting off the bus. I remember warning him there might be television cameras there but it was his decision and he staged his protest sit-in.

As I walked out of his room I remember pausing and saying, 'Gary, one day you might coach a team and you'll understand exactly what I'm doing now because you might have to do the same thing.' How ironic that was, with him eventually succeeding me as Kiwi coach.

I felt sad when I looked over at Gary sitting up there on the bus with the cameras on him. He should not have done that and I'm sure he kicks himself that he did, because the immediate result was a loss of respect from his fellow players and other people. I know being dropped rocked him hard, especially as it was the end of his international career.

Gary might still hold that against me to this day — I don't know. But I appreciated it when he asked me to coach his team when he brought a lot of Australians over for his testimonial match in Auckland. He knows he has my full support as coach of the Kiwis.

It is not easy to drop players, especially older players, but you can't afford to walk away from decisions like that. I never liked to embarrass players by making tough calls in front of others, or criticising individual players when the others were around. I would get them in a one-on-one situation, and I did plenty of that. There is nothing worse that seeing a coach bawl players out in front of a group and completely lose it.

Playing Henry Paul at hooker was not the only change from the team that beat the Kumuls. Kevin Iro was promoted from the bench into the centres, Richie Barnett returned from a thigh injury, John Lomax started at prop with Quentin Pongia moving into the second row, and Tony Kemp shifted from lock to stand-off half. I felt Tony's greater experience was needed there.

In the north of England they still talk about that semi-final at Huddersfield being one of the epic matches of all time. It was the first World Cup game to go into extra time and, as underdogs, we were given the wholehearted support of the Pommie fans.

Matthew Ridge had two opportunities to put an end to Australia's world dominance in the last two minutes of ordinary time. But he was well wide with a sideline conversion and then scraped the left upright with a snap field goal attempt.

There had been a moment's indecision, when the ball was first passed to Quentin Pongia, and he had to relay it to Ridge. That split second was enough for Brad Fittler to rush through and push Ridge on to his left foot. But he still struck the ball sweetly from 40 metres and for a long time it looked like it was going over. Sean Hoppe still swears it did. In fact, the ball was bending back and just brushed the outside of the upright as it went past.

That was the culmination of a sterling fight back by our blokes after Australia led 14–4 at halftime and 20–6 early in the second half. Steve Menzies had sprinted 70 metres, chased all the way by Hoppe, to score one of the most spectacular international tries by a forward. That would have broken the back of any team that wasn't rock solid but the Kiwis put all their frustrations from the French series, the losses in Australia, and the wrangle over payments, to surge back at the Aussies.

Replacements Gene Ngamu and Tony Iro made big impressions in the second half. It was probably Gene's finest game in a Kiwi jersey, while Tony did a lot of damage. Richie Barnett scored his first try for New Zealand to start the comeback, then Tony Iro stretched out from a tackle to score, and suddenly it was 20–16 with 10 minutes left and Australia tiring.

The crowd was right behind the Kiwis and there was near-panic on the Australian bench when English referee Russell Smith sin-binned centre Terry Hill for a professional foul. Hill was missing when Kevin Iro used all of his immense strength to squeeze over for a try near the right corner flag. If only Ridgey could have pulled off that conversion, or his field goal.

Extra time played into Australia's hands because their coach, Bob Fulton, had stuffed up. He had two subs who were not used in the first 80 minutes. Presumably he forgot about them in the heat of battle as we came back at them. So Australia had two fresh players available, and Hill to return after getting his breath back in the sin-bin. The Australian media probably thought it was a master stroke by Fulton but I wonder how they would have reacted if Ridgey had kicked that goal. Our bench was well and truly used up and the comeback had taken its toll. The break also gave Australia a chance to regain some composure before the start of extra time.

Matthew Johns was one of Fulton's fresh men and it only took him a few minutes to lay on a pass for Hill to race off and score. Brad Fittler put it beyond doubt by weaving his way through our exhausted defence. The fans gave both teams a standing ovation.

I couldn't understand Bob Fulton's reaction at the press conference. He gave the referee a verbal hammering after that game, yet he was the winning coach. It puzzled me because I was the losing coach and had shaken Russell Smith's hand and congratulated him on a fine performance. Fulton must have reported home too, because the Aussies have never forgiven Russell for something they think he did on that day.

Australia had lost to England in the opening match at Wembley. But they made no mistake when they went back there for the World Cup final, winning 16–8. It could so easily have been New Zealand's first and only World Cup because I'm sure we had the measure of England. The results when we did get to play them over the next few years would suggest that. We didn't bring home the World Cup and no one had expected us to do that. On the credit side, though, there were distinct signs we could trouble the Kangaroos given an even playing field.

Kevin Iro announced his retirement after the tournament but I asked him right away not to close the door too tightly. Happily, he was to answer my call for help in 1997 and give the Kiwis another couple of seasons. Our other centre, Richie Blackmore, had been outstanding throughout the World Cup and was named in many World XIII selections as well as being chosen as New Zealand's Player of the Year.

The World Cup also completed my initial two years as Kiwi coach. It was heartening to have the public support of former coaches Tony Gordon, Bob Bailey and Howie Tamati, who had all been cut from the job, when the media asked them if I should be retained.

The next appointment was supposed to have been made in December but I was grateful the New Zealand Rugby League put me out of my misery by reappointing me in late October, just days after we arrived home from England. What is more, I got my wish to be sole selector.

Chapter 8.
The empire strikes back

Great Britain mostly ruled the rugby league world from the first Lions tour in 1910 until Australia exerted its dominance of the modern game. Blessed with hard but skilled forwards, their strength honed in the mines and mills of northern England, clever halfbacks and fleet-footed outside backs, the British benefited from long having the most professional club competition in the world. Clubs could attract top players from Down Under and when transfer bans were introduced they switched their attention to the rugby union code. For decades New Zealand's amateurs did remarkably well in home series against British touring teams but it was not until 1984 that Graham Lowe's Kiwis achieved the first three-test whitewash over the Lions. New Zealand's more recent ascendancy can be traced back to the 1996 series.

It was total confusion over the first half of the 1996 domestic season. We had home series scheduled against Papua New Guinea and Great Britain but any chance of arranging a test with Australia to capitalise on the World Cup extra time semi-final was soon off the agenda because the national bodies were in opposing ARL and Super League camps. Instead, there was abrasive talk of the Australian

Rugby League fielding its own New Zealand 'All Golds' team so its players would still have international football despite the British and New Zealand leagues having gone to Super League. The ARL announced Bob Bailey would coach the All Golds with Sydney-based former Kiwis captain Billy Snowden as manager, and original Warriors chairman Peter McLeod in charge of team administration.

The ARL even went to the extreme of naming an Australian team to play the All Golds in Sydney and Auckland, with Brad Fittler as captain and, provocatively, eight Super League-affiliated players in the 17. Laurie Daley immediately said he wouldn't play against a New Zealand team that wasn't officially sanctioned by the New Zealand Rugby League and the other seven Super League players also pulled out.

They delayed announcing the All Golds for 24 hours, but when ARL-aligned players such as Jarrod McCracken and Jason Lowrie made themselves unavailable it was never going to get off the ground. That 24 hours became forever. Insults were being tossed backwards and forwards across the Tasman and in the midst of all that the Auckland Warriors gave their most dismal display of the season in losing to Balmain at Lancaster Park in Christchurch. It was all a promoter's nightmare and painful for true-blue rugby league fans to stomach.

The ARL finally played a 'test' against a team representing a few Fijian villages because the Fijian Rugby League had joined Super League as well. But just as mind-boggling were the happenings in the Super League trenches, with Graham Carden and others proclaiming all sorts of grand international events.

In late June Carden announced a proposal involving the Kiwis, Australia, Great Britain and Papua New Guinea playing a mini-World Cup in Auckland, Christchurch, Brisbane and Sydney, with subsidiary matches being arranged for the Junior Kiwis, New Zealand Maori, and New Zealand Residents. That release came out about the same time they were postponing and then cancelling an Oceania tournament involving a New Zealand XIII and the Pacific nations. It was replaced by a much smaller event in Auckland in early July.

If the Kiwi coach was baffled by all this, imagine how the public felt. All the while I had been planning for two home tests against the Kumuls and a three-test series against the touring Lions. At that stage there were plans for another World Cup tournament in Britain at the end of 1997 and I felt this programme would be ideal to build up for another crack at the Australians.

It was not until mid-August that Graham Carden, between court cases in Australia and a trip to England, confirmed we indeed had five test matches and that the Junior Kiwis would play curtain-raisers to all of them. The season was to last until the third Lions test at Lancaster Park on November 1, about the time they were usually rolling the cricket pitch. I was still hopeful of having the

Sydney-based Kiwis who had signed contracts with the ARL available for the tests, and in early September I dipped my toe into the waters by naming Craig Innes and Jarrod McCracken in a 40-man squad. Innes would have become a dual international in '96, no argument about that. He was playing the house down for Manly, but when he asked club officials about his situation they showed him newspaper reports quoting ARL chairman Ken Arthurson saying all ARL players were banned from the tests. Innes had thrived since joining Manly from Leeds. But Arthurson was the unofficial Mayor of Manly and that was that.

We weren't exactly flush with experienced backs because McCracken and Dave Watson were also with the ARL, Kevin Iro had retired, and Richie Blackmore and Tea Ropati were struggling for form. Henry and Robbie Paul were playing rugby union while Britain changed from a winter to a summer season under the Super League banner.

It was about then that I learned Tonie Carroll was eligible for New Zealand. He was born in Christchurch and had moved to Brisbane with his parents as a youngster. But Tonie, like Brad Thorn, had set State of Origin selection as his goal and was told he would not be considered for Queensland if he played for us.

Instead of Craig Innes getting a Kiwi jersey to hang alongside his All Black one, that distinction went to Marc Ellis, who was reunited with his old Otago rugby union mate John Timu. Marc was a replacement in each of our first four tests and then started on the wing at Lancaster Park when Richie Barnett was injured. Unfortunately for Marc, he lasted only about half an hour before he gashed a knee in a freak accident with a ground sprinkler.

Our customary deep reservoir of front-rowers had also been drained. Jason Lowrie, Brent Stuart and Terry Hermansson were with ARL clubs and John Lomax was not available for personal reasons. So big Grant Young, from the South Queensland Crushers, joined Quentin Pongia in the starting line-up and a youthful Joe Vagana debuted off the bench.

Some commentators were surprised that Richie Blackmore was partnering Timu in the centres instead of Ruben Wiki. But I had other plans for Ruben. I wanted him to come on fresh to take over from Mark Horo at lock forward, a tactic we had used in the World Cup semi-final the previous year. That worked fine against Papua New Guinea, but Ruben proved so valuable on the field that he was slotted back into the centres during the British series.

There was incredible drama over whether Matthew Ridge should play in the first test against the Kumuls after suffering a head injury during the ARL preliminary final against Cronulla. Despite Manly doctor Nathan Gibbs having cleared him for the grand final a week later, just about every medical man on both sides of the Tasman was making long-range calls on Matthew's condition.

Included was our own Kiwi doctor Stu Thomson, All Black doctor John Mayhew, and Wallaby doctor John Best. I had a chat with Stu Thomson and expressed confidence in Matthew's powers of recovery. When he went out and set up the shock try which took Manly to victory in the grand final everybody else shut up. As usual Ridgey did his talking on the field.

The Super League war was to affect our opponents too. When it first blew up the ARL signed British stars Jason Robinson, Gary Connolly and Lee Jackson, so they were barred from touring with the Lions. Papua New Guinea had to play without inspirational captain Adrian Lam, who was also in the ARL camp. Curiously, the ARL allowed Lam to captain the Kumuls against Britain in a home test on the same tour.

The ARL also threatened yet more legal action to stop the tests going ahead but that dissolved when Super League won its appeal in the Australian Federal Court. The case was being heard in Sydney while the Kiwis were in camp at Rotorua preparing for the first test. No one was happier to hear the news than Tony Iro. He had signed for Super League and would have been playing for the Hunter Mariners if their competition had been allowed to start in 1996. He was instead spending the season with the ARL-loyal Sydney City Roosters.

Our form background was not too flash, with the exception of the World Cup semi-final, and it had not been easy beating Papua New Guinea 22–6 at St Helens. But the '96 Kiwis put all the legal crap out of their heads and simply massacred the Kumuls. It took only about 20 minutes to establish mastery in the forwards and shake off five weeks of inactivity. Then they ran riot. The 62–8 result in Rotorua was surpassed by New Zealand's biggest ever test win, 64–0, at Palmerston North. But it was tinged with sadness because a calf injury ended Mark Horo's test career. Mark was so good for team morale that we arranged for him to stay with us throughout the British series.

Eleven of my Warriors reserve graders had their moments of international glory in Wellington when they beat the midweek Lions. I went to the game looking for someone to replace Mark Horo and had the bonus of watching my son, Shane, score two tries for the New Zealand XIII. Bryan Henare was probably most people's pick to fill the Kiwis vacancy and I surprised them when I took Logan Swann back to Auckland with me for the first Lions test. Tyran Smith went into the No. 13 jersey and Logan, who had never played first grade for the Warriors, joined the bench.

The Poms were written off in some quarters, and the TAB had us $1.28 favourites. I don't think their bookies knew much about the history between the two countries, or took into account the 3-0 whitewash Howie Tamati's Kiwis had suffered the last time we met. We hadn't beaten them in a series since 1984, and before that 1971. Twice in 25 years. Sure, the Lions had only beaten Papua New Guinea by two points at Port Moresby, but it was a completely different story playing them with Adrian Lam in tear gas territory and us playing them without Adrian Lam in our own conditions.

In lock forward Andy Farrell and scrum-half Bobbie Goulding the Lions could boast real talent around the scrum-base, and stand-off half Iestyn Harris was heralded as the new Jonathan Davies when he starred for Wales at the World Cup. Kris Radlinski and Anthony Sullivan were dangerous outside backs, and Farrell had Denis Betts, Adrian Morley, Paul Sculthorpe and Keiron Cunningham with him in the forwards. They were going to be tough all right.

Looking back now, I suppose we did a 'Tonga' on them at Ericsson Stadium. This time it was 12–4 to Britain with seven minutes to go. John Timu was our hero, with two quick tries off slick Gene Ngamu passes. Timu deceived the defence with clever footwork in one-on-one situations. And just as he had done against Tonga at the World Cup, Matthew Ridge converted both tries and kicked a last-gasp field goal for a final 17–12 scoreline. That one point enabled Matthew to equal the New Zealand test points-scoring record held for 40 years by Des White, and he broke it a week later.

Betts showed the Warriors fans who were there just how good he could be, scoring a magical try and playing brilliantly. British coach Phil Larder was not amused that Australian referee Bill Harrigan sin-binned stormy young second-rower Adrian Morley for a professional foul on Sean Hoppe just before Timu's first try. But the video tape shows we had them on the ropes for the last 20 minutes and Morley's action proved they were at breaking point.

British tour manager Maurice Lindsay, who was then chief executive of the English Rugby League, was also busy doing his sums. He didn't like what he came up with and sent 11 players home, reasoning that because there were no more midweek games they were surplus to requirements for the last 10 days. It was reported that team manager Phil Lowe learned of the dramatic move not from Lindsay but from a travel agent. Super League were paying the bills — and they reckoned there would never be a shortage of money! We used their problems as part of our motivation.

The second test at Palmerston North was another toughie. The Kiwis dominated early but were down 8–13 at halftime. This was the game when Ruben Wiki was restored to the centres and he was outstanding with two tries. John Timu played well again, and Gene Ngamu came up with the match-winner when he dummied his way past the defence from a scrum. It was nerve-tingling at 18–13 for the last quarter of an hour, especially when Syd Eru lost the ball over the British goal-line.

The result must have knocked some of the stuffing out of the Lions, while our blokes were getting stronger by the week and were ready for a big finale. In the previous eight tests between the Kiwis and Lions on New Zealand soil, extending back to 1988, the losing side had always been within a converted try of turning the tables. I called on the players to attack at Lancaster Park and they responded with a 32–12 result, a record-winning margin for us in 92 tests over 89 years. It was made all the better because it was achieved in my old home town and in the first rugby league test played on Christchurch's main sports ground for 76 years.

The Junior Kiwis had won all five of their youth internationals over the Junior Kumuls and Great Britain Academy, clinching their last one with a field goal by Scott Nixon, a younger brother of Mark, my former Canterbury captain. The juniors were coached by Lex Clarke, from Christchurch, who always had the ability to go on and become Kiwi coach if he had stuck to it. But Lex decided to pull out of the game. Lex and I had introduced match-up training sessions between the Kiwis and Junior Kiwis in test week and it really brought those youngsters on. Captain and front-rower Robert Henare, who later played for St George, and blockbusting winger Lesley Vainikolo were stand-outs for the junior class of '96.

So we finished the international season ranked higher than Great Britain for the first time in almost a decade. It was also a successful year for my Warriors reserve grade side, if not for the club's top team. With my tongue firmly planted in my cheek, I could also claim to have beaten the Brisbane Broncos twice in one day back in March.

Super League's proposed competitions could not go ahead because of a court ruling and everyone was lumped into the Australian Rugby League's 20-team Optus Cup. The pre-season was utter chaos because of the in-fighting between the two factions. As a protest, the Super League club chief executives decided to default their first-round matches.

The Warriors had been drawn against the Broncos in Brisbane. We therefore had the situation of two Super League clubs due to meet but with their respective chief executives hell bent on defaulting to each other! I doubt that has ever happened before or since in the world of professional sport. Most times they are trying to get any winning advantage they can cook up.

Early in the week I received a call from Gerald Ryan, who was then chairman of the Warriors, asking me to attend a meeting in the boardroom. I wondered what the heck I had done to incur the wrath of the board without even playing a game. So I hopped in the car and went straight there. The full board were around the table, and I was asked if it was possible to find two teams, with passports, to fly to Brisbane on the weekend. They wanted an answer by that afternoon. I told them they had to be joking, that it would be the toughest job in the world. But I promised them I would see what I could do. First, I went into chief executive Ian Robson's office and asked him if he knew what was happening. He told me he was aware of it.

'Who am I paid by?' I asked Ian.

'The Warriors board,' he replied.

'Well, in that case I want to do what they have asked. Do you have a problem with that?'

Ian, of course, was staunchly Super League but he was a politician too. He gave me a look that said 'Don't do it' while actually saying 'Yes, you have to do what the board wants'. It was pretty obvious he didn't want me to try. Deep down I think Ian held something against me for the rest of the time he was there because I ignored his signals.

Next I went into head coach John Monie's office and told him the same story about the board wanting me to find two teams to play the Broncos. To his credit, John, another Super League diehard, just said, 'Frank, you're paid by them, you do it if you can. I don't think it's possible, but you have to abide by their request.'

The New Zealand Rugby League office was the next port of call, and I got on the phone. By two o'clock that afternoon I had enlisted the Ellerslie and Otahuhu premier teams, with passports intact and all ready to go and play in Brisbane. Their coaches later told me that during the next two days their players trained better than they ever had and were really looking forward to it. But the Broncos went ahead with their forfeit and the Warriors were awarded the two competition points in both first grade and reserve grade.

The season did start for us a week later but the general atmosphere never got much better. There were so many distractions it wasn't funny. You never knew what would happen next. Secret meetings abounded, with and between players, meetings with Monie and Robson and the board, and a meeting between the squad and Super League's Sydney-based propaganda manager Trevor McKewen. So many things spoilt the game of rugby league in '96. It really took the gloss off it and by that time the general public was getting a bit edgy.

The critics panned the Warriors first graders for taking their fans on a roller-coaster ride. At one stage Monie's men lost four in a row, then won the next four. But they also dropped their last four games, against St George, Canterbury, Canberra and Brisbane, to finish eleventh of the 20 teams. The pressure was starting to build on Monie and a number of the big-name signings.

In some quarters John Monie's outstanding coaching record was being downgraded. It was claimed he inherited champion Parramatta and Wigan sides from other coaches and had big budgets to maintain them. But any coach still has to get a team, stars or not, working together and prepare them properly for the crucial games. It's okay to say Parramatta and Wigan were favourites to win their finals but the teams they were playing against couldn't have been too bad either to get that far. Just look at what Newcastle did to hot shots Parramatta in the first half of the 2001 NRL grand final. And how about the Sheffield Eagles' shock defeat of 'unbeatable' Wigan in the Challenge Cup final a few years ago? Both teams in a final invariably turn up with their confidence high from being on a winning streak and what happens in those 80 minutes is all that matters.

I can only speak from my own personal experience of John Monie and say I loved every minute working with him at the Warriors. I know John wasn't top of the popularity list with certain players in the squad. John had a policy that players were players and he didn't socialise with them because, among other reasons, he might have to sack them the following week.

Matthew Ridge criticised John in his book, comparing him unfavourably with his Manly coach, Bob Fulton. It is true, as Ridgey pointed out, that Gene Ngamu was one who suffered under John. We all have faults, and John sometimes was really negative in his halftime comments. What John didn't realise was that methods which might work with hard-bitten Australian professionals might not come over too well with a lot of New Zealand players. Gene was the worst affected.

I remember the start of some team meetings with the players sitting around, their heads already down and waiting to be barrelled. That should never happen. But for anyone to suggest John Monie did not have a good knowledge of the game is way off the mark. I learned a lot from him and appreciated his support.

We had held a meeting with the players and asked them what they expected of the coaching staff, and the message came back that they expected honesty. But when they were told the truth, at times some of them couldn't take the honesty. John had a very direct way of saying things and could be very sharp. Some of the New Zealand players found themselves in a professional environment for the first time and had not been treated like that before. It was a shock to their systems.

There were also stories floating around that John didn't understand Polynesians, to the stage where it was even suggested he was racist. That was totally wrong; there was no truth in it whatsoever. There is a certain way of treating certain players, not according to their race but as individuals, and John had a tendency to treat everyone the same. That's probably where he and I differed most. I prefer to treat every player differently because some can be given both barrels between the eyes while others need to be taken for a little walk for a quiet chat. That's the way it is, but John didn't believe in putting a comforting arm around anyone's shoulders. If he was in the mood to shoot it wasn't just one barrel, it was both, which is indicative of the system he was brought up in. I believe a coach should adapt himself to the players much more than to expect a whole group of players to try to adapt to the coach.

I don't think the rugby union recruits, John Kirwan and, more especially, Marc Ellis and Mark Carter, received the individual coaching they should have been given. If they were dropped from first grade they came down to me in the reserves. Marc Ellis arrived with the worst play-the-ball I have ever seen. We worked on it to get it right, and Marc was a very good pupil.

He and Mark Carter were crying out to be taught and I think they improved their all-round rugby skills while at the Warriors. But because of what they were paid the public expected them to be superstars. That was never going to happen overnight. In their defence, John Kirwan, Marc Ellis and Mark Carter were all men of exceptional character, whether from their rugby union backgrounds or their family upbringings. They wanted to learn but weren't really given the time.

The Warriors had lost Dean Bell, an inspiring captain in their first season, and lacked a bit of on-field direction because of that. The agreement with Dean had always been for one year but he had such a great presence within the team that, despite his age, retaining him for another year would have helped establish the club on a firmer playing foundation.

Ian Robson and John Monie stuck to that one-year deal, and so did Dean, who had business commitments in England and went back to coach Leeds before taking up his current development job at Wigan. Greg Alexander became captain. Greg was a smart footballer and good with the players too, but he didn't have Dean's mana.

About then the club started releasing some of the younger guys who Ian and John had signed on their whistle-stop, front-page-grabbing tours around the country in 1993 and 1994. John believed in having a regular clean out and bringing in new players. That's fair enough to a point, but what such a new club needed was some stability.

In contrast, my largely homegrown reserve grade side went all the way to the grand final after winning 15 of the last 16 regular season games and then beating Sydney City and Brisbane Broncos in the play-offs. John Simon, who was in the Roosters side we knocked off, was apparently being paid more than my entire team.

Those play-offs were the two best performances the reserves produced. Suddenly the guys who had lived in the shadows of the big names were getting a share of the limelight. Both games were shown on television in New Zealand, as we edged out the Roosters 19–18 and eliminated the Broncos 18–12. The win over the Roosters at the Sydney Football Stadium was a thriller. We led 16–0 at halftime but they stormed back to get in front at 18–17. Our captain, Aaron

Whittaker, kicked a long-range penalty goal but it was tense in those last few minutes. Our blokes still had plenty of force in their tackles but three of them had to chase down Nathan Wood over 70 metres in the dying seconds to make the game safe.

Nigel Vagana was the obvious star against the Broncos in the preliminary final back in Sydney a week later, scoring three tries against Tonie Carroll in the centres. Most of those Broncos went on to play first grade or into representative football, guys like Carroll, Petero Civoniceva, Michael De Vere, Syd Domic and Ben Walker. The fullback was lanky former Kangaroo Paul Hauff. But they couldn't catch Nigel, who scored two of his tries from halfway.

We were robbed in the grand final against Cronulla by a touch judge named Martin Weekes. Shane Endacott had put up a bomb and Doc Murray pounced on the ball to crash over for what would have been a crucial try. Referee Kelvin Jeffes was going to award it until he saw Weekes running on to the field. He was the only person in the stadium who reckoned a Cronulla defender had been taken out of play, but his imagination was enough to cost us a title in only our second season.

Cronulla won 14–12. The video tape clearly shows there was no interference, none whatsoever. That is all part of the game and you have to put up with it. But it was tough on those kids at the time. Nigel Vagana scored a beautiful try in the grand final to cap off a fine season for him.

The reserves had lost four of their first five games and everybody wrote us off. But our guys were still adjusting to the new world they found themselves in. Aaron Whittaker was inspiring as captain and goalkicker, playing in 24 of the 25 rounds. He should have been seen in first grade a lot more often than he was. Shane Endacott and Logan Swann played in 23 games and with Doc Murray, Bryan Henare, Iva Ropati, Aaron Lester, Nigel Vagana, Paul Staladi and Paul Rauhihi were the nucleus of a very good young team.

One of the fairytale stories was that of Dallas Mead, a forward who had been signed from Southland. For a rugby league player it's a long way from Invercargill to grand final day in Sydney. Another involved the Swann cousins. Before the year was out Logan Swann was a regular member of the Kiwi squad while Anthony Swann was a substitute in the last test against Great Britain. Neither of them had played first grade football.

It was great to be involved with the reserves and with the Kiwis having been unbeaten it was a very good year for me personally. But the political battles being fought in the background were damaging the game as a whole and it was all going to get crazier in '97.

Chapter 9.
In the hot seat

In late August 1996 Frank Endacott had replied to a journalist's query by saying the embattled John Monie should be allowed to complete his contract with the Auckland Warriors. 'It's a hard ask for a coach to go in there and deliver the goods in that tough a competition inside two years. I think John needs a third year and he's certainly got my total support,' said Endacott. By the end of April 1997, with the Warriors now competing in the Super League competition which had split away from the Australian Rugby League, Endacott was moving his gear into the head coach's office after Monie had been sacked. Endacott's Kiwis had just lost the first test of a widely spaced home and away series with the Super League Australians. His season could only get better, and, after a time, it did.

When the year started my red-letter day was going to be September 26, when we at last had a chance to confront the Australians at home. First, we played them in the inaugural Anzac test, when we salvaged some pride by recovering from a 0–20 halftime deficit to finish with a relatively facesaving 22–34 scoreline.

It was a game of one-offs, Tawera Nikau's one-match comeback and Stephen Kearney's acting captaincy because Matthew Ridge was sidelined with a shoulder injury. Henry Paul was to be second-choice fullback until he withdrew injured, so Richie Barnett was moved there from the wing and Daryl Halligan took his place.

We were competitive in the opening 20 minutes before making blunder after blunder in the second quarter. Stacey Jones sparked our revival, scoring the first try and having a hand in all of the other three, but Australia was always out of range. It was my fourth year as Kiwi coach and we still hadn't played them in front of our own fans. I knew if we could get them over here we had better than a 50 per cent chance of victory and tried to explain that to a succession of New Zealand Rugby League boards. But they were invariably dazzled by the dollars the Australians reckoned they could draw through their turnstiles.

In my seven years we only met them at home five times. We won three of those and it was oh so close in the 1999 Tri-Nations final. Too often we conceded that advantage, yet were playing before smaller crowds in Australia than we could command in New Zealand. I genuinely believe the Australians were worried we were becoming a force, so conceded us nothing.

Friday, September 26 was marked on my calendar from a long way out. We beat the Aussies 30–12 at North Harbour Stadium, a new test venue. I could only concur with Australian captain Laurie Daley's comment that 'there was no way we could contain the Kiwis, every time I lifted my head there was a wave of black jerseys running at me'.

The result was really satisfying, especially as we were given no show when Australian coach John Lang had the luxury of picking his fully match-fit team from the Brisbane, Cronulla, Canberra and Penrith teams which had contested Super League's Telstra Cup semi-finals. Alfie Langer was ruled out with injury and replaced by Paul Green. But they regained Darren Lockyer, Steve Renouf, Bradley Clyde and Shane Webcke, who had all missed the Anzac test.

Matthew Ridge came back for us and it was great for him to beat Australia seven years after switching codes. Tawera Nikau pulled out for the last time, but Kevin Iro rescinded his retirement to fill the gap caused by Ruben Wiki's broken arm.

Stephen Kearney put it into words afterwards, attributing the result to three years of team building as well as the discipline and professional attitude of the Kiwis on the night. During the week I had replayed videos of our tries in the Anzac test and the World Cup semi-final, then concentrated on getting our defence right on the training paddock. In the end we scored six tries and conceded two to Lockyer.

Richie Blackmore returned from Leeds to produce a blinder. He was cutting them in half with his tackles, even knocked Bradley Clyde cold in one bonecruncher, and the Aussies were not keen to run at him after that. Logan

Swann wore the No. 13 jersey for the first time after being a substitute in his five previous games. In the dressing room Logan passed the comment that test football seemed to be fairly easy, now that he could count six wins from six appearances. Between them Blackmore and Swann silenced any possible questions about Tawera Nikau being missed.

The Iro brothers carved them up and Stacey Jones and Syd Eru crossed for two tries apiece. Our little men were just as effective as the big blokes. John Lang, whose Cronulla side had lost the Telstra Cup grand final to Brisbane the previous weekend, was heard to mumble he had 'had better weeks'. Inevitably, some knockers argued the Australians were picked only from the Super League competition. But so were the Kiwis. It was not to be long before the Aussies were again claiming they could choose three or four sides of test standard. They just failed to prove it that night at North Harbour.

A month before the test, New Zealand Rugby League president Gerald Ryan and his board showed enough confidence in me to extend my contract into a third term, rather than wait until it expired in November. Ryan announced I had been retained for an additional 12 months after former Kiwi captain Mark Graham offered his services. His mate, Graham Lowe, had reckoned I was overburdened by simultaneously coaching the Warriors and the Kiwis, and Ryan rebuffed that by saying my success with the Warriors was the reason he had supported my reappointment. Ryan had just stepped down as Warriors chairman but had been in England for the club's three World Club Challenge games.

Matters were to come to a head in 1998 but the sniping had already started from Graham Lowe and Mark Graham. I publicly challenged Mark to compare his coaching record with mine, and did a little research. Although he had been on the staffs at Manly, North Sydney and the North Queensland Cowboys, Australian statistician David Middleton listed Mark's only official appointments as being with the Norths President's Cup team which finished sixth in 1994 and the Norths reserve graders who were tenth in 1995. The Warriors had then won 10 of their last 12 Telstra Cup and World Club Challenge games since I had taken over from John Monie.

In June Graham Lowe had listed Mark Graham, Mike McClennan and Graeme Norton along with myself as possible Kiwi coaches in his Sunday newspaper column. It was the start of a propaganda campaign pushing his old mates, whether they were qualified or not.

A few weeks later former Kiwi hardman Brent Todd replied in his *Truth* column: 'I can't believe all the talk about Frank Endacott getting axed as coach of the Kiwis. What crap. Just take a look at Frank's record and see what he's achieved and then weigh it up against the blokes tipped to take over. Honestly, the likes of Mark Graham, Mike McClennan and Graeme Norton don't measure up.' Toddy fired another salvo under the headline 'Marked Man: Lowe using Graham to gun down Endacott' in a column which appeared the day my reappointment was reported in the daily newspapers.

The demise of John Monie in April could be traced back to the change of chief executive two months earlier. Monie's greatest ally, Ian Robson, resigned in February under pressure from the Warriors board and went off to join Super League in Britain. He was replaced by Bill MacGowan, who arrived from a soccer and business background. It was MacGowan, under instructions from the board, who gave Monie his marching orders. At that stage the Warriors had won only three of their nine games, and Monie's departure was announced after a loss to the North Queensland Cowboys anchored the club at the bottom of the 10-team Super League competition table. It transpired his head was already on the chopping block before we went to Townsville.

I had no inkling I was going to be offered the head coach's job, nor even that they were considering a change. We were in Townsville before the Cowboys game when Bill MacGowan told me Monie was on borrowed time and the board wanted me to take over the reins. The circumstances were quite hilarious, really.

Bill asked me to go around the corner with him to have a cup of tea on the morning of the match. We sat down and he was about to offer me the job when we realised Graham Lowe and Graeme Hughes were sitting at the next table. Some polite chat passed between us while we waited for them to go so we could get down to business. I had heard rumours but can honestly say I had no knowledge of what was up until that moment. Like everybody else I was aware of the increasing pressure being heaped on Monie by the public, media, players and, maybe most significantly, the club's major sponsor. Brian Blake, the chief executive of the DB Group and a Warriors board member, had even publicly blamed a drop in DB Bitter sales upon the disappointing performances of the Warriors.

Meanwhile, the reserve graders had won four and drawn two of their eight matches and were right on course for the play-offs again. Gary Kemble took them over from me, and coached them to a second consecutive grand final.

The researchers had come up with the stats that John Monie's Warriors first grade teams had played 52 matches, won 26, and lost 26. But from season to season the win-loss ratio slipped from 13–9 in 1995, to 10–11 (not counting the forfeit by the Broncos) in 1996, to 3–6 in 1997. When Monie's sacking was confirmed on the following Tuesday, Bill MacGowan said player frustration and public expectation had been contributing factors. Brian Blake denied that DB Breweries had anything to do with it, adding that MacGowan had made the hard decision expected of a chief executive.

It all meant I had five days to prepare the first grade team for the next game, which just happened to be against the Brisbane Broncos. It took some rapid mental adjustment. While I had aspired to coach at first grade level, it was then probably the furthest thing from my mind. The previous week I had been busy preparing the Kiwis for the Anzac test in Sydney. I must admit, though, I had been wondering about my future at the club. John Monie and I had an original understanding that he would work for three years and I would then succeed him if the board wanted me. I thought three years would be enough but the rules were changing a bit and it seemed John was keen to take up an option for a fourth year. I made it known if that was the case I would probably be heading to England in 1998.

I'm sure that didn't have anything to do with what happened. Instead of me, it was John who went to England. He was snapped up by Wigan but couldn't replicate the success of his first term at Central Park, and later moved on to the London Broncos.

My first grade debut coincided with a historic moment for the Warriors. It was the first time they fielded a side comprised entirely of New Zealanders and, of course, it was under a New Zealander as coach. It wasn't anything I planned. Denis Betts pulled out with a hip injury and the rest had just fallen into place on form.

Other people have noted that some of the gloom which had descended on the club lifted during that first week after the coaching change. Matthew Ridge had written the senior players, aware that the younger guys were intimidated by John Monie, and had told Bill MacGowan there were problems with the coach. Ridge said there was relief all round when John told them he had been made to resign.

Actually, Ridgey, or rather his body, wasn't a lot of use to John, me or the Warriors in '97. He played in only nine of the 18 Telstra Cup games and mustered only 48 points because of various injuries. We had to rely on part-timers Gene Ngamu and Marc Ellis as goalkickers, and missed Ridgey's experience, leadership and downright mongrel, as well as the points from his trusty boot.

Graham Lowe had come out in a newspaper column suggesting that instead of being a lifeline the Warriors coaching job could become my noose. He claimed he had spoken to Bill MacGowan and offered to coach the team free of charge for the rest of the season provided they appointed me for the following year. Only he knows what his motives were. He predicted I would find the top job a lot tougher than I expected but I can't remember developing ulcers because of it.

There was no dream start to my first grade coaching career, though it looked deceptively easy when Bryan Henare made a big bust over Kevin Walters and Sean Hoppe ran 90 metres to score under the bar. We were 6–0 up after a minute and a half. After leading 12–10 at halftime, Allan Langer and Walters outsmarted us.

There was a three-week break then for the Super League version of State of Origin, involving New South Wales, Queensland and New Zealand. While that was going on I negotiated a deal with Bill MacGowan which was to have kept me at the Warriors until the end of the 1999 season. Two and a half years seemed time enough to put my own mark on the team, and there were to be performance reviews three times a year to keep everyone on their toes. Bill had no problems with me continuing as Kiwi coach and Gary Kemble was officially made reserve grade coach for the rest of the '97 season.

My good mate Ruben Wiki wasn't much help when he produced an outstanding individual display as Canberra beat us next up. There was another setback when we lost to the Perth Reds at the WACA on the first leg of a five-game trip around the world, taking in our three World Club Challenge matches in England and a stopover at Penrith on the way back to resume our Super League campaign.

Both Stephen Kearney and Matthew Ridge missed that Perth disaster, which left us a long and lonely last and gave us plenty to think about on the plane to England. I was sure the time overseas, in a touring situation away from all the distractions in Auckland, would help us regroup and salvage something from the season even if the finals were already out of reach.

Being so low on the Super League table, we were drawn against the leading British clubs in the World Club Challenge. Bradford was the top side in England, St Helens not far behind and Warrington about the middle of the table. The odds offered against us by the British bookies and back home in New Zealand were too attractive to ignore. Officially we weren't allowed to bet but we fancied our chances and there were a lot of smiling faces after we beat St Helens 42–14 at Knowsley Road.

Bradford was unbeaten until we got to Odsal Stadium. Although Syd Eru was sent off for a high tackle before halftime we hung in there until Gene Ngamu put winger Paul Staladi away for the winning try just before the end. Syd should never have been ordered off and it was laughable he was subsequently suspended from the game at Warrington. But Tea Ropati ran away for four tries and we scored more than 50 points.

We still had to keep winning, and by sizeable margins, to qualify for the World Club Challenge play-offs. Our fans at Ericsson Stadium could hardly believe what we did to Bradford and St Helens in the second round. Bradford was blitzed 64–14 and St Helens thrashed 70–6. The Australasian clubs were dominating. But it was not all one-way traffic as Canberra found out when they crashed against the London Broncos in England.

The decision to take our return game with Warrington down to Christchurch backfired on us. It was bitterly cold at Lancaster Park and George Mann led a brave Warrington defence as they held us to a 16–4 win. It cost us the points differential needed to be awarded a home semi-final against the Brisbane Broncos.

First, we had to get rid of Bradford in a quarter-final, and this time it was 62–14. With few exceptions, the British clubs let themselves down in this competition. Since then the best have shown they can outplay the finest Australian clubs in one-off matches. St Helens beat the Broncos in the 2001 World Club Challenge between the respective champion teams, and this year Robbie Paul inspired Bradford to a big victory over the Newcastle Knights.

In our '97 semi-final we went close to downing the Broncos. My diary entry after that game reads: 'Fantastic, committed performance'. The Warriors led 16–10 into the final quarter before the heat and the Broncos got to us. Kevin Walters and Ben Walker came up with late tries to clinch it at 22–16, and they went on to beat surprise finalist Hunter Mariners and bank the million dollar first prize money.

The improved form had been carried into our late-season domestic club games, starting with a second-half resurgence at Penrith. Down by 6–24, we got up to 22–26 and almost pulled off a win. That was our seventh consecutive loss in the Telstra Cup, either side of the English excursion, and under two different coaches. So we weren't exactly odds-on favourites to topple Cronulla, not with the Sharks just coming off a 32–6 victory over the Broncos. It was a real cliff hanger, not a classic, but just the tonic we needed when we held on to win 11–8. Matthew Ridge made a welcome return, as did the immensely talented Awen Guttenbeil, but Ridgey aggravated a calf injury and was sidelined again.

An 18–8 win over the Rams at Adelaide Oval would have lifted us off the bottom of the league, until news came through that North Queensland had upset the Hunter Mariners to retain the status quo. Our World Club Challenge home matches followed before we took a hammering from the Bulldogs and then completed our Super League season with high scoring wins over Perth and North Queensland. We had clawed our way up to seventh.

Ridgey contributed two tries and five goals against Perth before doing another disappearing act. This time he was cited by the judiciary for twice using his infamous feet-first try-saving technique. He accepted a one-match ban to be available for the second test at North Harbour. Stephen Kearney, who had accepted a new contract which was to last until after the 2000 season, had another blinder against the Cowboys and Marc Ellis was his dazzling best in snaring a hat-trick of tries.

There was good news for the other Warriors teams. The reserves qualified fourth for their play-offs and the under-19s did even better by winning the minor premiership. Gary Kemble's reserves then knocked over Cronulla, Perth and North Queensland to make another grand final. They were always expected to battle against a Bulldogs outfit that had cleared out in the regular season, and were up against it in losing 12–40.

The careers of some of the reserve grade forwards were moving in opposite directions. Jerry Seuseu was the team's Player of the Year and earned a fulltime contract for 1998, while discarded test prop Grant Young and former first grade crowd favourite Hitro Okesene were on their way out of the club. Their experience in that last season benefited the younger guys.

The under-19s won 13 of their 18 regular season games under coach John Ackland to take the minor premiership title ahead of Penrith, which has a vast junior development programme, on points differentials. And they did it without sensational winger Lesley Vainikolo, who wanted to keep his career options open and stuck to local football with Mangere East. The Warriors Colts beat Penrith 27–12 in the first round of play-offs, only to lose to them 18–22 in the grand final. Forwards Ali Lauiti'iti and David Solomona, plus Monty Betham, who was then playing at stand-off half, were signed to protect them being poached by other clubs.

The future of the Warriors was looking rosy through the deeds of the lower grade teams. But the great Super League boast about providing semi-professional football for our best young players was about to be snuffed out. It is significant that Lex Clarke's Junior Kiwis had beaten the Junior Kangaroos at Sydney on Anzac Day and lost by only four points in the return game five months later. There were 11 Warriors among the 21 players used in those two games, but only Betham and Lauiti'iti were still with the club in 2001. However, we never lost many players we really wanted to keep. It irked me when adverse comments were made about our junior development policy. I believe it was the best in the Australasian competition and we proved that with the successes we enjoyed in reserve grade and the under-19s. I still believe to this day we were threatening to get that good the Australians just couldn't wait to get us out of there because they could see us being a major threat for years to come.

The worst decision that ever went against the Warriors was the abandonment of the reserve grade and colts competitions. Bill MacGowan and I said that publicly at the time and it has been repeated by other people since. Bill and I worked out ways to include our other teams in Australian competitions. We were prepared to assist our opponents with accommodation in Auckland. All they had to do was cross the Tasman once each in a season and we could have gone over there every second week. But the Australians were not keen to play us, even with such favourable financial terms.

It would have benefited the Warriors more than any other club to have retained the reserves and under-19s, and introduce the under-17s who had also been included in the Super League blueprint. Not only were the juniors abandoned but reserve grade was also cut. Some of our most promising talent was left stranded in Australia. Now there are dozens of young New Zealanders taking off to Australia each year to try and make it, only to get lost in the crowd over there. They find jobs, girlfriends, a new way of life, and are lost forever with no compensation to their former clubs and provinces.

It's good that the New Zealand Rugby League introduced national competitions in 2002 for the 18s and 16s, but you can't compare a few weeks of football with what the Australians have in place to develop their kids. Over there they have fiercely competitive representative football from the age of 15. The gap could get bigger. I think the Bartercard Cup competition is the best we can possibly do and I applaud it. It's a damn good concept. But instead of bringing in new teams and keeping the number at 12 for the 2002 season the NZRL should have reduced it to 10, or maybe even eight, to further lift playing standards. Twelve is too many. All the Auckland clubs and some unproven provinces wanted to be involved and because of the vote-catching policies of those who make the decisions they have had their way. An eight-team competition would be more intense and better for those Warriors waiting in the wings. It's no good for them if you get to the stage where teams are winning 60–0.

At the end of '97 Bill MacGowan and I knew we could not do much to bolster the squad. We in fact had restraints put on us by a board that was wading through an alarming set of financial records. We were trying to prune contracts and didn't have a pot of gold to go out and buy players like many other clubs. But we were delighted to get Kevin Iro and Tyran Smith for nothing from Super League when the Hunter Mariners went through.

We also signed Quentin Pongia. It still needs to be clarified that we did not give Lesley Vainikolo to Canberra as any part of an exchange deal for Pongia. Some people labelled that to be the worst 'deal' the Warriors had made. Lesley Vainikolo was never ours to trade to anybody. We spoke to Lesley's manager, who was a member of his family, and did everything we could to sign him. Any suggestion of a swap is rubbish, as they were completely separate negotiations. Lesley was going to Canberra regardless. Canberra offered him something like double what we could afford, so we couldn't compete on that basis. Lesley also saw Canberra coach Mal Meninga as his boyhood hero and wanted to go play for him. With that combination of good money and hero worship we were never in the race. The North Queensland Cowboys, through Tim Sheens, actually offered Lesley three times more than we did and still he went to Canberra. Even the doubters must realise it's significant that when Mal Meninga finished up at Canberra after the 2001 season Lesley went off to join the Bradford Bulls. But some people don't want the facts to get in the way of a good story.

Quentin Pongia was available because he was keen to return home and because Canberra was prepared to release him, apparently because of his poor judiciary record. We were in the market for a tough prop, went for him, and got him. Reports we spent over $450,000 on Quentin were just rubbish. I am not prepared to reveal details of personal contracts but he was paid only what he was worth on the market at that time.

The critics always talk about so-called bad deals the Warriors have made. Bill MacGowan and I signed Nigel Vagana from Warrington on one of the best deals you would ever make. We got Nigel, who was the leading try-scorer in the British Super League despite playing for a lowly placed team, well under budget, but that was never mentioned. To be fair to Nigel I think his subsequent transfer to the Bulldogs was a smart career move. Being at an old-character Australian club has installed something extra, a bit of bite, to his game. He has always been without peer at sniffing out tries and his defence is much firmer than it used to be.

David Solomona was an enigma when I was at the Warriors. I can understand that people are puzzled why he didn't make it in Auckland yet has thrived with Sydney City and now Parramatta, so much so that he has played in two grand finals and Gary Freeman promoted him into the 2001 Kiwi squad.

I believe I knew everything about the young David Solomona from A to Z. As a coaching staff we would discuss week after week how we could improve him, especially trainer Bob Lanigan. His work ethics, or lack of them, meant we could not play him in first grade. I would stand on the white line at our fitness shuttles and tell Solomona he must put his foot on that line. But he would pull up short every time. He was always looking for short cuts and that didn't impress me. I always knew Solomona had as much ability as any player I have seen, and he has proven that. But you don't just get into a team on natural ability alone. If you haven't got the proper work ethics you don't get into one of my teams at all. Solomona would drive Bob Lanigan mad. Bob would try everything he knew to get weight off him and get him properly fit.

Solomona was inclined to hang his head too easily. Obviously, the best thing he ever did was head for Australia and get out of his old environment. Since he arrived at Parramatta he has matured under the Brian Smith regime. But it still suits Solomona's game to go hard in short bursts off the interchange bench. He can have you pulling your hair out because of his compulsion to pass the ball every time he has it. He will get one magic pass away that might be the pass of the year, but his next three will hit the deck while the commentators are still raving about that first one. We were trying to get away from mistakes at the Warriors, not increase them.

Denis Betts had also arranged to finish up at the end of the '97 season. He had only shown glimpses of the form that made him a legend in his native Wigan. But Betts will not be the last player who could not adjust to the style of football in a different hemisphere, as any number of Australians and New Zealanders have learned when tarnishing big reputations in England.

Having separate ARL and Super League competitions obviously alienated many true blue rugby league fans and turned off people from outside the game. I think we all welcomed the news there would be one 20-team National Rugby League competition in 1998. Even that good news was bad for some, though. Among the casualties were expansion clubs Adelaide and Perth, where so much spade work had been done and was wasted. Somehow the NRL wasn't as 'national' as the competitions it had replaced.

Nor would the gaping wounds, many ending life-long friendships in Australia, be healed overnight. Those who had benefited most from the big boosts to their bank balances and assets were the players. That's if you don't count Sydney's legal fraternity. It was clear most clubs would experience difficulties for years to come, as they strained to pay off the inflated and ongoing contracts signed at the height of the war. The Warriors were no different in that respect.

But 1998 loomed as something for me to look forward to. The chance to try and lift the Warriors up the points table was only half the attraction. There were also to be three tests against a united Australian team, two of them at home, leading up to a three-test tour of Britain. Little did I know it was going to be a year which, despite bringing considerable success on the international scene, made me feel I was lumping a sack of coal around on my shoulders while trying to present a positive image for the sport.

Chapter 10.

1998: The worst of times

None of Frank Endacott's predecessors as Kiwi coach had taken on the workload he willingly faced, indeed relished, in 1998. New Zealand was to confirm its place in the international rankings by playing a three-test series against the reunited Kangaroos, then undergo a three-test series in the Lions' den. Those assignments alone were not unique. But Endacott was also approaching his first full season in charge of the Auckland Warriors as the Australian Rugby League and Super League clubs got back together again. Despite a resounding Anzac test win over Australia and unbeaten run in Britain, Endacott admits he derived little enjoyment from it all. It was not the coaching duties that wore him down – only one test match clashed with the Warriors season – but rather it was the political posturing as the vultures wheeled above the vulnerable Warriors. When the Auckland Rugby League put up the 'for sale' sign, they swooped.

The task ahead of the Auckland Warriors had not been made easier by the introduction of the 20-team National Rugby League competition. Some of the supposedly weaker links had been cut from the previous year and it was clear that numbers would be further reduced in the near future. Many clubs saw 1998 as a season for survival, but we backed ourselves to be competitive.

We were expecting, after our promising finish in '97, to have a big year, and ultimately recorded wins over five of the top 10 teams. But it didn't pan out that way, and nor did it start at all well when Tyran Smith had a shocker with his hands and Terry Hermansson scored the try which broke our back in an 18–24 loss to South Sydney at home. Then after trailing the Knights 4–6 at halftime in Newcastle, we not only collapsed to lose 4–33 but also had Quentin Pongia suspended for four matches.

After a heartening 25–24 defeat of Sydney City in the third round, the video referee awarded St George centre Mark Coyne a try even though he didn't know he had scored as the Dragons pipped us 24–28 at Kogarah. So it went on, with the first of two wins over eventual third place-getter Melbourne, then a heavy loss at North Sydney aggravated by Stephen Kearney's subsequent suspension.

We weren't too far into the season before injuries took their toll. The suspensions of Pongia and Kearney overlapped, and Gene Ngamu, Syd Eru, and Shane Endacott were all simultaneously out with serious injuries. Zane Clarke, plucked out of the local Wellington competition, was playing hooker, Matthew Ridge was switched to stand-off half, and then I had to summon Aaron Whittaker up from Christchurch to fill in on a week-to-week basis.

Even with all the comings and goings the inconsistencies were disappointing. I am not surprised the fans were confused with our crazy form line. It confused me too. In the tenth round we beat the Bulldogs 20–6 at Belmore, the Warriors' first win in Sydney for two years, despite being down to 11 men when Jerry Seuseu was sent off and Matthew Ridge sin-binned. Referee Steve Clarke erred in dismissing Seuseu, who was later cleared.

Ridgey's sin-binning sparked the incident in which he was accused of spitting at a young Bulldogs fan who was yelling at him over the fence. Ridgey was a volatile player who walked a tightrope, sometime falling to the left, sometimes falling to the right. He got off-side with a lot of referees and the judiciary because of how he played the game. The spitting incident cost us a lot of time, money and disruptions to our training schedule before the charge was dropped through lack of proof.

Keeping the Bulldogs try-less had been a positive, and we were almost on a roll when we beat Canberra 25–14 at Ericsson a week later. That was Lesley Vainikolo's homecoming and we played on his nerves by kicking high to his wing. He dropped a Stacey Jones bomb for Nigel Vagana to score, then failed to handle a Matthew Ridge kick and Sean Hoppe scored. We knew Vainikolo was better than that but gambled that all the controversy about his departure and publicity about his return in a Canberra jersey would prey on his mind. Mal Meninga took him off during the game.

In mid-season we went on a real roller-coaster ride, down 4–12 to Parramatta after referee Matt Hewitt disallowed two tries in a display which led to his demotion to reserve grade, up 15–14 over Penrith in Auckland when Gene Ngamu kicked a vital field goal, down 16–18 to Western Suburbs at Campbelltown, up with wins at home against St George 31–14 and away over Melbourne 24–21, then down again in losing 14–17 to Illawarra at Ericsson. It was mind-boggling stuff, for the coaching staff as much as the fans.

The impressive victory over St George had our supporters, and critics, asking why we could beat top teams one week yet lose to those near the bottom the next week. I guess no one has yet unearthed the answer to that one. It was the likes of North Queensland Cowboys and Wests Tigers that prevented the 2001 Warriors from climbing further up the NRL table than eighth, despite Daniel Anderson's side beating six of the seven clubs which finished above them.

We were happy to take the wins as they came along. Tea Ropati proved a success at lock forward against St George, Joe Vagana had one of his vintage games, and young Joe Galuvao filled in most ably for Matthew Ridge at fullback. Stacey Jones was experiencing a mixed season behind a pack that was seldom at full strength. But Stacey and the forwards lifted against the Dragons and even two brilliant Nathan Blacklock tries could not make the result close.

Years later Radio Sport was still replaying commentator Allen McLaughlin screaming 'It's a miracle' after the sensational finish to our win in Melbourne. Quentin Pongia stripped the ball from rival forward Russell Bawden when the Storm only had to play out time. As the siren sounded a bomb went up, it rebounded from Syd Eru, and was passed to Tony Tatupu. There was chaos when Tony scored. Melbourne players claimed obstruction and video referee Peter Filmer watched what for us was an agonising eight replays before awarding the try.

The escape meant we had won five of our last seven matches and expectations were rising again. But the momentum was halted by a poor performance against Illawarra at home. The only New Zealander to catch the eye that day was Craig Smith in the Steelers' front-row. He had his name entered in my notebook for the end-of-season tour to Britain, but that was the only benefit I got from a game that could have been won with a reliable goalkicker. Matthew Ridge was already missing, Gene Ngamu got hurt early, and Stacey Jones duffed a couple of simple shots.

We simply could not afford to lose to Gold Coast at Carrara Stadium in round 18, but we went to great lengths to do just that. We sank without trace with hardly a whimper. Gold Coast had won only three games to that point yet led us by 18 points by halftime. We recovered sufficiently to trail 18–23 but then conceded another eight points and that was our lot for the season.

It was the lowest feeling I experienced while at the Warriors. In my diary I made the comment 'Are you brain dead?', as the theme of my halftime bollocking. Then I added: 'The worst effort of the season, too many mistakes, ball control pathetic, no one wanted to go forward, our attack was too flat.' We had a side which was capable of beating Gold Coast by 30 points but that was the killer.

A Stacey Jones field goal was the difference in a 21–20 defeat of Balmain at home as we did another circuit of the roller-coaster. Syd Eru was knocked out for the season with a knee injury to make our 20–22 loss at Adelaide even more nasty. Kevin Iro had performed erratically all season but his two tries in a storming display was all too much for North Queensland when we beat them 34–18 at Ericsson.

The season just melted away after that. Souths completed a double at our expense by winning 20–18 at Sydney, two of their tries coming while Brady Malam was in the sin-bin. The Broncos' defence was too strong despite a gritty effort in losing 4–16 at Brisbane, and we finished in farcical fashion against Manly in front of 12,000 home fans, who deserved better for their perseverance.

Manly did us up good at 38–12 but not before both Nigel Vagana and Stacey Jones, two of the slickest finishers in the game, lost the ball after brilliant lead-up work put them across Manly's goal-line. Someone wrote that the wasted opportunities fittingly summed up our season, and they weren't wrong.

The team we hoped would make us competitive wouldn't have run onto the field together more than once or twice. Stacey Jones and Logan Swann lined up for all 24 games, Stephen Kearney played 21, but Matthew Ridge and Quentin Pongia had only 18 apiece, Gene Ngamu 17, Kevin Iro 16, Sean Hoppe 15, Syd Eru 13, Tyran Smith 10 — and five of those were off the bench.

Marc Ellis appeared only twice in first grade before returning to rugby union in mid-season. Marc was struggling with the game of rugby league, partly because he had other things on his mind. His television work was a distraction and there was heavy public pressure for him to perform after all those figures about players' salaries were published. Marc never stopped trying and he wanted to learn. Unfortunately, the harder Marc tried the more mistakes he seemed to make. He wasn't suited to the tight defences in league. In the rare 'open' games he was in his element, such as when he scored three tries against the Cowboys. Generally, you don't get too much space against Australian defences. Marc was more in his element in rugby union, which is ironic

The undefeated 1994 New Zealand Residents after beating Australian Residents at Brisbane's Lang Park.

Not just pretty faces. Most of these Steelers women's club touch players went on to gain provincial and national honours.

The best of both worlds, having just been appointed to coach the Kiwis and the Auckland Warriors reserve grade team.

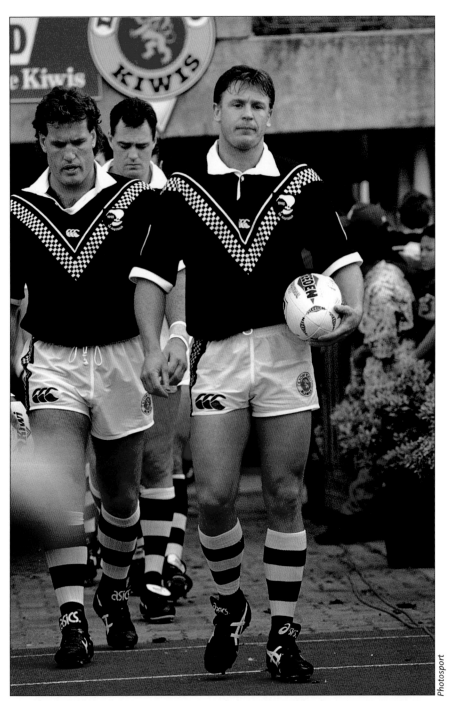

Serious business. Kiwis captain (and current coach) Gary Freeman leads
Brent Todd and Daryl Halligan out for the drawn first test of the 1993
Australian series.

Matthew Ridge in typically combative pose with Manly in 1994. Has he just given someone a spray? Or is he just about to?

Tawera Nikau taking the ball up against the 1991 French team at Christchurch in one of his all too rare test appearances.

Great bloke, great captain. Duane Mann's international career was cut short by a selection panel split decision in 1995.

It took the 1995 World Cup Kiwis 73 minutes to recover from this Tongan war dance and rescue an unlikely victory at Warrington.

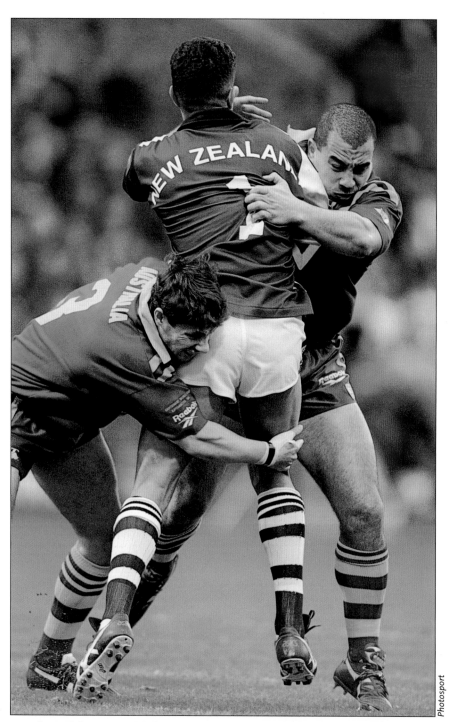

Matthew Ridge gets a lift from Kangaroos Mark Coyne and Jim Dymock during the dramatic 1995 extra-time World Cup semi-final at Huddersfield.

considering there are four more men on the field. He adapted back quickly when he went to North Harbour.

On the credit side, Jerry Seuseu started only once but he was a replacement in another 16 games. It is pleasing to see he has gone on to make the Kiwis and be the Warriors' Player of the Year in 2001. Ali Lauiti'iti was also destined for big things and was taken to Britain at the end of the year as part of his learning curve.

We had some fair wins and a lot of losses were by margins where the bounce of the ball or the 50–50 decisions going in your favour can make all the difference. But the reality was we finished fifteenth of the 20 teams. Four of the sides under us, Adelaide, Souths (twice), Gold Coast and Western Suburbs, had wins at our expense, cancelling out our victories over play-off teams Melbourne (twice), Sydney City, Canberra, St George, and Canterbury. At least we escaped the 60-point thrashings that even some top title contenders suffered, but that was scant consolation.

The sniping increased as the season progressed, most of it coming from Graham Lowe and Malcolm Boyle, who were among those lobbying to buy the club from the Auckland Rugby League. It was more than a coincidence to me that every shot was fired in the week before a major match. For example, the infamous 'Assignment' television programme about league and the Warriors was aired just before the Kiwis were to play a series-deciding test match against Australia.

I was an admirer of Graham Lowe when he was coaching the Kiwis. I was in awe of him, as were most coaches coming up through the system. He did a great job with the New Zealand team and I'm the first to respect that. But when I first took over the Kiwis I was given warnings about Lowe poking his nose where it wasn't wanted. I couldn't understand what they were saying and couldn't see it happening to me. But I got to know exactly what they were talking about. Lowe could never give it away and let the new coach do his own thing. The constant sniping was something I didn't need. With his profile in the game, and mine, I think if we had combined forces it would have been very good for rugby league as a whole. I never once came out and bagged Lowe to start an argument. But I was guilty on a couple of occasions of retaliating. Some of his criticisms were getting pretty pointed and it was time to bite back. The bagging I put up with from him in 1998 was nothing less than disgraceful.

I have no doubts whatsoever that Graham Lowe was doing it to undermine Bill MacGowan, myself, and the players at the club for one reason — to sway public opinion against us with the objective of buying the club at the lowest possible price.

I don't know whether it was personal or just because I happened to be the Warriors coach. Sometimes I took it personally because the shots were directed at me and I had to reply to them. It was always my name in his newspaper column, or Bill MacGowan's. Some I let go through to the 'keeper but others had to be answered. In June I told a journalist: 'Lowe is talking as though he has already bought the club. Someone should tell him the Warriors are not yet even for sale.' This was in response to statements made by Lowe that he had invited Australian legend Wally Lewis to be chief executive and former Australian Rugby League chairman Ken Arthurson to become a director, with former Kiwi captains Mark Graham and Hugh McGahan in mind as coach and football manager, respectively.

A press release just happened to be issued by Arthurson, who was then chairman of Manly, saying the Warriors 'desperately needed Graham Lowe's experience and expertise'. The release was reported to have come from the public relations company owned by Malcolm Boyle, who was Lowe's partner, along with the Tainui Trust, in a consortium seeking to buy the Warriors from the Auckland Rugby League and its clubs.

Of course, all that was orchestrated, and once again it was timed to coincide with a big game. If Ken Arthurson was so keen on saving a club with Graham Lowe's help I suggested it be Manly, where they had previously worked together. As it turned out, Manly was merged with arch rival North Sydney to form the Northern Eagles, based up on the Central Coast, but only until that unholy alliance fell apart late in the 2001 season.

Lowe's so-called 'dream team' to rescue the Warriors were all his old cronies. Arthurson had lured him from Wigan to coach Manly. Lewis was his Queensland captain when Lowe coached the State of Origin team. Graham was with him in the Kiwis, Manly and North Queensland camps. McGahan succeeded Graham as Kiwi captain in 1986, Lowe's last season.

When you analysed it, Lowe had lost the plot. What credentials did Lewis have as a chief executive? He couldn't even attract top players to the Gold Coast when he was their coach. I also questioned Mark Graham's coaching pedigree. At Manly, Lowe had all the pin-up boys in the competition, a huge budget, and still did not make a grand final. They cleaned up when Bob Fulton returned. And these blokes were going to take the Warriors to the top. Lowe replied to my criticisms by saying I was paranoid, then started rattling through all the names again, Arthurson, Lewis and company. I can't recall Arthurson ever turning up as a Warriors director, and Lewis' worth as a chief executive will forever remain a mystery. Lowe also denied Mark Graham was lined up to coach the team and blamed that on media speculation. Not surprisingly, it turned out to be the only accurate claim in his original story.

I also tried to protect the players he was getting at. Lowe had no reason to talk publicly about the salaries of our leading players. He would not have liked his salary being discussed, or his spending while he was at the Warriors to be made public. To go on, for instance, about Matthew Ridge being paid too much money showed he had a very short memory. When Lowe was at the North Queensland Cowboys, he offered Ridge a lot more money than he was paid at the Warriors. Ridge made the comment he wouldn't go to Townsville at any price. If you are going to snipe at people you have to make sure you don't leave yourself as a target.

Public debate about the club being sold was a big enough problem for the players to get their heads around without direct input from vested interests. When we went to Brisbane to play the Broncos in August the match programme quoted Lowe as saying, 'If we are successful (in buying the club) we will be making substantial changes to the Auckland front office.' That does a lot for a side's confidence when the odds are already stacked against it. Changing a club's ownership means new people in charge of the team and contracted players being given the flick.

The king hit was the 'Assignment' programme on Television New Zealand in October, screened on the night before the third test against Australia at North Harbour Stadium. Perfect timing if someone was trying to prevent the Kiwis from clinching our first test series victory over Australia for 45 years. We had won the Anzac test at North Harbour six months earlier, lost the second test at Brisbane the previous Friday night, and were trying to pull off the toughest task in rugby league.

Word was leaked in time to ensure the programme had a maximum audience, and must have had the Warriors', and rugby league's, detractors rubbing their hands with glee. The Kiwis actually had a training session scheduled for the test venue at the time the programme was shown — we always did that 24 hours before a test to get accustomed to the conditions — but the players could not help but be distracted by the furore.

Promotions for the show featured Lowe claiming Matthew Ridge was 'earning $56,000 a month'. Ridgey was laid up with the chest injury he suffered in Brisbane and which caused his abrupt retirement from international football. He was seething, having just decided to direct all of his energies towards the Warriors in 1999. Lowe had already alienated the man he most needed on his side the following year. Smart move that.

New Zealand Rugby League president Gerald Ryan commented that because the consortium had not then bought the Warriors they had no right to discuss confidential issues in public. Stephen Kearney voiced the players' concerns. But there was no way the programme was going to be withdrawn after all the free publicity for Television New Zealand. I hope their ratings justified the dirty game they were playing.

Not only did Lowe take a stab at Ridge's salary, he also reckoned the player he himself had signed for Manly from an All Black trial in 1990 was 'a little bit out of control'. Lowe had already upset Ridge by saying he could not continue his television work. Now he came up with the comment: 'It appears to me Matthew is more interested in the dollar than his playing performance.'

Lowe compared the higher paid players' alleged earnings with the average annual wage of most New Zealanders. He targeted Ridge, Stephen Kearney, Sean Hoppe, Stephen Kearney and Syd Eru, suggesting he would be seeking to place them with other clubs because the Warriors could not afford to keep them. In another promise that never materialised, Lowe announced his intention of signing top rugby union players and named former All Black Ofisa Tonu'u as a target. Didn't he know the other code had turned professional?

As for me, the viewers were told I had no future at the club. Lowe said he had lost confidence in me during the year because the Warriors were performing badly and I refused to drop players who deserved it. According to Lowe, I wasn't tough enough to do the job.

Comments like that really bugged me, and a lot of other people, because they simply weren't true. It was nothing short of a joke. I have dropped players all my coaching life. But I don't drop players for the sake of it, because we suffered a two-point loss in a game in which we competed well enough to win. What happens if you drop proven players, replace them with younger players, and get thrashed? The knives come out again. You have to take the park with your best available team and I always did that. In the confines of a small squad you don't have too many options.

Should I have gone through Lowe's selections from the season he was coaching North Queensland, and asked why he made or didn't make certain changes? He didn't exactly have a good year in Townsville. I would have preferred he had spoken to me personally — but that would have deprived him of his public stage.

I can remember Lowe ringing me at home in Auckland and asking me out in his boat on Sydney harbour if I could stay over for an extra day or two during one of our trans-Tasman trips in '98. It hurt to realise later he was already plotting my downfall. How can you trust a man like that?

One television reviewer, with no apparent rugby league affiliations, was amazed Lowe would involve himself in the Assignment programme while New Zealand was engaged in a test series with our arch-enemy. The Wellington Evening Post said: 'If Lowe set out to undermine Endacott's preparation with the

Kiwi team on the eve of tonight's test match with Australia he couldn't have picked a better time.' The reviewer said Lowe should have refrained from commenting until after the match. 'Instead, Lowe made crystal clear his lack of respect and regard for Endacott as a coach, saying he would be sacked as soon as Lowe was confirmed as co-owner of the struggling club. Lowe must have known that Endacott would hear these comments, but can't have cared.' Even a television scribe knew more about backing New Zealand's national team to try and win a trans-Tasman series than someone who had spent years trying to achieve that very goal.

In the end it wasn't Lowe's television antics that beat us. Wayne Bennett's Kangaroos gave one of the smartest team performances I have seen, and that was enough. Most writers were kind enough to say we had played as well as we had in winning the Anzac test when Bob Fulton was in charge of the Kangaroos. It was to the immense credit of our players that they were not thrown completely off stride by the Assignment programme.

Unfortunately, Lowe wasn't finished. We still had three tests to play in Britain. While we were there — nicely timed between the second and third tests — he struck again with an almost full-page story in the Sydney *Sunday Telegraph*. Copies of the article were soon coming out of our fax in England. There were photographs of his now familiar targets, Ridge, Kearney, Pongia, Hoppe and Eru, with sums of money printed underneath. The big threat in the story, as always, was contract cuts to 'save the much maligned Warriors from financial ruin and further public embarrassment in New Zealand'. At least by then the sale had been confirmed, Mark Graham was installed as coach, and former Auckland journalist and Super League publicist Trevor McKewen had been named chief executive.

Probably the most significant paragraph in the whole story read: 'Now the whip is in [Lowe's] hand. Failure to turn around the club's fortunes will make him look silly.' Enough said. When Lowe got his opportunity he blew it, fell out with his mates, and was sacked by Tainui. Lowe never delivered anything he had promised.

Should the Warriors have been sold after that 1998 season? I believe the club needed an injection of cash because Bill MacGowan and myself were operating under real restraints. Bill was never given the accolades he deserved for his sterling work. I could see what was happening behind the scenes. He was making decisions that hurt him, having to put people off left, right and centre. We would have loved a bigger coaching staff around us but we couldn't afford it. The Auckland Rugby League never put anything into the Warriors.

I was never one for politics or getting involved with any of the syndicates that were hovering around. My feeling was if I was wanted, so be it, if not I would always survive. There was so much backbiting going on and so many rumours about different syndicates I just divorced myself from it completely and concentrated on the football side of affairs. The only time I breached those boundaries was to have a crack at Lowe every so often because I thought he had gone over the top. I don't believe for one moment we were the embarrassment he portrayed to the public, and he left himself open by criticising my coaching capabilities.

I had just beaten Australia in the best win the Kiwis had enjoyed for years, then went to Britain and broke a 91-year-old record by not losing a test. It wasn't too bad a year overall. I might have lost my job at the Warriors but there were more positives than negatives. Not too many coaches in professional sport avoid being sacked during their careers. It's a bit like being heavyweight boxing champion — not many of them retire undefeated.

If certain people had shown more patience, better results would have followed. There were too many hidden agendas, individuals working for themselves rather than the game. Rugby league is not short of people trying to do good work, but they are constantly cut down by other factions. It happens all over, not just in New Zealand.

Selwyn Pearson looked me in the eye on several occasions during '98 when he was Auckland Rugby League chairman and said, 'Frank, read my lips, I am telling you now that Graham Lowe will never own the club while I have anything to do with it.' So what was going on behind closed doors at that time? Pearson succeeded Gerald Ryan as New Zealand Rugby League president in 2001 and before long had become a virtual executive chairman.

It is impossible to speculate why Graham Lowe was still attacking the players after he had wrested control of the club and while they were touring Britain with the Kiwis. He just wouldn't leave it alone. I can't repeat the words expressed by the players about Lowe.

During the off-season Stephen Kearney went off to Melbourne and subsequently shared in their 1999 premiership triumph, and Quentin Pongia signed for Sydney City. Both took less money to get away from the new Warriors management. But Kearney's premiership ring is priceless and an everlasting trophy from a distinguished professional career. It's a shame Pongia suffered a serious injury after Kangaroo legend Arthur Beetson said he could make all the difference between winning and losing a premiership for the Roosters. Syd Eru played only twice for the Warriors in 1999, and Sean Hoppe lost his try-scoring touch with only two in 13 appearances.

Matthew Ridge was reappointed captain by Mark Graham but got on the field only 10 times. Ridgey would never have allowed his contract to be altered at his expense. The new owners were always going to find him a tough negotiator. Like most, Matthew likes a dollar and wasn't going to give any away. They claimed to have 'restructured' his contract, which probably meant paying him the same amount but on a different day of the month. Ridgey also got into a lot of strife in 1999, what with the business of handling referee Paul Simpkins, the facial he allegedly gave Lesley Vainikolo, and being sent off on a tripping charge in Melbourne. He hardly played but still got paid. Was this the discipline we were accused of lacking the year before? How ironic that six months after leaving the place Ridgey was dancing through the door again to terminate the contracts of Trevor McKewen and company. Ridgey is a smart man. He knew which side of the line to go and picked a winner in new owner Eric Watson.

It did not take me long to wonder how the Warriors would fare under the new regime, if the circumstances of my payout were to be taken as a guide. Trevor McKewen and the new owners were keen to settle up before I left on the Kiwi tour, so we completed negotiations the night before departure. The discussions went on for hours during the day and into the night with my solicitor, two solicitors from Tainui, and McKewen present around the table.

We agreed the cheque would be paid by 5pm on a certain date, a Friday, after I returned from England. Five o'clock came and went and there was no cheque. I gave them another hour before contacting my solicitor, who recommended I track down McKewen. So I rang his cell phone and found him in the Glenfield Hotel. He said he would have the cheque to me in an hour. Seven o'clock came and still no sign of it. He rang me back and apologised, the words a little more slurred since the previous time, and told me eight o'clock.

To cut a long story short, there was a knock on my door at 11 o'clock that night. Standing on the step was an Indian taxi driver wearing a turban. He just handed me the cheque, which was not even in an envelope. I thought if that's how professional they are then they are going to be in trouble. I am not prepared to divulge what the payout was. I don't have to. Just ask the next turbaned Indian taxi driver you flag down in Auckland how much I got paid. For the record, it was a fair settlement for both parties.

Graham Lowe was not the only one to get my dander up. In September there was an article about Tea Ropati in the Australian *Rugby League Week*, written by former Auckland journalist Jim Marr. It was a load of ill-informed rubbish and deserves a response.

I always admired Tea as a footballer and a person. I really liked him and his family. But he was suffering a lot of injuries when he was up for renewal of his contract. I had medical advice that told me not to re-sign Tea, and I should have taken it, but I didn't. Because of his long service to Auckland and New Zealand rugby league I offered him a good, fair deal. It wasn't the highest contract around but it was enough to cover his family's needs and was incentive-based so that if he played the games required it would be a very good deal from his point of view. What I did exposed my soft side, and then I was gobsmacked to read Tea's interview with Marr.

It claimed Tea had reacted with disgust, quoting him (in reference to Bill McGowan and myself), 'Last week they said they would give me a pittance to stay on, but this week they gave me the brush. That doesn't surprise me because it's typical of them.' Marr went on to criticise every aspect of the Warriors, right back to when they first kicked a football. He didn't mention how few games Tea had started in 1998 (10 of 24), that he was 33 years old, and medically unsound.

Tea had asked for $50,000, as he told Marr, and I offered him less. But he could have more than made up the difference in incentives if he was fit enough to play. Tea also overlooked something else. When he was laid up with his crook knees I offered to come around with a crew of players to mow his lawns and do his garden to help out. When I read things like that I wonder if I did too much for players at times. It was the case of a player not being able to accept that his career was just about over and not wanting to grasp the lifeline offered him.

Marr claimed at least two of the three groups then vying to buy the Warriors, respectively headed by Graham Lowe, Dean Lonergan and some Mount Albert officials, had told Tea he figured in their plans for 1999. Lowe must have been the odd one out because Tea didn't make his squad.

Twelve months later, after watching a women's test match at Leichhardt Oval in Sydney, I was going down to the players' tunnel to congratulate the Kiwi Ferns on their win when Jim Marr came running after me. I hadn't seen him since the *Rugby League Week* story on Tea Ropati and other articles that had included digs at me and the management staff. Marr asked me if there was any chance of getting the Kiwi touring team I was about to announce, promising to embargo it. I told him I wouldn't give him the time of day, let alone the Kiwi squad. One word led to another and I suggested he get lost. I don't know what part of the message he didn't understand but when he wouldn't go away I threatened to knock him over. He kept arguing so I took off my suit coat. Just when he was about to get one on the end of his beak Dale Husband and a television crew walked around the corner. To this day they don't know they were about two seconds from getting the scoop of the year on camera. Jim Marr finally realised how serious I was, and I haven't seen him since.

It had nothing to do with Tea Ropati, but his brother, Peter, also got on my wick on Sky Television. Peter was continually saying he had serious question marks over the defensive plan of the Warriors and wondered aloud whether they were being coached properly. It was happening too frequently so I rang Peter one day from Bill MacGowan's office with the telephone speaker on. The conversation went along these lines: 'Peter, I was interested in hearing your remarks the other night about doubting the coaching and defensive plans of the Warriors. We've got a training session at 10 o'clock tomorrow morning and I'm inviting you down to explain to the team what you mean. In fact, you can help with the session if you have knowledge that I haven't got.' After some stuttering, Peter said he had three appointments the next day and couldn't get there. 'Well, that's okay Peter, we'll make it the following day because I'm really interested in hearing what you are trying to get across to the public.' Peter told me he didn't think there was any need for him to attend a training run. After a little more discussion I told him he had shown me just how big his balls were.

In fairness to Peter Ropati, he contacted me after that call and we met in a restaurant in Royal Oak and chatted about our problems. I have got on with him all right since then. I just felt if he was making criticisms he should be able to back them up.

I mention this as an example of how people hopped on the bandwagon as a result of comments from Graham Lowe and company. I felt I had to challenge him before it got any worse. When you call their bluff you catch them out. Coaching is not as easy as they think.

It wasn't all over when I left the Warriors at the end of 1998, either. There was a racist slur in a *New Zealand Truth* article the following March. It wasn't a paper I bought but someone suggested I check out a story headlined 'Club Tackles Racist Rift', written by their sports editor Doug Golightly. There was a big photograph of Mark Graham and the caption in quotes: 'Racism at its worst'. Even though my name wasn't printed, I was absolutely livid at the implication that the previous coaching staff was racist and that Trevor McKewen and his mates had to restore credibility with the Polynesian community.

I went straight to my solicitor's office and told him I didn't care what it cost: 'Let's sue the pants off these bastards.' Writs were served on McKewen and *Truth*. The matter was raised when I met with McKewen over a number of issues, with Peter Leitch as a mediator. I could not believe the way McKewen turned on his mate Doug Golightly, claiming he got it all wrong and that he, McKewen, was misquoted. My solicitor recommended we go ahead with the suit, *Truth* accepted liability, they published a major retraction, and paid all my legal fees. I didn't want any money out of it.

McKewen obviously had a massive chip on his shoulder and was really pathetic when he barred me from watching the Warriors from the Ericsson

Stadium press box after some journalists invited me to sit there. It was probably the most childish thing I have struck in my life and became a joke among the media guys. Not that McKewen had the guts to try to kick me out on the day. Instead, he wrote me a letter.

There had been another petty incident involving McKewen when I happened to be in Sydney for the Warriors' first match in '99 and saw them beat Sydney City at the Football Stadium. This time McKewen made comments to Sydney reporters criticising me for not having wished the players the best of luck. Bloody hell, as the former coach I would never have gone near that dressing room. If I had, McKewen would probably have accused me of undermining Mark Graham when he was preparing his team. It wasn't my place to be there, and ethics told me not to go there. I was out of the Warriors and had just gone along to support them from the grandstand.

The David Vaealiki affair also blew up in McKewen's face. I was accused of taking one of their scholarship players and diverting him to Parramatta when they wanted him at the Warriors. The truth was I received a call from his mum in Christchurch. She said the family wanted to talk to me and see if I could find a Sydney club for David. I had signed him on a Warriors scholarship but they told me on three occasions they couldn't get any answers about his future from the new management. It seemed to them the Warriors just wanted him to hang around in case he turned out all right.

I knew David Vaealiki's value from when he was 15. He had the best attitude of any young player in New Zealand, was head boy at his high school, and had football ability to match his other qualities. I offered to talk to Parramatta on his parents' behalf after they assured me they had exhausted all avenues with the Warriors. I contacted Eels coach Brian Smith and told him about David, saying I believed he would be a first grade player and an international, that he was a fullback who could also play centre. Smith said he would sign David on my word.

Before that happened, though, Parramatta checked with the Warriors to make sure he was cleared, and only then, after they had already had enough chances, did McKewen and the Warriors. I went back to David's parents and recommended they fly to Auckland, meet Mark Graham and Trevor McKewen, look at the facilities and see if they wanted to change their mind. I wasn't getting a cent out of this, I was doing it for the kid and would have been equally happy if he had chosen the Warriors.

I picked the parents up at Auckland airport, took them to Ericsson Stadium, didn't hang around, and collected them at the end of the day. Their comments were they didn't like the atmosphere around the place, were not impressed with the people they spoke to, and asked me to go ahead with Parramatta. Forget all those other stories, that is the truth of it.

The rest is history. David Vaealiki was the quick learner I always knew he would be and soon broke into first grade for Parramatta. If he had stayed in Auckland he would have been farmed out to a local club. Brian Smith has told me on at least two occasions that was the best tip he ever had on a player. I just thought Smith, and the way he works with young players, was the ideal coach for David. In 2000 David travelled to Britain with my World Cup squad and was blooded against the Cook Islands. Gary Freeman played him at centre against the Kangaroos at Wellington in 2001, and David set up both Kiwi tries. He went on to play in that year's NRL grand final. He would not have achieved all that from Auckland club football. It was not the first time the Warriors started performing like trained seals once it was rumoured a player was going elsewhere. Until then they were not even interested in David Vaealiki.

The so-called rock solid consortium that bought the Warriors was soon having internal strife. It was later revealed that Graham Lowe and Malcolm Boyle contributed only token amounts for their shares, while Tainui paid millions of dollars. Tainui sacked them from the board before the 2000 season and by July McKewen confirmed Mark Graham's future as coach was 'unclear'. A whole Who's Who of potential replacements were mentioned.

Fortunately, the New Zealand Rugby League found in Eric Watson a man with the money and ambition to save the club when its future was very bleak indeed. Trevor McKewen threw in his lot with the New Zealand Rugby Union, and Mark Graham went off to try and show the Auckland Blues and then the Italian rugby union team how to tackle. From eleventh of 14 teams in 1999, the Warriors had slumped to second-last of the 14 teams in 2000. During Mark Graham's coaching reign they played 50 games, won 18, lost 30, and drew two.

Chapter 11.
1998: The best of times

In the midst of all the ructions buffeting the Auckland Warriors, the 1998 Kiwis achieved one of the finest and most dramatic test match victories in New Zealand rugby league history. Frank Endacott thus became the first Kiwi coach to scheme consecutive wins over the Kangaroos since fellow Cantabrian Jim Amos in 1953. It was a magic occasion at North Harbour Stadium when Endacott's men overcame tremendous odds as a near capacity crowd went wild. The Australians, fielding their first united team since before the 1995 World Cup and under the command of revered coach Bob Fulton, were stunned.

Just to keep me on my toes during the summer some members of the New Zealand Rugby League board had revisited the old business of whether I should be 'assisted' by a selection panel. It seemed to me that the results achieved over the previous two seasons had justified my becoming a sole selector in 1996. We had won six of our seven tests, including three over Great Britain and one against the Australians.

President Gerald Ryan again backed me. A few of his colleagues apparently thought the unfortunate on-off availability of Tawera Nikau would not have happened if there had been a selection panel, and had even suggested I might favour Warriors players because of my dual coaching commitments. Those arguments just didn't hold water, sanity prevailed, and by the end of February I could concentrate on beating the Aussies. Not that you can ever completely beat our cousins from across the ditch, not off the field anyway. With test time looming, the Kiwis had to go through the annual high jinks with the National Rugby League judiciary. This time they got our two most experienced forwards. Quentin Pongia copped a four-game suspension, which meant he would be lacking match fitness for the Anzac test. But Stephen Kearney was fated to miss the test altogether when he was stood down for three weeks.

We would have worn Kearney's suspension had Kangaroo prop Paul Harragon not come up before the judiciary the same week, not on one charge but two. Harragon was deemed to be innocent of one offence and allowed to change his plea to guilty on the other. Then they got out the damp bus ticket, suspended him for one match, and effectively wished him all the best for the test against the Kiwis. With justice like that we figured if we had appealed Kearney's sentence he would have got life.

Losing Kearney was not our only problem. There was real doubt about who would play hooker and stand-off half with Syd Eru, Gene Ngamu, and their Warriors understudy, Shane Endacott, all injured. Then Kearney's replacement, 18-year-old Tony Puletua, damaged an ankle and lost the chance to displace Kurt Sorensen as New Zealand's youngest-ever test forward. John Lomax and Robbie Paul couldn't reach Auckland until the Tuesday, and Henry Paul flew in on Wednesday, only two days before the game. Had Henry been delayed en route, the next option was Aaron Whittaker. Then playing for Halswell in the Canterbury club competition, Whittaker was that close to becoming New Zealand's last test player selected from domestic football.

Some of our Australian Rugby League-aligned players were back too. Terry Hermansson was recalled for the first time since my first tour to Papua New Guinea in 1994, and Jarrod McCracken was not only on deck after a three-year absence but had been transformed into a specialist second-row forward. His 15 previous tests were in the centres but at Cairns in '94 I tried Jarrod as a back-rower and Parramatta followed that lead in '97.

When the squad assembled it had a patched-up appearance and early trainings were sloppy. Thoughts of positioning Matthew Ridge at stand-off half were soon discarded. So Ridge reverted to fullback, Richie Barnett to the wing, Robbie Paul was slotted into stand-off, and Henry Paul drew what might have been regarded as the short straw at hooker.

Meanwhile, Bob Fulton had the 'problems' of choosing Andrew Johns at scrum-half ahead of Alfie Langer, and naming Laurie Daley as captain and stand-off with Brad Fittler at lock forward. All the other stars were there, Wendell Sailor, Steve Renouf, Mat Rogers, Rodney Howe, Paul Harragon, Steve Menzies. It was the strongest Australian team we played while I was coaching the Kiwis.

At least all of our comings and goings had confused the Australian camp. Daley was busy fielding questions about how he would go about marking Ridge at stand-off. The pieces of our jigsaw fitted together perfectly late in the week and I went public 48 hours out predicting we were going to beat Australia by attacking them. We had quite a little family gathering really, with the Paul and Iro brothers and cousins Joe and Nigel Vagana in our 17. No one gave us any chance. We were something like $5.50 on the TAB head to head odds and the Kangaroos were unbackable. Centrebet in Australia was giving us 30 points start.

After our final team meeting, manager Gary Cooksley and I were convinced the Kangaroos were in for a whale of a game. We could tell by the players' attitudes they were ready for a huge effort. It actually became much more than that. For about 30 minutes of the second half we had only one sub left on the bench. It was the most courageous performance I have ever seen from a Kiwi team.

We lost John Lomax after 28 seconds when he pinched a nerve in his neck and was taken to hospital to be X-rayed. He heard most of the game on radio. Richie Barnett broke his left hand after half an hour when we were 2–12 down but ignored the pain to return and help shore up our defences in the closing stages. Jarrod McCracken also disappeared into the changing room to have stitches inserted in a gash above an eye, and both Quentin Pongia and Tony Iro needed medical attention during the fierce forward clash.

Make no mistake, the Aussies were hurting even more, both physically from the battering they took and mentally from being haunted by the 22–16 result on the scoreboard as they were trudging off. It wasn't a dirty game, no way, just the smashing of bone on bone, and flesh on flesh. Some damage was inevitable.

Though we were still behind at halftime the Kangaroos were getting stressed. Laurie Daley wasn't just making conversation when he admitted to Matthew Ridge he was 'knackered' as they walked off for the break. A gleeful Ridge reported the news to the dressing room, which further encouraged our blokes to go back out there and belt them all over again. Legally, that is. It was the toughest test match I was associated with.

Our bench, Joe and Nigel Vagana, Hermansson and Kevin Iro, was magnificent that night. We scored four tries in all and they got three between them. Kevin Iro monstered the Australians to get across twice and Terry Hermansson stormed over the top of two would-be tacklers for the most memorable try of his whole football career. Sean Hoppe also touched down from one of several handling mistakes made by Darren Lockyer, who had replaced Robbie O'Davis at fullback. The pressure on Lockyer was immense. He must have had nightmares of big Richie Blackmore, Ruben Wiki and Kevin Iro charging down on him for a long time.

I told Ruben as he was walking down the tunnel, 'Enjoy the first 20 minutes in the centres because you will be playing the rest of the game in the forwards.' Ruben had been a replacement lock in three tests but I didn't want him to dwell on the prospect of spending an hour there against this mob. He just gave his stock reply about being happy to play anywhere. Ruben had no choice as others fell about him, being drafted into the second row and even to hooker for a few scrums. I thought Ruben had his best game for New Zealand, and that is saying something. His defence was chilling at times, and he really pounded the Australians.

Kevin Iro produced one of his great games too, living up to the nickname of The Beast they had given him at Wigan. His first try cut the deficit to 6–12 by halftime. Although he scored his second try out near the wing, he was actually playing in the forwards by then. Nigel Vagana went on to make his debut when Richie Barnett broke his hand, and was immediately tested by a bomb to the in-goal area. Nigel stood firm and moments later Quentin Pongia, an inspirational forward leader, burst upfield in the move which led to Kevin Iro's first try.

Logan Swann was the quiet achiever of the pack, topping the tackle counts and playing the full 80 minutes because there was no one left to replace him. The Paul brothers were simply dazzling with their footwork and uncanny understanding of what each other was about to do. 'Backyard footy' I think they call it. They might have been wearing numbers six and nine on their backs but the Australian defence had the devil of a job reining them in.

All of the clichés were tossed around, about pride and passion, guts and determination, and the Anzac spirit, but they were really deserved. The players were conscious some cynics had sought to downgrade our '97 test win by saying Australia wasn't at full strength, ignoring the fact that we didn't field our top team either. We knew there could not be any doubts this time.

When Kevin Iro went over for the match-clinching try two minutes from fulltime the whole stadium went berserk. Even Bob Fulton was almost gracious in defeat at the media conference, crediting the combinations we started putting together in 1995 with having much to do with this victory. Ironically, Fulton didn't know there really was something he could have grumbled about. Before the match I persuaded the very obliging ground staff at North Harbour to bring the dead-ball lines in to something a little less than the minimum allowed. The width was borderline too. We played the game on a postage stamp without the Australians realising it.

BEING FRANK

As far back as the previous September I had called for a three-test series on consecutive Friday nights. We got the three games, but had to wait until October to complete the series. As one of my predecessors, Bob Bailey, found out after his memorable 1991 win in Melbourne, a big gap between tests plays into the hands of the Australians. They have time to lick their wounds and come back all the stronger. October tests also mean the Kangaroos can be picked out of the top three or four teams in the club finals while most of the Kiwis have been sitting on the sidelines for up to six weeks. Of the 1998 Kiwis only Richie Barnett, Ruben Wiki and Jarrod McCracken were involved in the NRL play-offs.

Nor did it take Great Britain long to ignore the International Federation ruling that October was to be kept free for test matches. Their Super League play-offs now extend through to the end of that month. In an incredible about-turn, the federation decided international duties had precedence over club commitments and then acceded to Britain's request for an exemption!

New Zealand Rugby League president Gerald Ryan received another of those hollow promises that it wouldn't happen again. I reckon Henry Paul summed it up accurately when he said from Wigan that the whole affair 'sucked'. We were deprived of Henry's services, but at least Bradford had the decency to get knocked out early enough for Robbie Paul to play.

You would also think the Kiwis would be safe from the Australian judiciary once the club season had ended, but that was far from the case leading up to the second test in Brisbane. John Lomax was suspended for a high tackle while playing for North Queensland in August. Instead of suspending him for a specific number of games the judiciary stood him down until a specific date, October 17. That just happened to be the day after the third test.

They tried hard to get Joe Vagana too. He was cited twice before they looked at the video tapes and saw there were no cases to answer. Then they got him on a third one when the Warriors played Brisbane, for something the referee didn't see, the linesmen didn't see, and the television viewers didn't see. I had to rewind the match tape four times to pin down the alleged incident. Apparently someone had tipped them off and they went to the television channel and asked for different angles on it. On the fifth angle they decided Joe was guilty and he got three games, which left him nicely underdone for the last two tests. He missed the final Warriors match and our two warm-up fixtures against New Zealand Residents.

Meanwhile, Dean Pay, who was in the Kangaroo first test team, had been responsible for several high tackles in Parramatta's quarter-final against North Sydney. They sent him a warning letter telling him not to be a naughty boy or they might have to do something about it. Contrast that with the treatment they gave Lomax and Vagana. Pay was probably even more perplexed when they decided he wasn't needed for the test matches anyway.

We also lost centre Willie Talau, first test hero Terry Hermansson, and back-up props Jason Lowrie and Craig Smith to injuries, and Richie Blackmore was stranded in the British play-offs with Henry Paul. Joe Vagana and Quentin Pongia were our only proven props still standing so I brought in 20-year-old Parramatta front-rower Nathan Cayless. He was a real smoky to most people but Stephen Kearney had mentioned Nathan's New Zealand heritage to me a couple of weeks earlier. I went home and watched a few Parramatta tapes. You could see the kid had what it takes and Brian Smith gave him a big wrap, which was good enough for me.

I named a squad of 23 to prepare for the two tests and the British tour, then whittled it down to the test side. Without Richie Blackmore our only specialist centres were Kevin Iro and Ruben Wiki. Instead of being able to switch Ruben into the pack, as we had been doing successfully, I had to consider what to do if Kevin or Ruben were injured. The logical move was to recreate Jarrod McCracken as a centre but fortunately we did not need such emergency measures. It again emphasised the lack of depth in certain positions when some players were not available.

The most significant change in the Australian line-up had nothing to do with the players. It was the coach. Bob Fulton resigned in August because his wife, Ann, was ill and he wanted to concentrate on his Manly club duties. Wayne Bennett took Fulton's place and that was to prove critical. Bennett rearranged the whole side, dropped some of Fulton's favourites, and included nine of his Brisbane Broncos who were fresh from their grand final win over the Canterbury Bulldogs.

I knew they were going to be a lot more difficult to beat, that we would have to come up with different tactics to combat a more flamboyant style against players who knew each other inside out. Bennett's approach to the game was vastly different to Fulton's, who based everything around big, strong, tough forwards. We could match them physically and always had a chance. As soon as Bennett took over everything changed. We were in for a more open game, designed to suit the Australians.

The Kangaroos, as ever, were odds-on in the betting and this time they lived up to that rating in what was a brawling match. Gorden Tallis set the tone when he spear-tackled Jarrod McCracken into the Suncorp Stadium turf in the opening minutes. It was all on. Unfortunately, we were the ones who copped the wrath of English referee Russell Smith. The penalty count against us was 11–3 at halftime and 16–5 overall.

BEING FRANK

I wouldn't say I enjoyed the night. Sitting with manager Gary Cooksley and Lion Breweries representative Gorden Gibbons, I was getting chipped by Tony Durkin, an Australian reporter. Durkin was accusing me of sending the players out to indulge in intimidatory tactics. Tony's a good bloke and I got on well with him, but I had such a gutsful of his remarks I told him if he opened his mouth once more I would close it for him. He never said another word to me until he apologised after the game. So it was very nearly the Battle of Brisbane in the grandstand too. A lot of what our players were doing was retaliation. The Kangaroos weren't saints; it was coming from both sides and the atmosphere was fairly heated.

They won 30–12 after leading 14–0 at halftime, and to make matters worse Matthew Ridge left the field in agony with severe chest and shoulder injuries. He never played for the Kiwis again. It was a sad way for New Zealand's most prolific test points-scorer to exit the international stage.

The dressing room was like a morgue after the game. You could have heard a pin drop, but not because we were feeling sorry for ourselves or even for Ridgey. At fulltime Jarrod McCracken was advised his two-year-old son Chad had been seriously injured. Chad ran into the path of a car at Port Macquarie and was in intensive care. The news stunned us all and we felt terribly sad for Jarrod. Fortunately, subsequent scans and X-rays revealed there had been no permanent damage. After Jarrod recovered from the initial shock, Gordon Gibbons drove him through the night to be with his family. Looking on helplessly as Jarrod tried to deal with his emotions put the loss of a football game into perspective. All members of the Kiwi camp took up a collection and bought wee Chad a new bike, complete with crash helmet.

The Kiwis hadn't deserved to win. Our handling was poor in the wet and there was little to cheer about. Sean Hoppe dashed 95 metres to score from one of his special interceptions. Joe Vagana was put on report for a shot on Steven Price, so we cited Tallis for his spearing of McCracken and no action was taken against either of them. All in all, it had been a classic case of a match-hardened team having the measure of one that was very much short of a gallop.

We had less than a week to recover from the beating and find a new captain, fullback and goalkicker. I guess Matthew Ridge could claim to be worth three men, for those jobs respectively went to Quentin Pongia, Richie Barnett and Daryl Halligan. Gene Ngamu had dropped back to fullback when Ridge was hurt at Brisbane but there were more options leaving him on the bench. We played Barnett at fullback when Ridge missed the '97 Anzac test and I liked the way he could defuse bombs and make ground from kick returns. Quentin became captain because he led from the front and would take the game to Australia.

However, Bennett and his troops were ready for us. Graham Lowe had told the world the night before that I was to be dumped as Warriors coach, and he had a lash at five of our players. It must have amazed the Kangaroos, if they were into current affairs programmes on state television, being able to sit back and watch a former Kiwi coach taking pot shots at the current one in front of the whole nation.

We held the Kangaroos for more than an hour but they would have beaten any opposition that night at North Harbour Stadium. Bennett had them at their very best and they were ruthless. It was a great game of rugby league and both teams shared in the standing ovation as they came off the park. We were praised for our commitment and for twice fighting our way back into contention, and I have no doubt we performed well enough to have beaten the Fulton-coached side we met back in April. But these Kangaroos were red hot as they raced away to their 20-point margin.

Afterwards Bennett challenged anyone to recall a better international try than the one Darren Smith scored after the ball passed through 14 sets of hands. The attack went from the right sideline to the left, then back to the right corner again, yet just about everybody who handled the ball was knocked over in a strong tackle. We just ran out of defenders. Victory in the series completed a unique treble for Bennett and his captain, Alfie Langer, who had already won the NRL grand final and the State of Origin series.

At least we could redirect our frustrations towards mounting a successful tour to England. No one was more disappointed we could not clinch the trans-Tasman series than Quentin Pongia, whose dislike for losing was even greater when he was captain. You could feel his determination to beat the Poms spreading through the ranks. They were all aware New Zealand had not won a series on British soil since 1971 and believed they had a real chance to grab a piece of history. Ces Mountford and Graham Lowe had both coached Kiwi teams to draw test series in England during the 1980s, and Tony Gordon's side lost 2–1. But the most recent tour in 1993 had produced a disastrous 0–3 loss with the smallest losing margin being 17 points.

It has been jokingly suggested that I had a co-selector for the touring team. With Matthew Ridge gone and both Willie Talau and Richie Blackmore injured, we needed to bolster our outside backs and goalkicking resources by taking Daryl Halligan with us. Daryl had already disrupted his family's holiday plans by playing in the third Australian test, when he scored a try and kicked four goals, and had gone back to Sydney saying he would have to check his availability with Linda, his wife. So I picked 21 players, and Linda completed the touring team when she told Daryl he could go.

It was British coach Andy Goodway's turn to draw his players from the Super League club finals, and he included nine of the winning Wigan team in his first test 17. Among them were dangerous winger Jason Robinson and experienced centre Gary Connolly, who had both missed the 1996 Lions tour to New Zealand because they had ARL affiliations.

We sent plenty of youngsters. Nathan Cayless was 20, and Tony Puletua, Lesley Vainikolo and Ali Lauiti'iti were all 19. Cayless and Puletua had already shown how good they were against Australia and I would not have hesitated in playing Vainikolo and Lauiti'iti if the need had arisen. Primarily, Lesley and Ali were there to learn, and it did not take long to discover they were doing just that. I'll never forget opening the door to their room on the day they received their first Kiwi pay packets. The notes were spread all over their beds and they were taking a video of the occasion. As tourists they were terrific.

We won the first test 22–16 at Huddersfield, and some Englishmen still claim Australian referee Bill Harrigan robbed them of a draw. This match was raised again when the Aussies and Brits had their big dispute over who should control the deciding test of the 2001 Ashes series. Some recollections of the incidents were woefully inaccurate.

Jason Robinson had been awarded a dubious try three minutes from fulltime to give the Lions a sniff at getting on level terms. They roared back and as centre Keith Senior jumped for a high ball he was tackled by Robbie Paul while still in the air, and bundled into touch. They were crying for a penalty try but Harrigan made the correct decision by only giving them a penalty. The incident happened in the field of play and there was no certainty a try would have been scored. Conveniently, they overlooked the fact that Robinson was given the fastest try in the history of video refereeing. When you watch the replays it is unclear whether Robinson or Daryl Halligan, who had shown his deceptive pace to keep in the race, touched the ball first. But it was blatantly obvious that neither had control of it. I presume the British video ref just got caught up in the excitement of the chase.

Also forgotten in England were the interventions of the local touch judges which directly led to two of Great Britain's scores, a penalty goal and a try, while turning a blind eye to some British errors and illegal tactics. Harrigan's penalty count was 3–10 against us. We deserved to win the test, probably by more than six points. Tony Iro had also reached the goal-line only for Harrigan to rule he was held up without consulting the video referee. Maybe he knew it would be a waste of time.

Henry Paul had been pawing the ground waiting to pull on the Kiwi jersey since Wigan had denied him permission to play against Australia and made the Lions pay. Stephen Kearney and Joe Vagana claimed the tries which shunted us

12–2 ahead at halftime, then the Paul brothers sent Stacey Jones away to score, and Kearney set up another try for Robbie Paul.

Big Joe's try came after the halftime hooter. The Poms hesitated when they heard the signal but Richie Barnett was still in the act of playing the ball. Joe charged out of dummy half, stepped around the startled markers, beat fullback Kris Radlinski, and dived over in Gary Connolly's tackle. The locals didn't like that either but Harrigan reminded them the game doesn't stop until the referee blows his whistle.

That effort took a bit out of Joe and as he was huffing and puffing his way towards the sheds he asked Harrigan, 'How long have we got for halftime?' Harrigan replied, 'Oh, the normal 12 minutes Joe, is that all right with you?' Joe nodded and said, 'That's all right Bill, so long as it's the same for both teams.' Bill looked a little puzzled.

Andy Goodway, the British coach, had been playing funny games with his selections before the first test, naming a squad, reducing it, and then not announcing his actual team until an hour before the match. Everyone was surprised he sat Iestyn Harris on the bench and played Andy Farrell at stand-off half. Harris proved to be one of Britain's best players when he went on after 25 minutes. So we expected Harris to start in the second test with Farrell reverting to his specialist lock forward role, and they did just that.

We had not played as well as we should have in the first test, turning the ball over too much and having to make a mountain of tackles in the second half. I emphasised control in the build-up to the second test and Goodway helped our motivation by voicing an opinion the Kiwis had not been as daunting as he expected.

The Brits were getting up to other tricks too. During the haka at Huddersfield some genius played 'Land of Hope and Glory' over the sound system. Between tests Goodway and his staff compiled a video of supposed first-test refereeing controversies and sent it to Bill Harrigan. I bet Robinson's 'try' and the touch judges' contributions were left on the cutting room floor.

The fans sitting up through the night at home to watch the second test telecast from Bolton were probably in despair when we were 8–16 down at halftime. But there was complete calm in the dressing room during the break and a really positive attitude that we were going to come back and grab the match and series. The players went out and blitzed the Lions with 28 unanswered points in one of the most convincing performances you could wish to see. That 36–16 scoreline entitled the 1998 Kiwis to be ranked alongside the original 1907–08 All Golds and Lory Blanchard's 1971 Kiwis as the only ones among 14 New Zealand touring teams to win their test series on British soil.

Other records were broken too. It was New Zealand's biggest test win, and highest score, in Britain, and for the first time New Zealand had beaten Great Britain in five consecutive tests. Sean Hoppe also became the most prolific Kiwi test try-scorer when he sprinted half the length of the field after a crunching Ruben Wiki tackle spurted the ball from Iestyn Harris' grasp.

Stacey Jones laid on tries for Stephen Kearney at Huddersfield and Richie Barnett at Bolton with his little blindside kicks, just one factor in him being named Man of the Series. Barnett's try was vital to our second test comeback and was not awarded until the video referee had viewed it several times from every conceivable angle. Barnett was a revelation in that second half, his broken field running adding a whole new dimension to our game plan. After scoring twice himself, Barnett set up Henry Paul for the last try.

I felt humble when I read later that Quentin Pongia had dedicated the win to me, although I didn't need him reminding one and all I would be on the dole queue when I got home. 'Frank's had a bit of an up-and-down year, like myself, with the Warriors not doing so well,' he said. 'To have that win is something we gave Frank. It was thanks for what he does for our side and for what he does for us as players.'

Andy Goodway didn't show any grace at all in defeat, claiming his side had lost the match rather than been beaten by a better team. I wonder what game he was dreaming about when our blokes were putting five tries through their defence in the second half. Goodway claimed 'key incidents' had turned the game in New Zealand's favour but wouldn't elaborate.

There were stories circulating that centre Paul Newlove refused to take a pain-killing injection Goodway wanted him to have. Newlove and his club refused so he didn't play. We were just happy to give New Zealand something to celebrate after the All Blacks had lost five tests in a row, and our soccer, netball and hockey teams were beaten.

We had a few beers on the bus going back to our Leeds hotel and the boys rang Matthew Ridge to give him hell for not being there. The phone was passed around among all of us to stir Ridgey up a bit. But knowing we had won the series was not enough. We set our sights on being the only New Zealand team to be unbeaten in Britain.

During the week Tony Iro came to me before I had selected the side for the third test and suggested new front-rower Craig Smith deserved a jersey. I had actually been wondering how to fit Craig into the team as a reward for his exceptional training efforts, and Tony must have sensed it. Tony offered to stand down, and as it turned out he was the logical one to miss out. Craig came off the bench and did a great job for us.

With two minutes of ordinary time to go at Watford we were seven points clear in the third test, yet were held to a 23-all draw when the Lions struck back with a converted try and scrum-half Tony Smith's first-ever field goal. It was disappointing but we at least had the consolation of achieving that unbeaten record. We blew it after being awarded a penalty about 20 metres from their goal-line. There were two options, to kick for goal or just tie the ball up, put on one of our scoring plays, and keep them down their end of the field. Instead, the ball went out to Stephen Kearney, who tried a fancy play on the first tackle and we lost possession. They got away from us, Tony Smith scored the try and Andy Farrell converted. Smith chipped over his field goal in injury time.

The draw was all the more annoying because the Kiwis were the better team in yet another comeback. Britain led 10–2 at halftime and they were playing well. Then Stacey Jones unveiled his rare attacking skills, the Paul brothers ran in three tries between them, and suddenly we were up by 12 points. In the end we paid the penalty for relaxing, and that can be fatal at this level.

Captain Pongia felt the players had unconsciously let their guards down after clinching the series, hence the slow start, but ultimately it was that one spilled ball which cost us a clean sweep. Quentin also reckoned he was going to try and twist my arm to stay on as Kiwi coach. He must have succeeded. Weeks earlier, all too aware I had no future at the Warriors under the new regime, I had signalled my probable retirement from the Kiwi job. To my way of thinking, the national coach should be coaching a first grade team. NZRL president Gerald Ryan told me then to wait before making any rash decision.

In January 1999 the NZRL board reappointed me for another two years, through to the Millennium World Cup in a deal that included other work for the league to keep me gainfully employed. An early stalemate in negotiations, when some radically inaccurate salary figures were bandied about in the papers, was eventually broken during a long meeting with deputy chairman Wayne Morris in Christchurch.

It was heartening some of New Zealand's best known sports columnists, all of them with strong rugby union backgrounds, came out in support of me and the Kiwis in 1998.

After our Anzac test win over Australia Ron Palenski wrote in the *Dominion*: 'If ever there was a test of the resolve of a team, this was it. If ever there was a test of Frank Endacott's ability, this was it. If ever there was a team that needed to dig deep into reserves of strength, this was it. It became the most complete of wins, all the more satisfying because of its unexpectedness.' Ron was kind enough to say it ranked alongside the great Kiwi victories, and in time 'may prove to be the best of them all'.

In the aftermath of our wins in England Ron Palenski penned another piece praising the manner in which the Kiwis had responded to the 'messy' sale of the Warriors, 'and worst of all the kick-and-tell grandstanding of the new owners in their contrived television documentary. Freed of that sour environment and able to concentrate solely on planning and executing winning league, Endacott and his players were able to show what playing with pride and passion can do'.

On the eve of the second test in Britain, *Sunday Star Times* columnist Phil Gifford, wrote 'a first series victory in Britain since 1971 would be a perfect finale for a man universally recognised as one of the nicest guys in New Zealand sport'. He went on to criticise Graham Lowe and Malcolm Boyle for their public attacks on me and the Warriors, saying, 'Endacott may have been knocked out of the Warriors but his work with the Kiwis should provide a much sweeter memory of his coaching career.'

Former All Black halfback Chris Laidlaw, referring to my Warriors sacking, commented: 'Having just pulled off a stunning series victory against the British, New Zealand coach Frank Endacott deserves rather better than that. He has been a convenient prey for the various predators hovering over the game for a season or two now. You would have thought that any coach who can post a test victory over an Australian team that are virtually unbeatable, then pull off a stylish series win over an accomplished Great Britain side, must be doing something right.

'But Frank's problem is that he wore two hats: a hard hat to avoid falling debris from the boardroom of the Warriors, and the more refined plumage befitting a national coach. Somewhere in between he has come unstuck. Coaching the Warriors must provide as much job satisfaction as flying the lead plane in a kamikaze squadron.'

It's nice to have support from unexpected quarters. At least that sack of coal across my shoulders had become increasingly lighter during the British tour. We flew home a contented team, though a lot of the players still had their battles to fight with the Warriors.

Chapter 12.
Video nasties

Rugby league can claim to have shown rugby union the way in many spheres, such as professionalism, World Cup tournaments, any number of rule changes, interchange players, video referees and the like. It took league's administrators a surprisingly long time, however, to set up a union-style Tri-Nations tournament involving the big three, Australia, New Zealand and Great Britain. Then, after an apparently successful prototype in late 1999, the format was dropped. Ironically, by the end of that one-off Tri-Nations series Kiwi coach Frank Endacott was wishing rugby league had never embraced video referees. But first there was another Anzac test to be played in Sydney.

Even though we lost the Anzac test at Stadium Australia, I rate that 14–20 defeat as a great performance by the greenest New Zealand team I coached in my seven years. We effectively had a whole side sidelined for one reason or another in the weeks leading up to the match, yet nearly snatched a miraculous win.

The list of unavailable players fills a page in my diary. Matthew Ridge and Daryl Halligan were officially retired but I would have approached them because we needed a goalkicker. But Ridge was suspended and Halligan was nursing a broken jaw. Kevin and Tony Iro had already committed themselves to the Cook Islands for the 2000 World Cup and a lot of experience went with them.

Stephen Kearney and Nigel Vagana were also suspended, Kearney in bizarre circumstances. His dangerous throw of Gorden Tallis while playing for Melbourne against the Broncos would normally have cost him only two games. But the Storm fought the charge and his penalty points soared from a basic 250 to 515, forcing him out of four NRL games and the Anzac test. Even Tallis said he felt terrible about it and Melbourne chief executive Chris Johns was reprimanded for commenting, 'We might as well start wearing skirts.'

In an ironic twist to Kearney's suspension, Melbourne coach Chris Anderson had just been appointed to coach the Kangaroos in place of Wayne Bennett, who was fully occupied dealing with the Brisbane Broncos' poor start to the season. Anderson had even been on Kearney's defence team. Melbourne was refused the right of appeal and, as usual, the Australians ignored the New Zealand Rugby League's protest that the Kiwis were being unfairly penalised.

Craig Smith, Richie Blackmore, Quentin Pongia, Tony Puletua, Syd Eru and John Lomax were all injured, and Sean Hoppe was still finding his legs again after coming back from injury. We couldn't consider Awen Guttenbeil or John Temu either. Among the missing were four test captains, Pongia, Ridge, Kearney and Lomax. Pongia assembled with the team but when he failed a fitness test Jarrod McCracken was our choice to lead the side. Although McCracken, like Pongia, had been a firebrand in his younger days, he had matured into a leader and was doing a fine job as Parramatta co-captain with Dean Pay.

There was the usual spat with Bradford about Henry and Robbie Paul. I thought I had an agreement with Bradford coach Matthew Elliott but his club's officials objected and the International Federation appeals committee (comprising two Australians and a Pom) again favoured club over country. The Pauls arrived in Sydney on the Tuesday.

New Zealand won and then partly lost the refereeing wrangle. Australia originally offered us a panel of three, all of them Australians. The NZRL plumped for Englishman Russell Smith, who had controlled the three trans-Tasman tests the previous year, but Australia trumped that by giving the whistle to Smith's countryman Stuart Cummings. There was to be one touch judge from each country and, interestingly, a video referee apiece, a compromise that ultimately proved costly for the Kiwis during the Tri-Nations later in the year.

I wonder how many national coaches in other sports have to put up with the politics that have plagued international rugby league. In the middle of the refereeing tug-of-war some alert scribe wrote they would fill Stadium Australia if the curtain-raiser was an all-in wrestling match between NZRL officials, led by

Gerald Ryan, and their Australian counterparts, fronted by David Barnhill. Ryan's opinions on Australian referees were colourful and well known, and Barnhill endeared himself to New Zealand radio listeners by blurting out: 'It doesn't matter if Mickey Mouse referees the game, Australia will still win.'

Australia's only apparent problem was Craig Gower, but Anderson had the luxury of replacing him with Andrew Johns, the game's best player. After claiming Gower had a groin injury, then denying accusations he had been guilty of anti-social behaviour, the Australian management finally admitted police had been called after Gower exposed himself to a woman in a Sydney hotel.

Meanwhile, we were out on the highways and byways seeking a team and called up five new caps in 19-year-old Lesley Vainikolo, Matt Rua, Willie Talau, Richard Swain and David Kidwell. Vainikolo was languishing in reserve grade with Canberra but the Anzac test turned his career around and he never played for the second XIII again. Talau missed the 1998 British tour because of injury, Kidwell was showing good form in the Parramatta centres, and Rua and Swain were outstanding defenders in the Melbourne pack. Old mates Jason Lowrie and Terry Hermansson were reunited, Lowrie for his first test since the 1995 World Cup.

I have no idea why New Zealand has not won a test match in Sydney since 1959, in the days when they played at the Cricket Ground. That last win was achieved even before Stacey Jones' grandfather, Maunga Emery, and Jarrod McCracken's father, Ken, made their test debuts. The Sydney Football Stadium had come and gone as the regular test venue and now we were heading to Stadium Australia. I felt confident that was a good omen because the Kangaroos had not played there as a team either. Australian officials promised us 50,000 spectators and delivered about 20,000.

It was understandable the Kangaroos were only paying $1.14 to win on the New Zealand TAB and we were at $4.75. Despite all that I was delighted with the way our players trained leading up to the test. We were all keeping our fingers crossed for Henry Paul's goalkicking, but he was on target at practice under the critical eye of the master, Daryl Halligan.

We went so close to upending them. The spirit of the players was strong through all our trials and tribulations, and stayed that way on the field as we matched their three tries. Mat Rogers proved the difference with four goals against one by Henry Paul. We rattled them by using short kick-offs and other little surprises, and played well enough to win. Richie Barnett had a try denied after Darren Lockyer fumbled, the video referees apparently believing the ball was stripped from Lockyer in a two-man tackle.

Henry and Robbie Paul were at their brilliant best and the Australians were stretched to restrain them. But Henry was the subject of a serious injury scare when heavily concussed in a Gorden Tallis tackle near the Australian goal-line just before fulltime. There was a long delay while Henry was taken off on the medical cart. We almost had their defence stretched to breaking point and the injury gave them a welcome breather.

Both starting props, Joe Vagana, who seemed to enjoy receiving more game time than he was getting at the Warriors, and Jason Lowrie had barnstorming games. Apart from the rampant Tallis our forwards had the measure of theirs as Jarrod McCracken led a superb defence. But Wendell Sailor's try was a classic after perfect passes from Brad Fittler, Laurie Daley and Darren Lockyer, and Sailor also saved a certain try with a crunching tackle on Ruben Wiki.

It had been a highly encouraging performance leading up to the end-of-season Tri-Nations tournament. We expected many established players to return, while their inexperienced replacements had their confidence boosted by the close call at Stadium Australia.

I still held a vested interest in the Auckland Warriors because my son Shane remained on their playing roster. It was not easy for him having the Endacott name after what had occurred between myself and the club's new owners over the previous year or two, but he had always battled against a form of prejudice. Having your father as coach can be hard on anyone but I always had a policy of picking the best players regardless of their surnames. You inevitably still get some people who accuse you of bias. I treated Shane the same as every other player when I was Warriors coach. He never got a favour and mostly found it tougher than the other players, but never once complained and was always a true professional and worthy of his position. Shane was a team player, invariably among the top two or three tacklers and with one of the lowest mistake rates in the club. His only deficiency at stand-off half was in his kicking game. He never had any confidence in it.

When Shane was signed by the Warriors in 1996 I never even knew about it. Shane had returned home from playing alongside Tevita Vaikona and Maea David at Hull and performed very well for Canterbury against the Warriors Colts in Christchurch. John Ackland, the club's development officer, recommended Shane to head coach John Monie, who did the rest. I had no input at all.

Shane was in serious contention for the 1998 Anzac test, only to be one of the casualties on a disastrous day at North Sydney Oval. Shane was understudy to both stand-off half Gene Ngamu and hooker Syd Eru at the Warriors. Gene had played in all my Kiwi teams up to then but was already injured and out of the upcoming test. Shane started at stand-off against Norths but switched to hooker after only eight minutes when Syd broke his ribs. Shane played stronger and stronger in a losing team and would have been seriously considered for the Kiwis. But just before fulltime he crocked his knee when tackling big Josh Stuart and was sidelined for weeks.

After I was gone from the Warriors, Shane spent a season under Mark Graham and played in most of the games. He still suffered because of his name and I felt sorry for him. At the end of that 1999 season Shane decided to retire at the age of 28. He had an option in England with the London Broncos that Mark Graham had sorted out on his behalf, but felt that would be a backward step.

As a youngster Shane was head boy at Hornby High School and went on to gain a Bachelor of Science degree from the University of Canterbury, so he knew there was life after football. He's done very well in business and earned more money in two or three years than he ever did when he was playing rugby league.

The Warriors had opened their season, and their short time under the ownership of Graham Lowe, Malcolm Boyle and the Tainui Trust, on a sensational note in Sydney with Matthew Ridge ignoring a painful ankle to inspire a win over Sydney City. The game was also notable for an all-in brawl which led to the orderings off of Ali Lauiti'iti and Brad Fittler and the sin-binnings of Tony Tuimavave and Roosters fullback Andrew Walker. The Warriors lost to North Sydney at home in the next round, recovered to bury Manly at Brookvale Oval, then lost their next six games.

Only five rounds into the season Ridge, Nigel Vagana, Tuimavave and Peter Lewis were all under suspension. Lauiti'iti had pleaded guilty and escaped suspension because of his clean record, but the same old questions were being asked about the Warriors' discipline. The only difference was that the guys who previously asked the questions were now trying to find answers to them.

Ridge was hardly back from his three-week holiday for touching referee Paul Simpkins than he was out for another eight weeks for giving Lesley Vainikolo a facial. In that same Canberra match he was also charged with a reckless high tackle on Mark McLinden and tripping Laurie Daley. Even Graham Lowe was in strife, being fined $10,000 for giving his opinion of Simpkins in the wake of a loss to the Bulldogs.

No points for guessing the individual and team highlights of the Warriors' season. They produced one out of the box to rout Newcastle 42–0 on the occasion of Stacey Jones' 100th appearance. Ridge was back to contribute a try and seven goals and show what might have been. A week later Jones ran in four tries in a 60-point avalanche against Western Suburbs as the Warriors again teased their fans and completed their season with four consecutive wins.

By then my attention was centred on the upcoming Tri-Nations series and it was heartening that Melbourne and Parramatta, both with big Kiwi contingents, were in the NRL play-offs. They clashed in the preliminary finals, with Melbourne nudging out the Eels and Stephen Kearney enjoying a change of luck when cleared of an alleged high tackle on Jason Smith.

Kearney, Richard Swain and Matt Rua, along with Tawera Nikau, all shared in the Storm's stunning second-season premiership triumph. Sadly, Craig Smith had to be a loser when his St George-Illawarra side was beaten by a last-minute penalty try in the grand final. Smith was the best player in any team throughout the play-offs.

New Zealand had been the strongest advocate for the Tri-Nations, Great Britain was keen, but the Australians showed their usual lukewarm approach to international football. They were bending to their clubs again, claiming the November 5 final would give players too little rest before the early NRL start forced on them by the 2000 Sydney Olympic Games.

New NZRL general manager Gary Allcock was discovering just how mind-numbing it is trying to deal with a country where the tail, the National Rugby League, wags the dog, the Australian Rugby League.

For once our withdrawals were manageable, though we would have fielded an even more menacing forward pack had Quentin Pongia and Jarrod McCracken not been casualties of the NRL play-offs. But Craig Smith had been playing the house down and Matt Rua grabbed his chance to partner Stephen Kearney in the second row. Losing Pongia and McCracken meant finding another captain, and Richie Barnett took to the job as if born to it. We were still short of seasoned outside backs and after thinking about Australian-born Lee Oudenryn, who had qualified on a residential basis while with the Warriors, I preferred North Queensland speedster Brian Jellick. He didn't get to play in the Tri-Nations but scored four tries against Tonga at Carlaw Park. Jellick was the sole new cap but seven others had played only one test.

Chris Anderson oversaw a changing of the guard with his Australian team, perhaps because of his close call in April but also with an eye to the 2000 World Cup. Laurie Daley had been dragging a leg, Allan Langer admitted he had lost his desire at top level, and Glenn Lazarus was not going to rise to the occasion again. Then Gorden Tallis, Brad Thorn and Shane Webcke succumbed to injuries and our forward defections didn't look quite so serious. Buoyed by what had happened in the Anzac test, we rated ourselves as winning chances.

It was heart attack time again in the opening match when we clung to the remnants of a 24–4 halftime advantage to win 24–22. That first spell was about the best 40 minutes in my time as Kiwi coach but Australians are never beaten no matter what sport they are playing and we knew they would come back hard.

They steadily cut into our lead but when Mat Rogers converted their last try there were only 24 seconds left on the clock. Both teams had crossed for four tries, and this time Henry Paul had better goalkicking figures than Rogers. In fact, Henry was quite remarkable with his strike rate. I had asked him earlier in the year to get in plenty of practice and he did that, despite not being Bradford's first choice. In the three Tri-Nations matches and the test against Tonga he goaled 26 of his 30 attempts, including 11 in succession against the Tongans. Henry is a natural at just about anything he turns his hand, or foot, to, and stunned everybody except himself by kicking 35 successive goals for Bradford in 2000 and breaking Daryl Halligan's world record.

Stacey Jones was our Man of the Match against Australia, orchestrating all four of our tries and being pin-point accurate with his kicking game. Stephen Kearney ran over his Melbourne club-mates Brett Kimmorley and Robbie Ross for a try and was the link man for the most popular try of all, to Jason Lowrie.

It was Jason's first try at any level since we toured Papua New Guinea in 1994. He had been try-less through 129 first grade games and 12 previous tests, yet he knew exactly what to do when given the ball in a gap 25 metres from the goal-line. The widely used photograph of his post-try celebration was as dramatic as any I've seen in sport. By the end of the night's celebrations, Jason reckoned he had run 95 metres and sidestepped half-a-dozen defenders.

Some of our players had been out of football for nearly two months, so the Tongan test was designed to boost match fitness while Australia and Great Britain played in Brisbane. It was also part of a pledge by the more powerful nations to encourage rugby league in the Pacific, something the Australians eventually decided was a waste of their time and energy. We expected to beat Tonga easily and did just that, exorcising the ghost of our one-point escape at the 1995 World Cup. The prospect of an easy win was no reason for not playing another country.

There was some stirring going on behind the scenes, and by midweek before the test the Auckland Warriors, Melbourne Storm and Canberra Raiders were demanding their players be withdrawn. According to them it was not a real test match. That label apparently only applied to games against Australia and Great Britain. We were brassed off because the tournament was out of the club season and the New Zealand Rugby League had generously decided to donate all proceeds to children's hospitals in Auckland and Tonga.

It was hypocritical of the Warriors because they had released John Simon to play for the Australian Aboriginals against Papua New Guinea at Campbelltown the same weekend. Warriors chief executive Trevor McKewen claimed he hadn't been told about the Tongan test, yet the match promotion was in the hands of

BEING FRANK

Dean Lonergan, his club's own marketing manager.

We decided to play those who missed the Australian match, Brian Jellick, Terry Hermansson and Tony Puletua, so they could shake off the cobwebs of their long lay-offs. I rested Craig Smith, Matt Rua and Robbie Paul, who had all played through to the last weekend of their respective club competitions.

Murphy's Law prevailed when Stacey Jones had his arm broken in a collision with Joe Vagana as they tackled Tongan fullback Paul Koloi. It was an accident that could have happened to any player, anywhere, anytime. I have no idea what the great hue and cry was about. There would have been no difference in resting Stacey to resting any of a dozen other players who were in the same situation of needing another game under their belts. The test had been sanctioned by the International Federation, and Tonga had brought players from Britain and Australia. They were taking it seriously enough and we owed it to them to do the same.

Trevor McKewen regarded me as the biggest bastard in the world. But I didn't break Stacey's arm. McKewen raved on in the newspapers about it happening in a nothing game, and how it must never be allowed to happen again. Here we had a New Zealander sounding exactly the same as all those Australian and British club officials who put their selfish interests ahead of the game as a whole.

I felt as sick as anyone for Stacey and felt sorry for the Warriors when he was hurt. But the Kiwis also suffered because we lost him for the remainder of the Tri-Nations. The one person who never complained was Stacey himself. His good mate Joe Vagana felt bad enough about it for both of them. We enlisted Gene Ngamu, who was home from Huddersfield, paired the Paul brothers in the halves, and Richard Swain took over from Henry Paul at hooker.

The Lions were humbled 6–42 by the Kangaroos, their biggest defeat on Australian soil, and then we made them even more miserable by winning 26–4 and creating more records. The previous biggest New Zealand winning margin in 95 tests had been 20 points, at Lancaster Park in 1996 and Bolton in 1998. It was also my last test against Great Britain, which was to be split into the various home nations for the World Cup, and took my record to six wins and a draw. The hidings also cost Lions coach Andy Goodway his job.

Nigel Vagana had shaken off Brian Jellick's challenge for a wing spot by claiming three tries of his own against Tonga after replacing Richie Barnett at fullback. He almost had another try-scoring treble against Great Britain, but one was disallowed for a previous infringement. Nigel's first try, from an interception, completed a 14–0 halftime scoreline and his second was a 90-metre sizzler that killed off a brief British revival. Henry Paul fielded a chip kick just out from our own goal-line and Nigel left them all for dead.

It was a big night for the Vagana cousins. Joe was a human steamroller in a

Sharing a joke with John Monie at a Warriors function. He is still a good friend.

With Joan before setting off for a Warriors awards night.

At the awards with Stacey Jones, the finest Warrior of them all.

Craig Smith's wedding day in Wollongong. From left, Peter Leitch (the Mad Butcher), Craig, Quentin Pongia and myself.

'Arrested' on suspicion of plotting Great Britain's downfall during the 1998 Kiwis tour.

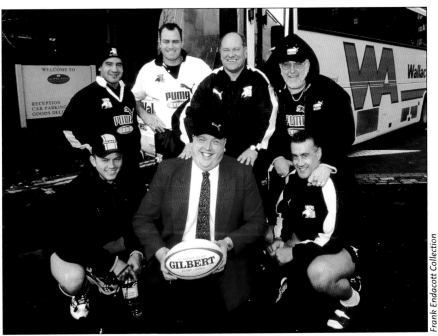

Our favourite British bus driver, Ian Durham, flanked by Henry Paul, Stacey Jones, Daryl Halligan, me, Peter Leitch, and Quentin Pongia.

The Mad Butcher

Dreaming of another test win. Kiwi manager Gary Cooksley and I fail to appreciate the scenery along yet another English motorway.

The Press

Happiness is holding a winning ticket at the Motukarara trots. Harness racing has long been a hobby of mine.

A perk of the Warriors coaching job. Being invited to join the Brazilian chorus line talent at Auckland's Sky City Casino.

Mark Horo, giving his usual 110 per cent against Papua New Guinea before injury cut short his comeback to international football.

Old rugger mates Marc Ellis and John Timu in league again during the 1996 international season.

Captain Matthew Ridge congratulates John Timu, a star of the 1996 home series against Great Britain.

Aaron Whittaker carries the ball during the 1996 reserve grade grand final. Logan Swann, Nigel Vagana, Aaron Lester and Bryan Henare are also prominent.

A Lion Red shower after beating the Australians in the 1997 test at North Harbour Stadium.

Advice for the new boy. Making a point to Lesley Vainikolo before his debut in the 1999 Anzac test at Sydney.

pack that monstered the big Brits, and he finished it off by scoring our last try. Jason Lowrie had another cracker, and Henry Paul bamboozled opponents who should have known him fairly well after all his years at Wigan and Bradford.

Great Britain's only try was awarded by referee Tim Mander after they couldn't make up their minds in the video box. It was the only time they really threatened our line, despite having topliners like Jason Robinson, Kris Radlinski, Iestyn Harris, Sean Long, Adrian Morley, Keiron Cunningham and Andy Farrell. The score flattered the Lions; we were fizzing at the time.

Before the Tri-Nations final I said the Kiwis were 'trained to the minute to run the race of their lives'. We were putting a lot of faith in our pack, with Joe Vagana and Craig Smith in great form, Richard Swain slotting in smoothly at hooker, and Stephen Kearney, Matt Rua and Logan Swann providing a well-balanced back three. Jason Lowrie and Nathan Cayless were the back-ups on the bench. But I predicted something else too, that the final would be so close it could be decided by one line break or one mistake. The previous six tests between our two countries had been equally shared and there was nothing between the sides in 1999. It was a great chance for us to win our first 'series' (loose as it might seem with the matches so far apart) since 1953, and to inflict Australia's first series loss since the Kangaroos toured France in 1978.

The Australian media also tried to saddle us with the responsibility of lifting the gloom that had descended over New Zealand because of the All Blacks' shock loss to France and elimination from their World Cup.

It was scant consolation to us that while the All Blacks were roundly criticised, the Kiwis were given credit for being so desperately unlucky in a match which rated with the very best for sheer drama and excitement. Wendell Sailor's late try won it for Australia at 22–20 but the game actually finished with Logan Swann held up over the Australian goal-line. It was that close.

It might not have been so close had it not been for a succession of baffling video referee rulings. My diary notes show that when we were down 10–14 at halftime I told the players that every 50–50 decision had gone against us and must turn around in the second half. Unfortunately, that didn't occur. We dominated the last 35 minutes and only needed a draw to carry off the Tri-Nations title after having won the opening game.

In the last minute Henry Paul chipped ahead, and two things happened. Henry was taken out in a late tackle by Australian second-rower Bryan Fletcher right in front of referee Russell Smith and directly in front of the posts. But the referee, touch judges Alan Caddy and Kevin Hawke, and video referees Tony Drake from New Zealand and Dennis Spagarino from Australia, all missed it. They were distracted by the ball rolling towards the in-goal area and the scramble that followed. Logan Swann got to grips with it and Smith signalled for the video referees to rule on a possible try. The ball was clearly well off the ground so it was never a try. But the video referees didn't notice what happened to Henry Paul and the penalty which would have drawn the match and won the Tri-Nations was never awarded.

A few days later I asked New Zealand Rugby League referees chief Kevin Bailey to take a look at the match tape, not that it was going to change anything. We had a meeting with the touch judges and Tony Drake, who by a weird coincidence had grown up across the road from our house in Emmett Street. They admitted to missing the late tackle. The touchies had not seen it live, and Drake said he and Spagarino were concentrating on the ball after it had been kicked.

It was the fourth contentious decision to be referred to the video referees. After only three minutes Mat Rogers clearly knocked on when palming down a Henry Paul pass, regathered, and ran 50 metres to score. Russell Smith obviously had doubts and went upstairs. Then the video referees took so long that they must also have initially been in two minds, yet the try was given. Advantage to the attacking side.

Ten minutes later Robbie Paul was tackled centimetres short of the goal-line but his momentum enabled him to roll his chest over the ball and onto the chalk. There was no double movement. Robbie had scored tries in England using the same ploy but the video referees had not seen it done and ruled it out. Advantage to the defending side. Since then tries have been awarded in the NRL in exactly the same circumstances.

After 27 minutes Henry Paul was held over the goal-line by Craig Gower and Darren Lockyer and stripped of the ball. Henry believed he could have rolled over and forced the ball if it had not been ripped from his grasp. Russell Smith considered giving a penalty try but took advice from his sideline and video assistants. We received only a penalty, even though Lockyer was sin-binned for the offence.

After giving the Aussies the benefit of the doubt on attack and defence with the first two calls, the video referees this time didn't have a penalty try button so signalled 'ref's call'. Up in the video box, Spagarino had control of the microphone, as he had done for the entire game. If Smith had been sure he wouldn't have asked for their assistance in the first place. Spagarino could have told him penalty tries had been awarded for stripping the ball over the goal-line.

Our players put all that behind them, and came back even after the Kangaroos increased their lead to eight points early in the second half. Henry Paul was in everything, having sent his brother away for our first try and finishing with six goals from seven attempts as the Australians blatantly conceded penalties from professional fouls when desperate and deep on defence. The referee eventually decided enough was enough and sent Darren Britt to the sin-bin. Joe Vagana made a dent in the short-handed Australian pack to put cousin Nigel over for the try which nudged us 20–18 ahead with 10 minutes left. We held that for five minutes, until Kangaroo scrum-half Brett Kimmorley struck. He was too quick for centre David Kidwell, beating him on the outside as the defence slid across field. Once Kimmorley got behind our front line we were in real trouble, and when Wendell Sailor ranged up in support the try couldn't be stopped.

Although the Kiwis lost the match they didn't lose any friends. I had old internationals coming up to me afterwards and saying it was one of the very best test matches they had witnessed. One or two of them were even a little emotional about how we had taken it to the Aussies.

Australia's general kicking game was better than ours and they were dangerous on the flanks with Rogers and Sailor scoring three tries between them. But the Paul brothers bluffed them around the rucks, Craig Smith and Logan Swann had mighty games in the forwards, Ruben Wiki gave their centres a rugged time, and Lesley Vainikolo was more than a handful on the wing.

It was another one that got away from us, and with it went my last chance to win a series over Australia. I would have loved the opportunity to play a full series at home but that hasn't happened since 1989. The Kiwis clearly respond to passionate home crowds.

On the day before the Tri-Nations final Gerald Ryan felt the need to put on his NZRL presidential hat and confirm my position was not under threat. It didn't worry me unduly but there had been rumours in Auckland that I was not assured of taking the team to the World Cup, despite being contracted through to the end of 2000. And this after we had just beaten Australia and put a record winning margin past Great Britain. Gerald was a stickler for the letter of any agreement and told the media he had heard two names being bandied about as potential coaching replacements, but he wouldn't name them. I had a fair idea where the rumours started but had no wish to get into a slanging match on the eve of such an important final. Funny about the timing yet again.

It's disappointing the concept of the Tri-Nations series wasn't carried on. In New Zealand it was a fantastic success: the public thought so, the players thought so, the British camp even thought so, and why they never followed it up I'll never know. Apparently the Australians were not happy with the small attendance for their match against Great Britain in Brisbane. It's not hard to guess where a good idea died.

We certainly gained plenty of positives out of it and were looking to carry that feeling into the new millennium. Although I was in no hurry to make it official I had already decided Richie Barnett would retain the captaincy for the proposed Anzac test at home and then the World Cup tournament in Britain. Richie had proved a fullback really can lead from the front, and he was not reluctant to take a few hit-ups among the forwards in addition to his trademark kick returns. He showed courage in his front-on defence and in plucking bombs out of the air. Richie also had the advantage of being on the field for the full 80 minutes, while forwards are generally rotated in the modern game.

I looked forward to working with Richie again. I wasn't to know that the next time we got together the occasion would prove to be the lowlight of both our international careers.

Chapter 13.

Shocker in Sydney

Frank Endacott's Kiwis had established records for winning margins and highest scores in test matches against several countries. But in the 2000 Anzac test they suffered the biggest hiding ever given a New Zealand team when the Kangaroos won 52–0 in Sydney. The scoreline was a blow to coach and players, and to international rugby league in a World Cup year. The after-match reaction also brought the by now Wigan-based Endacott into serious conflict with members of the New Zealand Rugby League board.

Hindsight, they say, is a wonderful thing and if I was to claim now for the first time that the 2000 Anzac test should never have been played then it would have a hollow ring to it. But I can reveal for the first time that I strongly recommended to New Zealand Rugby League president Gerald Ryan that unless we were competing on an even playing field there was no point in playing the Australians.

The fax to Gerald was sent from Wigan on January 31, almost three months before the game, which had been scheduled for Good Friday, April 21, at Sydney's Stadium Australia. After a flurry of optimistic statements that the test would be staged at Wellington's new WestpacTrust Stadium, it had been announced in early December that the NZRL had 'reluctantly' relinquished home ground advantage. That was like a red rag to a bull as far as I was concerned. It seemed to me that the Australians had bluffed us again. New Zealand's share from the Stadium Australia business plan and budget was to be $500,000. There was more pie in the sky stuff about general manager Gary Allcock going to Australia to negotiate for a second test after the National Rugby League grand final and to lobby for three test matches as well as a Tri-Nations series in 2001. None of that ever happened.

What brought matters to a head was the latest fight for the services of the Paul brothers and Richie Blackmore. I had told the NZRL I saw no point in selecting them if they could not be in Sydney by at least the Tuesday morning prior to the Friday night test. My Wigan club had scheduled a Friday night match the week before the test and I wanted the players to be on the plane alongside me when I left Manchester on the Saturday morning. But with Bradford Bulls chairman Chris Caisley also being chairman of the English Super League a clash of interests was inevitable and there were no prizes for guessing who would win.

New Zealand was still banging its head against a brick wall quoting the International Federation clause that players must have five clear days to prepare for test duty. As far as the Brits were concerned the 'five clear days' started at fulltime of their previous club game and could therefore include a 24-hour air flight.

The Australian Rugby League was reported to be nervous about its predicted million-dollar gate if the Kiwis were forced to field a weakened team. They knew the Paul brothers had a certain exotic quality that was usually only seen in Australasia once a year. Just about everyone else running around in a trans-Tasman test could be seen playing in the Australasian club competition every week. Even the National Rugby League's new chief executive, David Moffett, had grandstanded about lifting the promotion of the Anzac test to the level of rugby union's Bledisloe Cup. But, to me, having the Australians on our side was even more worrying than being at loggerheads with them. At least you really knew where you stood then.

So I sent the following fax to Gerard Ryan at the New Zealand Rugby League office:

'Thank you for your faxes explaining the situation regarding the availability of the UK-based players for the Anzac test match.

'It once again shows a complete disregard to the agreement of all international nations to make their players available five full days prior to a test match.

'This happens every year at this time and I, like you, find it very frustrating listening to the fragile excuses given by certain English clubs not to release their players within the time frame.

'The fact is, Gerald, to compete with Australia we need to be close to full strength to continue our competitive nature and the success we have shown over recent years, and also our credibility.

'Gerald, I believe it is time to stand up and be counted. We have already given the edge to Australia by giving them what should be a New Zealand home test. Do we give them a further advantage by not having our full squad available until two days prior to the match?

'The Australians will always agree with the English because they see us as a major threat to their crown.

'I would strongly suggest we cancel the Anzac test if our players are not made available for the normal assembly date, but only after all channels have been exhausted to encourage the English clubs to see common sense on the issue.

'I know this is drastic action but I firmly believe New Zealand has been the victim of devious actions by Australia and Great Britain on far too many occasions and now is the time to stand up for what is right.'

I added a postscript, asking: 'Gerald, if [Bradford's] Paul brothers and [Huddersfield's] Gene Ngamu are not available and Stacey Jones still has a question mark over his injury, who would be our two halves for the test and who would provide the cover on the bench?'

Within 24 hours of Ryan receiving my fax, Australian Rugby League chairman Colin Love announced in Sydney he had written to Britain's Rugby Football League supporting New Zealand's stance over the Paul brothers and other players who might be required for the test. Love claimed the ARL believed the Anzac test would have the same profile in Australia within five years as the annual State of Origin series between New South Wales and Queensland. That in itself was an interesting comment, considering the Anzac test was scuttled only months after Love made his statement.

Despite the lobbying from Down Under, Bradford continued to insist Henry and Robbie Paul make themselves available for their club match against Salford on what was the Monday morning Sydney time. That meant they could not reach the Kiwi camp until late Tuesday night, jetlag and all, and that we would have only one serious training day before taking on the best team in the world.

When the International Federation finally got together, after the reluctant British had deferred the meeting, it was March and too late to pull the plug on the test because the venue, television and other contracts had been signed.

Naturally, the Australians did a massive backflip and sided with the Poms, just as I had predicted in my fax to Gerald Ryan. Once again Bradford had beaten the New Zealand Rugby League, with a lot of help from their friends, and the showcase test match between the sport's top two nations had been relegated behind what was expected to be a one-sided club game in England.

I have since been told the test match could not be played in New Zealand on Good Friday because of restrictions applying to such things as the selling of liquor on that day. But this was supposed to be the Anzac test, not the Good Friday test or the Easter test, and should have been moved to a different date without gifting Australia home ground advantage. Good Friday suited Australia's argument that they could not easily get players home from New Zealand for their Easter weekend club commitments. Once that home ground was given away everything started sliding.

By the end of March the Australians had their own referee, Bill Harrigan, polishing up his whistle for the occasion. All previous Anzac tests had been controlled by Englishmen Russell Smith and Stuart Cummings, and Smith had officiated in two exciting Tri-Nations matches the previous year. I could live with that concession at the time because I considered Harrigan to be by far the best referee in the world. But the Australians were again calling the shots. If this was a money-saving decision where was all that Australian confidence about a million-dollar gate?

It was becoming all too familiar with our casualties too. Quentin Pongia was sitting out a seven-week suspension, Ruben Wiki had broken an arm, Brian Jellick suffered a broken ankle, Richie Barnett, Nathan Cayless and Jarrod McCracken were in doubt because of leg injuries, and Stacey Jones had not resumed playing for the Warriors because his broken arm was taking longer than expected to heal. It was getting to the stage where I didn't want to answer the phone. At least the Paul brothers were playing with all of their flair at Bradford and Richie Blackmore zoomed back into calculations with Leeds after shaking off the groin problems which had dogged him for two years.

With so many top-liners in doubt the last thing I needed was New Zealand Rugby League board member Bernie Wood voicing the opinion that Quentin Pongia should not be considered for selection because of his judicial record. I thought West Coasters were supposed to stick together. Wood reckoned Pongia was a poor role model.

I have never had a more committed player in any of my teams than Quentin Pongia, whether it was for Canterbury, the Warriors or the Kiwis. Sure, his tackling style got him into trouble in Australia but Pongia never missed a test for New Zealand while under suspension, from his debut in 1992 through to when Gary Freeman left him out of the 2001 side.

If we allowed the vagaries of the Australian judiciary to dictate whose tackling styles were acceptable for international selection then John Lomax,

Jarrod McCracken, Stephen Kearney, Matthew Ridge and Dean Bell are just some Kiwis who wouldn't have seen much test service. Then there was their infatuation with Craig Smith's running style in 2001, when they suspended him twice for allegedly lifting his knees while ignoring everybody else.

From my point of view I thought Quentin Pongia was a safe bet for the Anzac test. The seven weeks on the sidelines would keep him fresh and, perhaps more important, safe from the judiciary. He would have two games back to get ready for the Aussies. Instead, the poor bugger went and tore a tendon in his arm. Pongia was so desperate to play for us that even when his Sydney Roosters club doctor told him he needed an operation and three months' recuperation he sought out Kiwi doctor Tony Edwards for a second opinion. But the diagnosis was the same.

He was one of eight Kiwis out for one reason or another. Jarrod McCracken and Nathan Cayless recovered from their earlier injuries, only for McCracken to badly bruise a leg and Cayless to break a thumb. Ruben Wiki (arm) and Brian Jellick (ankle) also had broken limbs, Logan Swann did a knee, Willie Talau sprained ankle ligaments, and Ali Lauiti'iti got himself suspended. Worse, Pongia, McCracken, Talau and Lauiti'iti became forced withdrawals in the week of the test, leaving precious little time to plug the gaps.

I had named a 19-man squad during the previous week, with Lauiti'iti, who had toured Britain in 1998 without actually playing, and Melbourne Storm stand-off half Tasesa Lavea the only prospective new caps. Lavea had enjoyed a meteoric rise but I had the Pauls in mind to compete for the No. 6 jersey and young Tasesa was included as a future prospect. Australian and Melbourne coach Chris Anderson backed my judgement by describing Lavea as a talented kid who might not yet be ready for the international stage. Unbeknown to Chris and myself, he soon had to get himself ready.

The days leading up to the test were a nightmare, as players came and went as if through a revolving door. On the Monday Willie Talau hobbled off. On Tuesday Quentin Pongia and Jarrod McCracken were declared non-starters. That night Ali Lauiti'iti was suspended for four matches.

We called Tony Puletua in from Penrith, and David Kidwell received a shock when he went to the Parramatta reserve grade team's training and finished up running with us. Kidwell swapped his Parramatta shirt for manager Gary Cooksley's Kiwi top and borrowed a Kiwi cap to keep the sponsors happy during an interview with a television journalist. The Pauls and Richie Blackmore trained for the first time on the Wednesday. Our first two days together were a complete waste of time. We did what we could with about a dozen fit players, waited for our plane to come in, and wrestled with various selection posers.

I considered making another plea for Kevin Iro to come out of retirement but he was too far away at St Helens.

In desperation we tried to enlist Christchurch-born Brisbane Bronco Tonie Carroll to play in the centres. But Australian officials told him he would never play State of Origin football again if he turned out for us. They completely ignored that Papua New Guinea captain Adrian Lam and Kiwi prop Craig Smith had played State of Origin for Queensland when it was convenient. There were double standards at play here.

We still finished up with 17 individuals who were all good players in their own right. But the team had a makeshift appearance, most notably with Henry Paul suddenly finding himself in the centres so that Richie Barnett could stay at fullback. Tyran Smith was first recalled to replace Logan Swann in the larger squad and then promoted into the starting line-up when there were so many more defections. Instead of a power-packed, forward-dominated bench, we were left with two backs, David Kidwell and Tasesa Lavea, sitting alongside Jason Lowrie and Tony Puletua.

The only joy in the build-up occurred on the Tuesday, when Soky's Rage, a horse I was racing in Sydney with Canterbury Rugby League development officer Jeff Whittaker, bolted in at Harold Park. Our training schedule prevented us from getting to the track but there were plenty of happy Kiwis watching the telecast in a local TAB. We would have been even happier if Peter Leitch, the Mad Butcher, hadn't told half the population of Parramatta that Soky's Rage was a good thing. There were queues lining up to back her, and the odds plummeted from 16:1 until she started favourite.

But on Black Friday (there was nothing Good about it) we were on a hiding to nothing, and we got that hiding from a typically ruthless Australian team. Mat Rogers had a ball, scoring 24 of their 52 points, and we were never competitive after the opening minutes.

We actually began strongly, with Joe Vagana reaching the goal-line before being penalised for a double movement by Australian video referee Colin Ward. Then Bill Harrigan wrongly ruled a forward pass when Vagana put Matt Rua into the clear with the goal-line beckoning. In the next set of six our defence collapsed, and Brad Fittler skipped through to open the floodgates.

The Kiwis made every mistake possible that night. Nigel Vagana and Lesley Vainikolo both misjudged high kicks and presented the Australians with soft tries. Fittler and Brett Kimmorley tormented our blokes with their kicking game. Our backs were disjointed because of the pressure the Kangaroos exerted on Stacey Jones and the Paul brothers. They showed up Henry's inexperience in the centres. Our forwards seldom went forward. Australia dominated possession.

Craig Smith and Stephen Kearney covered themselves in glory, and bruises, trying to stop the roll-on effects of Gorden Tallis, Rodney Howe, Shane Webcke and their mates. Matt Rua was concussed when he wore Chris McKenna's knee in a tackle. Poor Matt was probably the luckiest Kiwi because he couldn't remember much about the whole debacle.

Captain Richie Barnett was the unluckiest player after suffering the most sickening injury I have seen on a football field, and on his twenty-ninth birthday too. Richie had his head smashed in a full-on collision with a rampant Wendell Sailor, leaving him with multiple facial injuries and a broken jaw. He underwent emergency surgery and had 10 permanent plates inserted. Not many people expected to see Richie back in action during 2000, but his return to lead the Kiwis at the World Cup is one of the most inspiring and courageous stories in New Zealand sport.

Stephen Kearney came out publicly after the test defending Stacey Jones' kicking game, which wasn't a patch on those produced by Kimmorley and Fittler. Kearney was adamant the forwards had let Stacey down and should shoulder a fair amount of the blame for what happened. I promised the post-match media conference they would see a very different Kiwi team at the World Cup. We were humiliated and didn't like it. There were reasons but no excuses for such a shocker. The 52-point margin between the first and second ranked teams provided plenty of ammunition for those who had an axe to grind. The prophets of doom in the sections of the Australian media that cannot see beyond their own club competition suggested it was not even worth holding the World Cup.

We knew there would be some fallout after a result like that. But I wasn't prepared for what happened within minutes of fulltime. Just as I was going into the after-match function at the team's Parramatta hotel I was confronted by Bill McEntee, a New Zealand Rugby League board member who had obviously enjoyed the hospitality at Stadium Australia more than the game.

McEntee verbally abused me and said there was going to be a major inquiry into the Kiwi performance. We had a few heated words. It's not often the veins stick out on my neck but they did that night. There were seven or eight people around him. I turned towards McEntee and suggested the inquiry should be into why the board played the game after bowing to the Australians' every whim. He doesn't know to this day how close he was to getting one on his beak.

The official attendance at Stadium Australia was 26,023, about a quarter of the ground's capacity. Match promotion had been typically poor. I wonder how little of the promised $500,000 the NZRL actually received from the Australians.

Afterwards, I repeated my plea for the NZRL to get tough or forget about Anzac tests. It was interesting to note that the two national bodies abandoned the Anzac concept for 2001. That decision was supposedly by mutual agreement but you can bet it was an Australian initiative. Their media reported Australia wanted to pick the Kangaroo team from the State of Origin matches in May and June, so the 2001 test was shunted back to July.

Obviously the air had to be cleared between the NZRL board and me before World Cup preparations could be put in place. I had been informed just before the Anzac test that my mother was dying, so instead of going straight back to Wigan I was on a plane to Christchurch the next morning to see her for the last time. I spent two days with Mum, then caught a flight to Auckland which gave me time for a meeting requested by the board before travelling on to England that night.

We met for about an hour and a half and I made it crystal clear I didn't want to leave the boardroom until I had the absolute, unanimous support of every one of the seven board members in the room. I said if I didn't have their unanimous support they could have my resignation on the spot.

They all looked at each other and I could sense four were positive but that Bud Lisle, Bill McEntee and Bernie Wood were not. McEntee was obviously still hurting after the words we had in Sydney, and Wood kept making 'helpful' interjections until I asked him about his coaching qualifications. There was some pretty heavy discussion and questioning about the Anzac test, but when it was time for me to leave for the airport every one of them said they were totally satisfied and supportive.

I shook their hands, walked out the door, went down in the lift with general manager Gary Allcock, and my son Shane drove me to the airport. When I reached England I was told by the time Allcock had gone back up in the lift those three men wanted me sacked from the World Cup job. It would have taken no more than three minutes for them to show their true characters.

The other four, Gerald Ryan, Gary Allcock, Wayne Morris and Bob Haddon, had always been supportive. But with such a split in the ranks I decided then to finish up after the World Cup. When word leaked out about the meeting, Ryan said he would have used his casting vote to retain me as coach had it been necessary. He confirmed the board had been divided and that the meeting became acrimonious after I had left.

All of those years of bickering over player availability from Britain could so easily have been avoided, even by means other than a strong International Federation refusing to bend the knee to one or two selfish clubs. There were never more than two or three players involved and it would have been a simple matter for their clubs to have played their fixtures on Friday nights prior to Anzac tests. The Paul boys tried to put a brave face on dashing across the world to play Australia but it was Richie Blackmore's first time in 2000 and you could see how much it affected him.

It's not easy fending off Brad Fittler with one hand and jetlag with the other. When Australia made their short 2001 tour to Britain they made the mistake of departing too late and consequently lost the first test. By 2002 a lot of the leading British clubs were gravitating towards Friday night football on their own accord, with fewer games on Sundays. Maybe Gary Allcock and I were ahead of our time when we had suggested exactly that a few years earlier.

# Chapter 14.
Taking on the world

The Millennium World Cup, awarded to Britain after the rousing success of its predecessor in 1995, was to be the biggest rugby league celebration of all time. Sixteen nations competed in four pools, with matches in England, Wales, Ireland, Scotland and France. Despite the huge loss at Sydney in April, Frank Endacott's Kiwis were ranked second behind the Kangaroos. They were in a preliminary group with the Cook Islands, a Lebanese side comprised entirely of ethnic Australians, and Wales. The seedings dictated New Zealand would progress to meet France in the quarter-finals, with third-ranked England barring the way to the final at Manchester United's famed field of dreams, Old Trafford.

When it came to the crunch there was no challenge to my remaining coach when the New Zealand Rugby League board met in mid-May. Being based in Wigan and not likely to meet up with the Kiwis until a week before our opening World Cup match, I had recommended that Gary Kemble be put in charge of early preparations at home in conjunction with team manager Gary Cooksley. Kemble would then have joined me in Britain as my assistant. The board didn't quite see it that way. Graeme Norton was appointed project manager with

Kemble as his offsider. Neither accompanied the players to the World Cup.

I never had a problem with Norton's appointment but from comments by the players and staff it really was a waste of time. I was supposed to be informed weekly as to what was going on and heard nothing. They actually scrapped the last camp at Palmerston North without my knowing why. But I wasn't too concerned because the minute the team arrived in England I knew we would start doing it my way.

We had some good news in July when Tonie Carroll agreed to make himself available for the Kiwis. It helped our cause that he had signed to play for Leeds and was effectively making himself unavailable for any more State of Origin or Australian selections. Carroll loved playing for the Kiwis at the World Cup and I thought he would be a regular test player for years to come. But in 2001 he declined the chance of playing for Gary Freeman against Australia at Wellington.

There could have been some pressure exerted by Leeds because the test was in the middle of their season, or maybe he thought the dramatic recall of Alfie Langer for the deciding 2001 State of Origin match might enable him to go back for future games. That was a one-off situation, though. It would be a shame if Carroll's World Cup appearance was a oncer for the Kiwis because at 25 he still has much to offer.

The will-he or won't-he saga about whether Richie Barnett would play at the World Cup after his horrific injuries in the Anzac test occupied plenty of media time and space. I was in constant touch with Richie and his wife, Carrie, checking up on his condition, especially after it soon became obvious that the initial three-month recuperation period was very optimistic. As the months went by everyone, and I mean everyone, told me there was no chance he would be available. But for some reason I always believed Richie would be back, and kept telling that to people in England. Sure enough, he produced one of the great sporting comebacks of all time.

When Richie led the Kiwis onto the field against Lebanon at Gloucester it was exactly six months and eight days after he had been taken away from Stadium Australia by ambulance. That sickening crunch with Wendell Sailor must have required tremendous mental and physical powers of recovery, but in his first game Richie quickly tested himself by taking the ball up to the opposition. It was not long before he was showing us that old brilliant attacking style from fullback and an international panel chose him as the best fullback at the tournament ahead of Darren Lockyer and Kris Radlinski. No one had more reason to stay away from the World Cup. The injury cost Richie a grand final appearance with the Sydney Roosters, and he was putting at risk a new contract he had signed with the London Broncos. What's more, Carrie was due to have their first baby while he was away. No matter what was achieved at the World Cup, Richie's courage overshadowed everything else in my mind.

When the 23-man team were named in August, centres Tonie Carroll and David Vaealiki were the only new caps, but although they both had Canterbury connections they came from vastly different rugby league backgrounds. Carroll had been hardened by his State of Origin experiences, and was a product of the Australian system, while Vaealiki was realising all of the potential he had shown during New Zealand elite camps and as Canterbury's youngest ever senior representative. Vaealiki had one advantage over Carroll, though — he was far more familiar with the haka!

Tough nuts Quentin Pongia, Ruben Wiki, Nathan Cayless, Logan Swann and Willie Talau were on board again after missing the Anzac disaster but, sadly, Jarrod McCracken's career had been ended by injury.

We had heard reports that Sydney-based Samoan coach Darrell Williams was making overtures to some of our players for his World Cup squad — shades of Graham Lowe five years earlier. The Vagana cousins and Ali Lauiti'iti were all mentioned and we tried to warn Williams off.

Gerald Ryan was hopping mad when Williams, himself a former Kiwi and more recently a member of the notorious National Rugby League judiciary, included Lauiti'iti plus Tony Puletua and Tasesa Lavea in a 37-man squad a week before we were to name all three of them in our team. As I had told Williams back in April, he was farting against thunder if he really thought any of our players were going to change camps.

Just before the players were to leave for England the Auckland Warriors came back to haunt me. The club was changing hands again and players were concerned whether their contracts would be honoured. The Australian Rugby League Players' Association stirred things up and so did players' manager Simon Burgess, whose clients included Joe Vagana and Logan Swann. There were threats of a World Cup boycott spreading through the squad because of the wildly inaccurate stories being bandied around, and I spent long nights on the phone trying to sort it out. In the end I gave the players a deadline to meet or I would replace them in the team. All the players checked in, said they were available and had no problems, except for Joe and Logan. I contacted both of them and gave them until the next day to confirm they were coming to England, which they did.

Burgess actually flew to England, where he was negotiating with Bradford on Joe's behalf. He ran into Gerald Ryan, trainer Bob Lanigan and a couple of others in the foyer of our hotel and they told him to get lost, or words to that effect. Joe thought that I was one of those who kicked Burgess out of the hotel but I wouldn't even know what he looked like if I passed him in the street.

Burgess then rang me in my room. I respected he had a job to do and gave him permission to contact Joe. But I told him to get the business done as quickly as possible so Joe could concentrate on his duties with the New Zealand squad. I've heard Joe made comment that I had his contract but there was no truth in that whatsoever. I didn't care where Joe played. Presumably they all lived happily immediately after, Joe with his Bradford deal and a share in the grand final win over Wigan, and Logan because he stayed with the Warriors under their new management for a successful 2001 season.

Terrible weather beset the World Cup from the start and it was difficult to get combinations working smoothly in gale force winds and driving rain. The most pleasing aspects of a big win over Lebanon were Richie Barnett's two tries in a Man of the Match performance, and Tonie Carroll's double on debut. Three Lebanese players were later treated for mild hypothermia. The weather was obviously a lot worse than the average Sydneysider was accustomed to.

Four days later, at Reading, Richie Barnett crossed for two more tries as we scored a New Zealand test record 84 points against a Cook Islands side which featured Kevin Iro in the centres. Tasesa Lavea grabbed 32 points, another record, and this time it was David Vaealiki's turn to score two tries first-up.

We expected Wales to be a big step up after they had reached the semi-finals in 1995. But our 58–18 win at Cardiff's Millennium Stadium was easily a record in eight matches between our two countries over more than 90 years. Lesley Vainikolo made a massive impression with a try-scoring treble and Richie Barnett got two more. The overall display, however, wasn't as good as the score might have suggested. There were too many errors for my liking.

Stacey Jones was rested for the quarter-final against France at Castleford, and Robbie Paul enjoyed his chance to pull on the No. 7 jersey so much that he scored three tries in a 54–6 canter. Our forwards were rock solid in a match that marked Richie Blackmore's farewell to the Kiwis after a decade of service. The one-sided games were making it hard to gauge how well we, or the Australians in their own pool, were going.

Our semi-final, against England, seemed to be the tougher of the two, with Australia expected to beat the Welsh at least as easily as we had. But the pundits were wrong on both counts. While the Kiwis romped to a 49–6 victory, the heaviest defeat ever inflicted on England by any opponent, Wales amazingly led Australia into the second half until the Kangaroos were stung into action. Still, many described the 22–46 Welsh loss as a moral victory. Australia had beaten England by a comparatively modest 22–2 in the tournament opener, so the margin of our victory was very satisfying. On reflection, we peaked a week too soon. I thought it was just about flawless, the way we took England to the cleaners. A lot of homework had been done on their playmakers and everything we planned came off that night.

Lesley Vainikolo further enhanced his growing reputation as The Volcano with two more tries and Henry Paul was on target with eight goals and a field goal. England coach John Kear was kind enough to describe the Kiwis' performance as 'a bit special'.

Next day the Kangaroos got the fright of their lives, unfortunately. Any complacency they might have developed while thrashing the likes of Russia by 110 points was wiped away in the first hour against a remarkably determined Welsh side. At one stage Australia was down 8–20. It was 14–20 at halftime and the game was into its final quarter before the Kangaroos finally broke the Welsh spirit. The Australian players owned up to not showing the Welsh due respect, and you can bet their management cancelled any nightclubbing they might have had in mind for the week leading up to the World Cup final.

I was doing the live comments for the British Sky television channel at the match and was trying to hide my excitement. But when the Aussies came back to win I knew they would receive a major shake-up from Chris Anderson. Wales had done us no favours.

Although Russell Smith had seen fit to award Australia seven consecutive penalties in the second half against Wales he was our choice to referee the final. Australia was dead against Smith and naturally wanted their own Tim Mander or Bill Harrigan. The compromise decision, made by British-based Australian Greg McCallum, who was in charge of match officials, was for another Englishman, Stuart Cummings. I just expressed the wish that Cummings didn't allow himself to be intimidated by the Australians.

We were confident going into the final, though we tried to play it down. I wouldn't have swapped our forwards for any pack in the world despite the English bookies making Australia a warm favourite and their big men getting plenty of pre-match publicity.

It was inevitable the British spectators would get behind us if we were a winning chance, as they had in that 1995 extra-time semi-final at Huddersfield. There could be no better place to finish one's coaching career than at Old Trafford and, despite the continuing wet weather and lack of a British team in the final, 44,000 fans turned out. I must admit I had a lump in my throat.

There were some nervous players around the hotel during the week so we tried to relax them. Training went well until I noticed a bit of fatigue on the Thursday morning. I stopped that session to freshen them up approaching the game.

When we were on our way to the ground the heavens opened up and the rain poured down. It seemed to be a good omen for us. While the Australians had stayed overnight in Manchester we were required to travel over from Yorkshire. The police escort inexplicably took us through the backroads and got us there half an hour later than scheduled. We only had time to briefly look at the pitch, get changed, and it was game on.

The first half belonged to Australia and I am convinced that if possession had been equally shared we would have won. There were two things which contributed to the imbalance, a very good kicking game from Brett Kimmorley to give them field position, and a couple of balls we dropped to put ourselves under pressure. To go in at halftime trailing only 0–6 represented a great defensive effort.

As I glanced around the dressing room, though, it was obvious we had spent a lot of energy and were going to have our work cut out containing them. The Australians weren't breathing too hard but we were really struggling for air. To the players' credit, they went out in the second half and played their guts out. We scored a couple of tries to get us back into the game and after 65 minutes there was still only six points in it. But in the last quarter of an hour the defensive wall crumbled and the much fresher Australians took a severe toll. You look at a 12–40 scoreline and say it must have been a thrashing but in this case it was nothing of the sort.

Our blokes got caught out on their left flank two or three times. They were buggered, they had put such a strong defensive effort in and couldn't see the 80 minutes out. The Kangaroos were right on their game after that scare against the Welsh. If they had cruised through their semi-final the way they had cruised through their earlier games we would have been the ones to catch them off guard.

I remember the strained expressions on the faces of the Australians before the kick-off. They seemed very uneasy about the match, and knew if there was one team in the world capable of beating them it was the Kiwis. I had never felt so confident as I did that week. I really believed it was going to be our World Cup. But we never had the ball or the field position to capitalise on their self-doubts. Our kicking game wasn't good but it did cause an amusing interlude. Henry Paul had been given specific instructions to pepper Mat Rogers, who sometimes can be a bit suspect under the high ball. Rogers had his hair bleached blond so was standing out like a beacon on his wing. The plan was to keep the ball away from big Wendell Sailor over on the other flank. Yet every kick Henry put up was going down Sailor's throat.

At halftime I told Henry our kicking game was crap. 'I asked you to kick to

Mat Rogers. He's the wee blond bloke not the big brown bloke on the other wing.' Straight after halftime Henry kicked again to Sailor and I wondered what I was saying wrong. It wasn't one of Henry's best games in the Kiwi jersey but he has had plenty of good ones so you don't hold that against him. Meanwhile, the Australians were dropping precision bombs on Lesley Vainikolo and Nigel Vagana from a great height.

After the game Stephen Kearney, knowing it was my last time with the Kiwis, swallowed his own disappointment, stood up, and said some lovely words. Ruben Wiki came over and gave me his No. 13 jersey, which I will always treasure. It was all very emotional, leaving me with a hollow feeling as I left the dressing room for the last time. Majestic Old Trafford was a world away from that little wooden hut in Addington where it had all started.

Kangaroo captain Brad Fittler admitted later he had never been so nervous before any game, and coach Chris Anderson said he was still worried about the outcome into the final quarter. Anderson and Wendell Sailor both rated the Kangaroos as among the best to wear the green and gold, tributes to our performance which were no consolation at the time but mean something now.

Australia's extreme depth of talent was emphasised yet again when young Trent Barrett came on when our blokes were dragging their legs and immediately set up one try and scored another from 60 metres. Sailor grabbed two quick tries to tip the balance and laid on another with a grubber kick, while Fittler had his customary big-match impact.

Lesley Vainikolo really sharpened his finishing skills, completing the tournament with his ninth try and obviously planting some thoughts in the minds of Bradford officials. After his 2001 season at Canberra was ruined by injury, Vainikolo signed for Bradford. His next try on British soil was in the Bulls' 2002 World Club Challenge victory over the Newcastle Knights at Huddersfield. Tonie Carroll, who was already with Leeds, and Craig Smith were others to stand out in the final and Wigan snapped up Smith as soon as he wanted a change from the NRL.

Tonie Carroll's dedication to the Kiwi cause could not be questioned. About 10am the next morning I was in the middle of a television interview in a room at our hotel when the door was pushed open. Standing there was Tonie, obviously the worse for wear, with a can of beer in his hand. It was more than 14 hours after fulltime but he was still wearing his full Kiwi strip right down to his boots, mouthguard, and headgear. We stopped the interview and I asked him, 'Tonie, what's wrong?' He replied, 'Coach, I didn't turn up to play yesterday so here I am now, ready to play.'

It was a bloody funny interlude but I believe Tonie was being hard on himself because he had played well in the final.

At the post-match media conference I reiterated that having to tackle, tackle and tackle again in that first half was the winning and losing of the World Cup, that it had taken the juice out of our players and Australia made us pay for it. I had already told the players in the dressing room that I was proud of every one of them. You can never ask a player to go out and win for you, but you can ask them to go out and give their best, and they did that.

I was asked by a British journalist if I would consider coaching England or Great Britain once I had finished with the Kiwis, but laughed it off. There is no way I could imagine coaching against players I had been so close to for so long.

If it had not been for the run-in with those three NZRL board members after the Anzac test I might have continued to coach the Kiwis. Several times in the months leading up to the World Cup, Gerald Ryan offered me another two years in the job. It was certainly an attractive proposition but I had always said that if I didn't have the unanimous support of the board I was not interested.

I made no firm recommendation to the NZRL about a successor. A lot of names were being bandied about, including several prominent Australian coaches. While I said it was always best to have a New Zealander in charge, I conceded there might be a case to look overseas if the locals did not have the necessary experience. But I added a rider that if they were going to bring in an outsider they should also appoint someone like Gary Kemble to be his understudy for two years as a prelude to taking over as head coach. Gerard Stokes was another I mentioned because he had the distinct advantage of coaching on a week-to-week basis in the Bartercard Cup.

The board did not ask me to be any more specific than that so I wasn't going to poke my nose in where it wasn't wanted. But when they did appoint Gary Freeman from Sydney, they also made Stokes his assistant and a co-selector. They then returned to the old 1994–95 policy of having an Australian-based selector in Jarrod McCracken. Not much else changed, though. In Gary Freeman's first year he had to grin and bear it when British clubs refused to release players for the mid-season test against France in Auckland, while the Paul brothers again stepped off a 30-hour flight and went straight to training in the week of the Australian test at Wellington. That was Henry Paul's last test before switching to rugby union.

I loved just about every minute of my seven years with the Kiwis and appreciated what Peter Bidwell, in the *Dominion* newspaper, wrote about my relationship with the players: 'Even people with little interest in league were drawn to Endacott because of his warm, generous personality, strong record as Kiwi coach, and reluctance to become embroiled in the public blood-letting which is so much a part of rugby league.

'The burly Endacott was never one to back away from a scrap, but it was usually only after he had been provoked or was in defence of his beloved players. He was very much a players' coach, and they in turn were highly supportive of him. To see the Kiwis assemble in his hotel room in Sydney this year was like watching a proud father welcoming home his children. There was huge mutual respect between them. He gave them the confidence to play to the best of their ability.'

The calibre of player made my task so much smoother. I was also lucky to have excellent managers in Sel Shanks and Joe Diamond, Ray Haffenden and Bevan Olsen, John Devonshire and Gary Cooksley. It was pleasing to see Gordon Gibbons, who was so often with us as the Lion Breweries' representative, elevated to team manager under Gary Freeman. Terry Baker, from Air New Zealand, was an excellent travel manager and would have fully deserved the New Zealand Warriors' 2001 Clubman of the Year award. There were many, many great fans who popped up in the most unlikely places to support the Kiwis. But Peter Leitch, the Mad Butcher, was the type of supporter who would follow his team to the ends of the earth.

Chapter 15.
Top ten

From the 55 players who represented New Zealand during the seven-year term as coach, Frank Endacott was asked to select a top 10. He named them in no particular order, then increased the list to the entirely appropriate number of 13 by adding three others.

This was the hardest selection I have ever made. Over the years I was privileged to coach so many outstanding players, but there is a distinction between very good players and truly great players. In earlier chapters I praised the natural talent of Logan Edwards and sheer toughness of Brendon Tuuta, but their international careers were comparatively brief. My top 10 Kiwis are listed just as they came to mind.

Stacey Jones
Stacey Jones is the first name to spring to most people's minds when they think of the Kiwis and Warriors. As a 19-year-old, he took over from our most capped international, Gary Freeman, in difficult circumstances at the 1995 World Cup and has been an automatic selection, and one of the game's most popular players, ever since. It really was a cauldron at Warrington on his debut night as Tonga did everything but beat us. Stacey was never overawed. Despite the responsibilities lumped on him, he had such raw ability and such a positive attitude he was

always going to take the step up to international football in his stride.

Stacey is still going from strength to strength and when he retires it will be as one of New Zealand's greatest players. He has developed into both the off-field public face and the on-field backbone of the Warriors. The Australian clubs now realise Stacey is the player they have to subdue if they are to beat the Warriors. Australian publications are inclined to overlook, or underestimate, some of the Warriors because they are based in another country and are not seen as often as the Australian-resident players. But it is now commonplace to see Stacey listed among the very best halfbacks in the National Rugby League competition, along with Andrew Johns, Brett Kimmorley and company. It is obvious from comments made by Johns, arguably the best player in the world, and former champions Allan Langer and Peter Sterling, that the players themselves have the utmost respect for Stacey too. The prestigious 2001 Dally M rankings underlined all that, with Preston Campbell winning the title by one point from Andrew Johns with Stacey only one more point behind. Stacey effectively finished second because Johns was ineligible.

From the first time I saw Stacey at the national junior tournaments I knew he was going to make it. Stacey was very shy when he hit the big time, perhaps not surprising when most mothers just wanted to cuddle him. As his career has evolved, and with his experience of being co-captain and calling the shots for the Warriors, Stacey has come out of his shell. His impish sense of humour was always bubbling away just below the surface.

He might be small but Stacey is resilient, as his record of continuous service to the Kiwis and the Warriors shows, and he tackles above his weight. The broken arm he suffered against Tonga in 1999 saddened us all. Stacey, however, just got on with his rehabilitation and has bounced back better than ever. They still show film clips of that magnificent solo try at Penrith last year, when he used his eye for the gap, and his speed, serve, kick and retrieve, to leave the defence in tatters.

Ruben Wiki

One of the most reliable players I coached, Ruben Wiki did a sterling job for us in the centres before playing lock forward with equal effectiveness. He is well respected by the opposition, and had the strength and impressive physique which allowed him to be so versatile. I was lucky to be associated with Ruben in the Junior Kiwis and it was good that association carried through to the Kiwis.

Losing Ruben to the Canberra Raiders wasn't one of original chief executive Ian Robson's finest hours in the year leading up to the Warriors' entry into the Winfield Cup. Even though I was then reserve grade coach I was happy when the case was resolved in Ruben's favour and he was able to play in the environment he preferred.

I don't think it was reported in New Zealand but I was rushed across the Tasman to give evidence in the Canberra High Court when Ruben's future was being decided. Robson had rung from Canberra the night before and summoned me over for some reason which was never clarified. It was one of the longest days I ever put in. I flew out of Auckland at 8am, literally ran from the Sydney international terminal to catch a domestic flight to Canberra, took a cab to the court, was allowed to give evidence straight away because of my tight schedule, grabbed another cab back to Canberra airport, flew to Melbourne, and arrived home in Auckland at midnight.

To this day I still don't know the reason I was sent for. I was questioned by Ruben's solicitor and gave him such a glowing report he must have thought I was giving evidence on his behalf and not the Warriors. It was even suggested by the solicitor that Ruben looked on me as something of an uncle figure and advisor. I replied we had enjoyed a close association and said I had nothing but admiration for Ruben and his family. Ian Robson never told me what he thought of my contribution.

If anything has marked Ruben's career it has been loyalty to his club and country. He has played for the Raiders through good times and bad, never shirking whatever job they have given him from the centres to the front row. It was incredible that he still had the sharpness to revert to a midfield back position in the Kiwis while he was plugging a gap at prop for Canberra. It was the same with the Kiwis. It didn't matter what numbered jersey you tossed Ruben you knew he would give 100 per cent effort to honour it. He was a coach's dream. Whenever I would ask him to go into the forwards or return to the centres he would just say, 'I'll play anywhere.'

An amusing thing happened at Ruben's wedding in Auckland, when I was coaching the Warriors. Joan and I were sitting at a table with Laurie Daley, David Furner and their wives. Kevin Neil, the Canberra chief executive, finished his speech by saying he wanted me to know Ruben would always play for Canberra. Daley and Furner suggested I give an appropriate answer. I stood up, looked over to Kevin, and with the most triumphant expression I could muster told him that the lakeside signing we had all witnessed wasn't really a marriage register but a Warriors contract. It brought the house down.

Jarrod McCracken

Jarrod McCracken was one of the toughest and very best players I have seen. He had a certain aura about him. I first came across Jarrod as an 18-year-old playing for Auckland at the national tournaments and along with Bob Bailey and Laurie Stubbing selected him for the Junior Kiwis to play Australia. There were never any doubts about Jarrod; he impressed me as a world-beater from the start. Even though as a kid he was a bit rough around the edges he stood out from the others with his physique and attitude, and he always had a great sense of humour.

He must have made a similar impression on the Canterbury-Bankstown scouts when they 'discovered' him playing for Port Macquarie. The Bulldogs had gone to watch a centre in the other team, but he was completely outplayed by Jarrod and their scouts went into the Port Macquarie dressing room instead. As he developed his career Jarrod became a player the opposition feared.

Unfortunately, he was not always available to the Kiwis because of the Super League war. Jarrod was cruelly treated by the Bulldogs when they left him out of their grand final-winning team while the other so-called rebels, Dean Pay, Jim Dymock and Jason Smith, were all allowed to play. The Bulldogs didn't show much loyalty to someone who had been forced to withdraw from a Kiwi tour to Britain and France because he had ignored a chronic leg injury so that he could keep on playing on for the club.

Jarrod made a sensational start to his test career as a big, strong centre against France and Australia in 1991 and developed into one of the most rugged second-rowers in the game without losing any of the speed and ball skills he had perfected in the backs.

It was widely predicted that Jarrod had the size and robustness to move into the forwards, but he was adamant it would never happen. Only the next season he was wading into his work in the second row and loving every second of it. Jarrod never took a backward step, as we saw in his tussles with Gorden Tallis. Big Gordie was one of the most intimidating characters around but he stood toe to toe and eyeball to eyeball with him. If there was one player I wouldn't want to get into the ring with it was Jarrod.

Stephen Kearney

There have been few more accomplished forwards in modern rugby league than Stephen Kearney, and he could go on to become New Zealand's most capped international, providing the bloke who already holds that record keeps picking him. Stephen missed only three of my 35 tests, twice because of suspensions and once through injury, which shows how tough he has been and how proud he is to pull on the Kiwi jersey.

When Stephen was 15 years old he attended a national elite camp I was at. I can still vividly remember this kid sitting in the front row of seats asking all the questions. I took special note of that because I liked youngsters who wanted to learn as much as they could about the game.

As a 17-year-old he was playing hooker for Wellington and Syd Eru was playing at stand-off half. Cameron Bell, then the Auckland coach, and I sat down with the two of them and suggested strongly to Stephen he move to second row and to Syd, who impressed as a born hooker, to give up playing in the backs. Happily enough, they took our advice.

It wasn't all that long before Stephen was rising through the Australian ranks with the Western Suburbs President's Cup team. He walked away from a car accident one night and next day helped them win their grand final. And, of course, he was one of the strong men of a very powerful forward pack that carried the Melbourne Storm to their 1999 premiership.

I mark players down as being truly great when the opposition really rates them, and Stephen has earned the respect of all he has played against. He is the epitome of the true modern professional. He does everything right in his training and his diet, he's a very deep thinker, an intelligent bloke who is forever wanting to learn. Stephen will never stop learning, he's that sort of player. Sometimes he can be guilty of giving penalties away, but the positive qualities far outweigh that fault. He has one of the best off-loads I have ever seen in a footballer and is a menacing runner. So he can set his teammates up on attack, or run off them as a finisher.

Quentin Pongia

Quentin Pongia has one of the best motors I have seen in a rugby league player. He combines the 80-minute work ethic of an old-style prop forward with the modern expectations of being able to slip passes. Those skills were developed during his days as a second-rower on the West Coast and for the Riccarton and Linwood clubs in Canterbury before being taken up into the front row for his professional clubs and the Kiwis.

He is a player who has a love for the game and a hate of losing. Quentin will go down as a real tough nut, just like Jarrod McCracken. The tougher it was the better he went. It was never in Quentin's nature to take prisoners. But although his tackling style caused him to become all too familiar with the Australian judiciary system, he managed to space his suspensions so that they never caused him to miss a test match. Quite a feat that. Apart from resting him from one World Cup game, Quentin was missing from my teams only when he was injured.

On the successful 1998 tour to the UK, Quentin played right through the 160 minutes of the first two tests, something very few props in the world would have been able to do, and then complained bitterly when I brought him off in the third test. Quentin was also captain on that tour and deserves his place in history for being the first to not lose a test in a series in Britain. He might have been a man of few words but people were inclined to listen to all of them.

I first saw Quentin playing for Riccarton, which was then only a junior club, and rang Bob Bailey to tell him we had a prospect for the Junior Kiwis. Bob thought it was a long way to go to look at a forward running around on a suburban park in Christchurch but I managed to twist his arm. As soon as Bob looked at him he just muttered, 'He's in.' Quentin had come over from the West Coast at 16 or 17 and it was obvious even then he would be a great player.

Tim Sheens was fortunate to have Quentin Pongia and John Lomax as his props at Canberra and described them as the new breed of front-rowers. Canberra's previous premiership winning pair of Brent Todd and Glenn Lazarus were renowned for their uncompromising go-forward but Pongia and Lomax had more options and mobility from their days in the second row.

Quentin also gave dedicated service to the Warriors, and it was unfortunate that injuries plagued him after he had gone to the Sydney Roosters in 1999. But that was indicative of the way he played the game, so hard that something had to give occasionally. The injury cost him a longer term as test captain, but it was good to have him back in the team for the 2000 World Cup.

Craig Smith

I wish I had come across Craig Smith earlier in my coaching career. Craig emerged during the war between the ARL and Super League. Because he was with an ARL-aligned club he didn't come into calculations until the two factions were reunited and was a comparative latecomer to the Kiwis when we toured Britain in 1998. Craig appeared in only 11 tests for me but had the circumstances been different he would have played in many more.

You hear plenty of comments that prop forwards aren't the brightest people in the world but he doesn't conform to that image. Craig would be one of the most intelligent blokes you would ever meet, which explains why he went from Northland to high school in Brisbane on an educational rather than a sporting scholarship. He could have done really well in rugby union had old schoolmate Craig Polla-Mounter not persuaded him to try out for the Bulldogs. From there Craig went to Illawarra, the Dragons and Wigan.

Craig has a great off-load, an excellent knowledge of the game, and is a natural leader. And he maintains one of the highest work-rates I have seen. Craig is forever laying the foundation, ever going forward, and other players follow him. That's why he was captain of St George-Illawarra and it must have been a hard decision for Gary Freeman when he needed a new Kiwi captain in 2001. Nathan Cayless had age on his side, as well as a fine captaincy record with Parramatta, and Gary was probably looking for a long-term appointment. Craig would have been just as highly qualified.

We have had some fantastic front-rowers over the years. Whenever suspensions or injuries took a toll we could whistle up another couple of big, tough blokes who could be relied on to do a good job. But what Craig Smith and Quentin Pongia have done for the Kiwis in the last few years has been phenomenal.

I was tipped off about Craig Smith by Peter McLeod, who was manager of the Rest of the World team which played the ARL representative side during the split. Once Peter had talked about him I started taking a closer look and soon realised Craig was much better than I thought. He was a quiet achiever. On that 1998 tour to England he trained the house down. Because there were no midweek matches, just the three tests, Craig would be one of the few players to actually train his way into a test match. Craig was that keen he would be up at six o'clock every morning working with the gloves. Attitude-wise, you can't beat him. When I announced he was in the 17 for the test at Watford the other players all applauded. They really wanted him in there.

Henry Paul

My association with Henry Paul stretches back almost as far as that with Ruben Wiki. Henry came into the Junior Kiwis a year after Ruben, as captain for the 1993 tour to Britain and France. He was a specialist fullback on that trip but even then could play just about anywhere. Henry was a sensation on the junior tour, everyone in British rugby league who had seen him play were talking about him. Not too many could have stepped straight up to the Kiwis as Henry did when Howie Tamati called for a replacement on the senior tour.

Henry is such a talent. You never know what he is going to do, nor does the opposition. How could they, with Henry not always being too sure himself? From his younger days he has always had a special eye for the smallest gap, plus the footwork to open that into a yawning hole in the defence. He has become a more than capable goalkicker, virtually from nothing. It was typical of Henry that not too long after I asked him to practise his goalkicking, because we had just lost Matthew Ridge and Daryl Halligan, he went on to break Daryl's world record for consecutive goals.

During his test career Henry has played fullback, wing, centre, stand-off half and hooker. He started on the wing against France in 1995 to cover for an injury, and the appearance at centre was in a real emergency. He plays best at fullback, stand-off and hooker. Henry prefers stand-off but he was a revelation at hooker against Australia. His runs from acting half were electric and really shocked the Kangaroos.

You can see the enthusiasm that bubbles away in Henry. No matter how stressed he might have been when stepping off the plane from England in test week he would tear straight into training. It must have taken a toll but Henry never let it show.

He played especially well in combination with younger brother Robbie for Bradford and New Zealand. But they were different types. Robbie was more of a support player who would probably score more tries than Henry, but Henry would have created a good number of them. They used to feed off each other.

After Henry switched to rugby union, Robbie led Bradford to victory over the Newcastle Knights in the 2002 World Club Challenge. Robbie was still thinking of his brother during the post-match interviews and threatened to tease Henry about it, saying, 'I remember when he won that first Super League ring and would wear it around the house. So I went and got my '97 winner's medal and sellotaped it to my finger. Now I'll tell him he hasn't got one of these.'

Richie Barnett

Richie Barnett played for Auckland when I was still coaching Canterbury, and was subsequently signed by Cronulla. He always showed plenty of pace on the wing and made his Kiwi debut the same night as Stacey Jones at the 1995 World Cup. He had a good debut and would have been a regular even if he had stayed on the wing.

He has now emerged as one of the best attacking fullbacks in the game, and when I made him captain in 1999 he became an outstanding front man for rugby league. He was a pleasure to work with and I told the New Zealand Rugby League more than once that Richie would be a perfect role model to market the game.

Richie also enjoyed playing in the centres, and that desire had something to do with his transfer from the Sharks to the Roosters a few years ago. But I never really saw him as a centre. Instead, he showed enough on the wing for me to confidently put him at fullback when Matthew Ridge was missing, and give him the job fulltime after Ridge retired. Richie used to get up for those high balls with such confidence that, combined with his basic speed, I knew he would be a sharp attacker from the back. He proved to be an absolute success.

His comeback from a horrific injury in the 2000 Anzac test to lead the Kiwis at the World Cup was one of the most courageous things I have seen in sport. I really had a lump in my throat as I watched him lead the team out at

Gloucester. Everyone told me he wouldn't make it, everyone that is except Richie. We kept in touch and I always had the feeling from the tone of his voice that he would be there.

It would not have mattered to me if Richie had decided to be cautious and had withdrawn from the World Cup, because the most important thing was for him to get right again. He was more important to me as a person than as a player. But he felt confident about it, and so did I.

It's ironic that the last time I saw Richie he was cutting my Wigan team to ribbons for the London Broncos. I suppose he was one of the blokes responsible for me getting the sack. Richie was the best player on the park that day. We looked to have created a couple of certain tries, which would have won us the game. But Richie stopped them, and he caused us the usual problems with his broken field running. I had Wigan players come up to me after the game and admit that the homework we had done on him was 100 per cent accurate, but they just couldn't shut him down. He's a top player, and I won't hold that against him.

Matthew Ridge

There was never a more courageous player to pull on a footy jersey than Matthew Ridge. Sure, he was a handful in the early stages with his attitude and all that. I first selected Matthew in '94 when we toured Papua New Guinea and found him to be great company. He had badly blistered feet and couldn't do much training but wanted to play right or wrong. Matthew was critical to our team's success and the medical staff got him fit enough to play.

In '95, when Super League was started, Matthew was one of its high profile players and I thought it really affected him at times. Too much pressure was being put on him. Before a test match in Brisbane the whole team were training great except Matthew, who was pissing me off because his mind wasn't on the job. I sent the rest off for a quiet jog and told Matthew to stay with me. I told him we obviously had a problem, he didn't look interested, and I was 30 seconds away from making a vital decision on his international career. He looked me in the eye, patted me on the shoulder, and said, 'I understand what you're saying, leave it to me.' From then on he trained as good as anyone. His attitude changed immediately and I enjoyed working with him from then on.

Because he was around so long, Matthew was always an ideal player to bounce ideas off and talk about the opposition. But I always, repeat always, made the final decisions. We probably should have elevated Matthew to captain before he eventually led the team at the 1995 World Cup. I felt that was one of the best decisions I made, even if it was a little late.

Matthew obviously had the respect of the senior players and was a strong personality. When they had a dispute with Graham Carden about player payments during the '95 World Cup it was Matthew who led the charge on behalf of the team. He had plenty to say and maybe they had a good case. But that was never a mutiny. I would never have stood for that.

Some of the on-field and off-field strife Matthew allegedly got into wasn't his fault. When I was at the Warriors we asked the players to put down on paper any thoughts they had about where we could improve. Some of the comments indicated the Polynesian players weren't happy with Matthew over something he was reported to have said. But I supported Matthew because they were taken out of context. Sometimes you can make an innocent statement that can be interpreted by some as being racist. Matthew said the Island players were terrific in short bursts but didn't have the stamina to go a full 80 minutes. He got into hot water but wasn't wrong. The Polynesians are explosive and that's why they are so good at rugby league. Used right, they can be the most devastating players in the world. He meant no disrespect or malice at all. To Matthew's credit, he sorted it out with them.

Matthew's retirement from international football was sudden, when he got hurt in that second '98 test against Australia, and it left us searching for another fullback, captain and goalkicker. It was a pity he made his decision so quickly because he had a lot more to offer at the highest level. But he was riddled with injuries at the time and explained that to me.

Kevin Iro

There was a lot of competition for the top 10 spots and I have left some very good players out. Kevin Iro is included because of his big-match temperament. When it was the grand occasion he could go out there and turn a game, as the Australians found out on more than one occasion.

Kevin scored two tries against the Kangaroos at North Harbour Stadium in that famous '98 test win and that really broke their back. On his day he was a handful for any opposition. It was also Kevin who burst over for the try that tied the scores in the '95 World Cup semi-final and forced it into extra time. Few other players could have broken those tackles with so little space to work in.

Kevin is a nice guy, although he didn't say a lot and was media shy. He was a giant of a man for a centre and had exceptional balance and speed with it. He was often seen as a lazy player by many critics and at club level he could have been guilty of producing a number of mediocre games. But when it came to the big ones he could go out there and win it for you. That was obvious from his teenage days. In his first test he scored 20 points against Papua New Guinea in '87, then played strongly in the Kiwis' shock win over Australia at Brisbane a few

Graham Lowe and Malcolm Boyle, one-time Warriors owners who had their chance and blew it.

Former Warriors CEO Trevor McKewen. Wondering whether that Indian taxi driver delivered my settlement cheque?

Mark Graham, just another coaching casualty.

Meeting the media. It might not always be pleasant but coaches must always front up and be honest.

Captain and coach celebrate moments after our most satisfying win, over the reunited Australian team at North Harbour in 1998.

Stacey Jones and Jarrod McCracken with the spoils of victory.

Even Jason Robinson and another flying Lion couldn't stop Stacey Jones becoming Man of the Series in England in 1998.

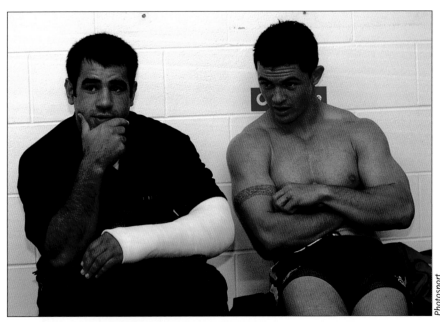

Stacey Jones with THAT broken arm, and Robbie Paul, who took over Stacey's No 7 Kiwi jersey during the 1999 Tri-Nations series.

Tonie Carroll's try got us up to 12-18 with 15 minutes left in the 2000 World Cup final at Old Trafford.

Big Wendell Sailor struck back with two quick tries to keep the World Cup for Australia.

Halftime pep talk for the Wigan lads during a match at Halifax.

The Wigan Observer

Another diary entry coming up here.

The Wigan Observer

Getting the message across.

The Wigan Observer

Welcoming Australian winger Brett Dallas to Wigan.

Receiving the English Super League Coach of the Year award in 2000.

Frank Endacott Collection

days later. As a youngster Kevin had a big start over most players because of his physique and natural speed and skills.

When he was at Wigan Kevin had the unique distinction of three times scoring two tries in Challenge Cup finals at Wembley, something that will probably never be equalled let alone bettered. Even though he finished his career with arch rival St Helens, the fans at Wigan still held Kevin, and his brother Tony, in high regard when I was coaching there.

And the rest . . .

There are always unlucky players in any selection, and I could make a long list of those who earned serious consideration. But there are another three who I reckon deserve a special mention — Daryl Halligan, Tony Iro and Sean Hoppe.

Daryl Halligan was one of the finest characters I coached. He was the perfect tourist, one who knew when to relax and when to train hard. Daryl was the greatest goalkicker of my time, ahead of Matthew Ridge, but he was much more than just that. There was a misconception, especially in Australia, that Daryl was only a kicker. But he was a much better all-round footballer than he was given credit for. Daryl had a knack of being able to con Wendell Sailor. We used to have a nice short-side play from a scrum, knowing that Sailor had a compulsion to leave his wing to take the man with the ball. Stacey Jones would run far enough to attract Sailor infield with Daryl powering along centimetres in from the sideline. A quick pass from Stacey and it was all over. Daryl never missed those chances. They claimed he wasn't quick but Daryl was deceptive and could sustain his pace over the length of the field.

More than once Daryl came out of retirement, disrupted his family's holiday plans, and came to our rescue when we were short of outside backs and a goalkicker.

I put Tony Iro into the same category as Daryl Halligan for being such an asset on tour. I played Tony off the bench a lot of the time for New Zealand and he was a real handful for any opponents. Tony was even bigger than Kevin, was strong, and knew how to score tries. Not many players have made such a seamless transition from the wing to the forwards.

While Tony was a high quality winger, he was simply devastating in the back row. It was his try which started the comeback against Australia in that epic '95 World Cup semi-final. Three years later Tony showed me how much character he had when he suggested Craig Smith take his place in the third test side even though he must have known it was his last tour.

Sean Hoppe was already a top winger for the Kiwis before I came along and was always on course to become our most prolific test try-scorer. In his heyday

Sean was as fast as any winger around and scored many length-of-the-field tries from breaks and interceptions. Those interceptions were dismissed by some people as being flukes, but Sean actually worked on perfecting them. There were too many to be flukes. They resulted from his anticipating what the other side was going to do.

After finishing at international level Sean fashioned a whole new career as a centre and occasional back-rower for St Helens. He had slowed up a little by then but was just as alert between the ears. Within two years Sean had won grand finals against Bradford and Wigan, a Challenge Cup final against Bradford on the hallowed turf of Twickenham, and a World Club Challenge showdown against the Brisbane Broncos.

 *Chapter 16.*
Ancient and loyal?

The inscription under the Wigan coat of arms proclaims that England's, and arguably the world's, most famous rugby league club is Ancient and Loyal. It is certainly old, the club having been formed in 1879 to play the only rugby code then in existence. Wigan was part of the Northern Union breakaway in 1895. Its association with New Zealand teams and players extends back to the pioneering 1907–08 All Golds. Wigan signed gifted Auckland back Lance Todd after that tour and later All Black forward Charlie Seeling. The sequence continued through Lou Brown and Len Mason in the 1920s, Ces Mountford and Brian Nordgren in the late 1940s, to modern stars such as Dean Bell, Kevin Iro, Frano Botica and Henry Paul. Wigan's recent coaches include New Zealanders Graeme West, Graham Lowe and Frank Endacott. But loyal? During the last decade Wigan has been ruthless in sacking its coaches. When Australian Stuart Raper replaced Endacott in May 2001 he became the seventh man at the helm in eight years.

As with all things at Wigan, my arrival and departure from the club both began with a telephone call from chairman Maurice Lindsay. Both times he issued invitations, firstly to turn around the fortunes of a club that was slipping down the Super League rankings, and secondly to drop into his office for a chat. Most coaches know what that means.

Career offers had been coming fairly thick and fast during 1999. Leeds chairman Gary Hetherington had approached me at the time of the Anzac test and I expressed my interest in coaching at Headingley. A few weeks later he rang to tell me the job had gone to Australian Dean Lance, who was a Super League coach on an existing contract and therefore a better proposition financially. Lance was to be the first Super League coach sacked in 2001. Leeds is a sleeping giant, an attraction to any ambitious coach.

There was also a call from one of New Zealand First party leader Winston Peters' off-siders to enquire whether I would be interested in standing for parliament at the national elections. I must admit I was tempted at the thought of trying to improve the teamwork at the Beehive. But while I was thinking it over Maurice Lindsay made me an offer I couldn't refuse.

I was sound asleep about 11.30 one night in November 1999 when Lindsay woke me up to ask whether I wanted to coach Wigan. I woke up pretty quickly. Lindsay said he had returned to the club to find it in a rut, with an atmosphere of gloom about the place. It just wasn't Wigan as Lindsay had known it during the balmy days when the Challenge Cup and other trophies were almost permanently housed in the display cabinet at Central Park. In the last game of the 1999 season the Wigan Warriors had lost to Castleford in the first game at their new pride and joy, the JJB Stadium. Worse, the fans had turned their backs when the players jogged across to applaud them for their support. That's the lowest thing that can happen. Fifth was simply not good enough for Wiganers.

Lindsay said the players were shuffling around with their heads down, that there was no enjoyment in the club at all. I knew coach Andy Goodway had been given the bullet, and Lindsay asked me if I would go over on a one-year contract and try to turn the club around. I said I would love to, and we negotiated terms over the phone the following day. He faxed me his offer, we made a few adjustments, and it was a good, clean deal. I left on January 2 and discovered Lindsay had not been exaggerating. You could feel a bad atmosphere about the place.

New Zealand Rugby League president Gerald Ryan and general manager Gary Allcock gave me their blessing, although I did hear there were some rumblings from board members that I would be too far away to properly fulfil my duties as Kiwi coach for the Anzac test and World Cup. I could understand their concerns but our preparation was so far down the track that it wasn't going to go off the rails in a few months. I knew what players I wanted for the World Cup.

Soon after I arrived at Wigan I told the players to leave their training gear at home and took them to Dublin for three days. We got right into the Guinness and bonded quickly. I got to know the players and they got to know me. You tend to let your feelings out much quicker over a few beers. Despite an emergency landing at Manchester airport on our return, with ambulances and fire engines on the alert, the feeling in the Wigan club from that day was nothing short of fantastic. Everyone wanted to play and there was keen competition for places. We wanted to go out and turn things around, and did. At the end of the regular season Wigan had to beat St Helens at Knowsley Road to clinch the championship and we demolished them 42–4. We made the grand final, only to lose to St Helens at Old Trafford. I was fortunate to be voted British Coach of the Year ahead of two Australians, Bradford's Matt Elliott and St Helens' Ian Millward. It was a great accolade, but I had a good team to coach and attitudes were totally positive.

It didn't help, though, that Wigan was an early Challenge Cup casualty in both seasons I was there. The change to a summer season means the cup is now played at the start of the season instead of being the climax because the final is still held in late April or early May. Wigan, by tradition, starts slowly and we had the misfortune to draw away ties at Hull in 2000 and St Helens in 2001.

Times have changed since Wigan had the only fulltime professional squad and won seven consecutive cup finals at Wembley up to 1995. Some people around the place have not been able to adjust to the fact that Wigan can't buy all the best players in the world.

Hull had been enjoying a resurgence under Shaun McRae's coaching in recent years, joining Bradford, Wigan, St Helens and Leeds among the really super clubs in Super League. Playing Hull at The Boulevard in a cup tie is about as tough as it gets. We were tipped out of the 2000 cup soon after I arrived and the ride home down the motorway was not pleasant. Our supporters were giving it to us when their buses drew up alongside ours, and the coaching staff decided it was best to make out we were asleep.

Losing to neighbour and arch rival St Helens is akin to a capital crime in Wigan. Some of the supporters would forgive you if you lost to every other team in the country, so long as you beat St Helens in the cup and league. But most Wigan people expect to win every week, and win well. They have rugby league and soccer teams playing out of the same stadium. Wigan's rugby league coach knows anything less than 50–0 will not be totally acceptable, while his soccer counterpart always needs five clear goals to earn a pass mark. It's all so unrealistic.

In 2000 we played 28 league games and lost only three. How many first grade teams, anywhere, can claim a record like that? And when we lost one of those games I was 12,000 miles away with the Kiwis.

The expectations are a hangover from all the success Wigan enjoyed in the late 1980s and early 1990s. I spoke to the supporters' club and some of the fans about it. They were living in the glorious past. In those days a fully professional Wigan team were playing what amounted to semi-professional opposition. Now every Super League team have a fulltime playing staff. The genuine supporters understand all this, but the fringe fans who only come to the big games are still struggling with it. Those who turn up every week are the best in the world, really lovely people who understand you can't win every time you take the field.

We were really confident of beating St Helens in the 2000 grand final, but after we clawed back from being down 4–17 to get up to 16–17 there was a crucial decision which went against us. Lee Gilmour made a copybook tackle to force a St Helens player into touch, all in one movement, but referee Russell Smith penalised Gilmour. From the next set of six we were defending, instead of being on attack at the other end. One tackle was missed and that was the game as St Helens pulled away to win 29–16 with another converted try in the last minute.

I believe it is always an achievement to make a grand final, especially from fifth the previous year. But even though we were the most consistently successful side over the entire season we finished up without a trophy. They only play for two trophies now, instead of five, so Wigan's display cabinet can never be as full as it used to be. To make it worse, St Helens went on to beat the Brisbane Broncos in the World Club Challenge in early 2001. To some Wigan folk that was an itch they couldn't scratch.

No team have a divine right to win. Dean Bell wrote in his book that when he played in those great Wigan teams of the 1980s all they had to do was hop on the bus to collect the competition points. In the Super League era even the bottom team can rear up and bite you in the bum if you have not prepared well enough, especially on their home grounds.

By August of my first season Maurice Lindsay showed enough confidence in me, and satisfaction with the way things were going, that we signed a new two-year contract which was to have taken me through to the end of 2002. I was absolutely rapt with that because I was convinced we had the squad to win a grand final, and so did the rest of the staff and the players. But two results which would have been regarded as no more than hiccups at other clubs prompted Lindsay to get rid of me, an action seen in most places as a panic response to what was not a major problem. After we lost to London Broncos in London, always a difficult away match, I started hearing rumours coming through from

Australia, of all places, that my position was not as secure as it should be. Those leaks could have come from only one person, Maurice Lindsay.

I know how Lindsay works. If he wants an idea to spread he first leaks it. If he did it to put pressure on me all he did was piss me off. Stuart Raper, an Australian coaching at Castleford, was already being mentioned as a possible replacement. Yet when we went to London we were in first place. Ironically, it was my own Kiwi captain, Richie Barnett, who was most responsible for London beating us. I had never put more homework into any individual as I did on Richie before that game but he was dazzling with his broken field running and saved two tries with brilliant defence.

Then we played Wakefield Trinity at home. They were considered to be a danger after beating Bradford the previous week. We thrashed them by 50 points but the rumours still persisted. Salford was the next stop, and turned out to be the end of the line for me. Young prop Ricky Bibey was sent off early in the second half and we lost 30–31. The scores were locked at 30-all when our stand-off half, Matthew Johns, hit an upright with one field goal attempt and was then wide with another. Just before fulltime Graham Holroyd won the game for Salford with a 40–20 kick to gain field position and then the fatal field goal.

It was one of those games that got away from us, an awful effort, and no one was more brassed off about it than me. My wife, Joan, felt it too. She was sitting up in the grandstand with Mick Hannan, who worked in the Wigan office, and she said to him, 'That'll be Frank gone.' Mick told her not to be silly but she knew more than both of us.

Wigan never plays that badly twice in row and there was always going to be a rally the next week. There was no next week for me. That Salford game was on a Sunday, and Maurice Lindsay's second career-defining phone call came on Monday morning. Before going to his office I told Joan to prepare for the worst.

I would have preferred Lindsay to have spoken to me during the fortnight between the London and Salford games but, curiously, he was hard to find. If we had been losing games hand over fist I would have understood. But we were still third in the league, had the best defensive record, and the second best attack. I was absolutely sure we would have been in the 2001 grand final, and won it. Under Stuart Raper, Wigan did go to Old Trafford. But Bradford ran away to a record 37–6 victory in Henry Paul's farewell to rugby league. It could have been so much different. We had played Bradford four times in 2000 and they never beat us once. I knew more about the Paul brothers than anyone in Britain.

When I went into Lindsay's office he looked pretty upset and said he couldn't see us being there at the end of the year. I told him he must be joking. Then he said he doubted we would even be in the top five and I couldn't help laughing.

I tried to reassure him but Lindsay had already made up his mind. He felt he had to do something and only he knows why. There was no indication that the players, staff or fans were restless. There had only been those mysterious stories coming out of Australia and it seemed there was more to it than basic rugby league results.

Before I left that last meeting I turned to Maurice and said, 'There is one thing I need to know. Are you going to replace me with a better coach?' He looked at me and said, 'No'. I couldn't work that one out.

One fairly strong theory emerged before we left England. A number of media people and some good, solid fans suggested to me that I was taking the limelight away from Lindsay. I don't know how much substance is in that idea, but I notice that since I have left Lindsay has again been making all of the statements on behalf of Wigan. When I was there it was me. So he is back on top again, where he likes to be.

The results had been good until those blips at London and Salford. We began by beating Warrington 34–6, won 24–8 against Stuart Raper's Castleford side at Castleford when I started young Phil Jones at stand-off half and he scored three tries, then thrashed Leeds 42–6. Guys like legendary Wigan winger Billy Boston were saying that was the best display they had seen from a Wigan side for years. We beat Halifax away in the wet to make it four wins from four, and drew 22-all with world club champion St Helens. Our only previous loss was 24–35 at Bradford two days after we played St Helens, and we easily accounted for Huddersfield before going to London.

I had done all my experimenting and told Lindsay the best times were ahead of us. It was logical that it would take time for our new halfback pairing of Adrian Lam and Matthew Johns to settle in. They had their first game together in the cup tie at St Helens, and Johns had great difficulty adjusting to English conditions. I wasn't surprised he stayed only one season.

But that's the Wigan way. The club had two coaches in 1999 and two in 1997, so maybe I didn't do too badly lasting a season and a half. Another New Zealander, Graeme West, won every trophy on offer and even beat the Brisbane Broncos in the World Club Challenge but still got sacked. Now it's spreading. I left about a third of the way through the 2001 season but Dean Lance at Leeds and former Kiwi Gary Mercer at Halifax had already been shown the door by their clubs.

I don't think there was any hint of player power. It was a tight-knit team and we got on well. Denis Betts was the only one who could have had a beef. He might have thought that for such a high profile player he was coming off the bench in too many games. But that continued to be his lot after I left and Betts retired at the end of the season. Maurice Lindsay always told me he never asked players about anything, and I'll take his word on that.

No, I am sure it was Lindsay's decision and his alone. He made his fortune as a bookmaker and likes to play the odds with people as well as horses. One of the leading English journalists told me the day I was sacked that they hadn't seen any reason to speak to Lindsay when I was so readily available. Now Lindsay is back in the limelight and doing all the talking again. Maybe I suffered because of my popularity with the media. Dave Hadfield wrote in the *Independent* that I was the 'latest sacrifice to Wigan's expectations' and BBC Sport headlined it 'Happy Frank Just Another Victim'.

My whole career rested on a few little things that can happen to any team in any sport. Against London Broncos we had a clear two-on-one situation, something we had worked on that week, only for Richie Barnett to knock down the pass from Paul Johnson to an unmarked team-mate, and two of our other players lost the ball over the goal-line. Then at Salford Matthew Johns was so close with a match-winning field goal, before Graham Holroyd's field goal sank us. They are hardly the fault of the coach sitting in the grandstand.

The trouble with Wigan is that all the other clubs have a board of directors, but not Wigan. Wigan has Maurice Lindsay and that is a dictatorship. You get all the views and feelings of only one person and have no one else to rebound them off. I had an honest discussion with Lindsay every week, and enjoyed them. He can be delightful company to talk to and as a host. But when he had a complaint to make about team selections it was always after the event, with the benefit of hindsight.

In the 2000 grand final I played Jason Robinson at fullback and put young David Hodgson on the wing. Hodgson scored an 80-metre try yet Lindsay virtually blamed him for losing the game. It was ridiculous. One try was scored down his wing but someone inside him missed the vital tackle. When I saw that same David Hodgson playing for Great Britain in the third 2001 test against Australia at Wigan I knew my decision was justified. I could see the potential in the kid. He was only 19 and a real speed merchant. It's also interesting that Jason Robinson has been starring at fullback for the England rugby union team. I wonder what Lindsay thinks about that.

I spoke to Robinson several times when he was being wooed by the English union. Obviously there was a big financial gain but he felt he had done everything in rugby league. He went for the challenge as much as anything. I certainly didn't want to lose the fastest player over a short distance I had ever coached. He was a great professional, a great bloke with it, and he went with our blessings.

If Lindsay wanted a 'yes' man, I'm afraid I am not one of them. He didn't even like Dean Bell sitting with me at games but wouldn't tell me why.

BEING FRANK

Ancient and loyal? Many true supporters came up to me after I was sacked and apologised for the wording of the Wigan motto, saying, 'We are ancient but unfortunately we are not always loyal.' There is not a week goes by that I don't get calls from Wigan people, players or staff. In the two days after I left the club I received 300 cards and calls, despite having an unlisted phone number.

The most emotional aspect of my leaving was telling the players. The room was like a morgue. On the same night Neil Cowie, the big prop, rang me at home and said a few of the boys wanted to have a beer with me at a local pub. When I arrived I found the entire squad was there except the four who were playing reserve grade the following night. We finished up at 5.30 in the morning. They also organised a surprise going-away the night before Joan and I flew out, with more than 100 players, staff and their wives.

It must be said in fairness to Maurice Lindsay that he honoured every clause of my contract. Most of the previous coach sackings had led to acrimony but my settlement was finalised and paid out in four days. Money is no object at Wigan, not with a backer like multi-millionaire Dave Whelan. He also owns the Wigan soccer club and recently bought the Orrell Rugby Union Club. I see Lindsay has also been put in charge of Orrell and that Whelan is prepared to invest £10 million there. I don't think the Wigan fans are going to like that because they are died in the wool league people.

Anyway, Lindsay would not have had to beg Whelan for the money to pay me out 18 months early, then agree to terms with Stuart Raper, and compensate Castleford for pinching their coach. Raper was already sitting in what had been my office before the next game. Not surprising that, considering Lindsay had been courting him even before we had gone to London as league leaders.

It is not often rugby league tops the sports news on the BBC and Sky but it did the day I was sacked. Both channels came around home for interviews soon after the announcement was made but they couldn't find Lindsay for a few days. I told the news media I was astounded and disappointed but accepted the chairman's decision. There was no point in making waves. They tell me Lindsay was on Radio Sport in New Zealand lauding me to the heavens so much you would have thought he was hiring me not firing me. I think he had leaked so much to certain media sources that he couldn't go back and had to flex his muscles.

Funnily enough, the day before we left England Lindsay's personal assistant, Mandy, rang and said Lindsay wanted a word with me. Lindsay came on the line and said, 'Frank, I just want to tell you that you were great for this club.'

From my point of view, it wasn't me, but we, who turned the club around. Billy McGinty, the assistant coach, was never in Lindsay's plans for further advancement and has since gone to Sale rugby union. I could not have had a more honest and hard-working assistant than Billy, who was an ex-player at Wigan. I had good staff all around me, in trainer Nigel Ashley-Jones, an Australian who came to us from St Helens, and former Kiwi captain Dean Bell and Brian Foley as development officers in charge of scholarships.

Despite what happened, being at Wigan was a marvellous experience. It's just a shame Maurice Lindsay stopped something that could have been really momentous. Lindsay was in his element again last off-season signing up internationals Craig Smith, Jamie Ainscough and Julian O'Neill. He might talk to the coach about signings but it's Lindsay who makes the final decisions.

Lindsay was even speculating (leaking ideas again) about signing Andrew Johns after he completes his Newcastle Knights contract in 2004. He likes to give the impression that he is three steps ahead of the next man. Other clubs can only wonder how Maurice negotiated Wigan an extension on the salary cap limit from £1.8 million to £2.3 million. Lindsay claimed it was to honour existing contracts yet he continues to sign new and expensive recruits. But I must commend him on getting a player as dedicated as Craig Smith.

I hope for Wigan's sake that Lindsay takes notice of what has happened at Bradford since Super League started in 1996. The Bulls have stuck with their coaches even though Matthew Elliott didn't win any major trophies until his last year before going to Canberra. But Elliott was doing an excellent job rebuilding his squad and the administrators showed patience. Now Brian Noble has taken over. He beat Wigan in the 2001 grand final and in March 2002 became the first Bradford coach to win at Wigan's JJB Stadium. It was sad to read on the internet that the Wigan fans booed their players and coach.

Wigan also must take care of captain Andy Farrell to prevent him burning out before his time. Farrell led the Great Britain Academy against the Junior Kiwis in 1993 and has captained his club and country since he was about 21. If there are any off-field promotions to be done Farrell is the first one asked and he doesn't often refuse. It's taking a toll. On the field he is responsible for the leadership, ball distribution, goalkicking and a lot of tackling, you name it. When I went to Wigan I wanted to make Farrell more of a runner, off the halfbacks, but we had injuries that first season. It would have happened in 2001, once Adrian Lam and Matthew Johns were settled.

In fullback Kris Radlinski, Wigan has a player as professional as any I have come across, while hooker Terry Newton will go on to better things so long as he keeps away from the judiciary. He is a real tough nut and a quality hooker-cum-forward. Wigan's junior development system is also producing some classy youngsters, and I hope they are given every opportunity.

The British club competition is obviously not as strong overall as that in

Australia. While the chance of lowly placed clubs upsetting the big guns is always present on their home grounds, they cannot sustain the intensity and by season's end the top five will always be disputing the championship. My old mate from Christchurch Whetu Taewa shared in the biggest Challenge Cup final upset of all time when Sheffield Eagles beat Wigan at Wembley in 1998. But you otherwise have to go back to Halifax in 1987 to find a winner other than Wigan, St Helens, Leeds or Bradford.

There is not much between that quartet, and Hull has made big strides lately. Bradford's new assistant coach, Karl Harrison, learned early that you have to keep your feet on the ground. After Bradford rolled the Newcastle Knights in the 2002 World Club Challenge, Harrison publicly speculated about the Bulls going through the season unbeaten. Next weekend Leeds knocked them out of the Challenge Cup, and Harrison had his wrist slapped by head coach Brian Noble. One week later Bradford bounced back to win at Wigan. It's all about preparing properly, physically and mentally.

There are quite a number of players in the English Super League who would more than hold their own in the Australian National Rugby League. But a lot of others just aren't good enough to deserve being fulltime professionals. Import quotas should also be reduced. A lot of the Australians, more so than New Zealanders, go to Britain after their use-by date has expired and are simply topping up their superannuation funds. You can't blame the players, just the club officials silly enough to sign them.

Most of the clubs in the lower half of the Super League standings are also walking a financial tightrope and must be forever careful they don't fall over. While Wigan is spending its £2.3 million, and the other top clubs their £1.8 million, some of the lesser lights would be lucky to get into seven figures at all. It is not an even playing field.

Fortunately, rugby league doesn't have the spectator riots that have plagued British soccer. There is a fine line between passion and fanaticism. Rob Harris, a New Zealand physio who was with the Auckland Warriors and Wigan, went to work for Manchester City and would sometimes toss me some tickets. I went along to watch City play Manchester United at Old Trafford. Because I was with the City fans I was frisked on my way in and then penned in for the game. We had to wait until United's 90 per cent of the sell-out 68,000 crowd had dispersed, then were released through two lines of police in the direction they wanted us to go.

Millwall fans are among the worst. They played Wigan one night at the JJB Stadium and wrecked it, attacked the cops on horseback and everything. It was like a battleground. Fortunately, the rugby league supporters haven't lowered themselves to that level.

You can run into an idiot in any crowd, though, as Dean Bell and I discovered at Wakefield one day. We were heading for our seats when someone on the embankment spat on Dean. He spotted him and was trying to get at him with me clutching my coaching diary in one hand and straining to hold Dean back with the other. Then this same guy deposited a gobful on my jacket. Next moment I've shoved the diary onto Dean and he's trying to prevent me from climbing over people to get to this clown. We suddenly realised that the television cameras could be around and it wouldn't be a good look for Wigan or the game if we were giving this yob what he deserved. The Wakefield club later sent us a letter of apology.

The phantom expectorator got what was coming to him as well, but not from us. After we had beaten Wakefield Trinity by 50 points the same idiot was so incensed he jumped the fence and punched one of his own team's players. Wakefield banned him for life.

Chapter 17.
The weakest link

Legendary Australian coach Jack Gibson, who is almost as famous for his one-liners as his many on-field triumphs, said back in the 1970s, 'Rugby league must be a great game to survive the people who run it.' Many would contend that still applies today. Having coached at every level from schoolboys to the World Cup, and in the major domestic competitions of Australia, Great Britain and New Zealand, Frank Endacott has experienced the very best and very worst aspects of the game's administration. The term 'shooting itself in the foot' has been applied to few sports as frequently as the rugby league code.

There is nothing wrong with rugby league as a game. The fact that rugby union has pinched so many of our innovations, modelled so many of its rule changes on rugby league, and signed so many of our coaches since it turned professional proves we must have something special. But rugby league has never been able to break out of its traditional strongholds. It is the national sport in Papua New Guinea, the premier football code in New South Wales and Queensland, and the 'rugby' preferred by most people in the north of England. In New Zealand the Warriors have given rugby league a national awareness as never before but the domestic scene is not as healthy as it should be.

There have been some radical fluctuations in popularity, and the Warriors carry an unfair burden because they are on television every week. Too many people relate the state of rugby league in this country to the result of the Warriors match the previous weekend. Television has made players such as Stacey Jones household names far beyond what are traditional rugby league households. But if the Warriors are not winning many television sets are turned off and the game as a whole is said to be in a slump. That's a tough price to pay.

The more Bartercard Cup games they can get on television the better. The competition provides our domestic players with valuable exposure, which benefits their prospects of being seen by professional scouts and gives viewers the chance to associate themselves with their local teams. What our sport in New Zealand needs is heroes, and players these days are only going to get that status by being on television. It's a similar situation with the Kiwis. We play too few test matches at home these days. Apart from the Warriors' contingent, our international players are attached to Australian and British clubs and are seen in the flesh by their young fans only when playing for the Kiwis or as the 'enemy' when lining up against the Warriors.

More than 20 nations were involved in the 2000 World Cup and the qualifying competition that preceded it. Many of the 'national' teams represented small pockets of enthusiasts, while the Lebanon side the Kiwis played was comprised entirely Australian residents who qualified because of their ancestry. I don't think it made the lead sports story in the Beirut daily newspaper.

Rugby league's growth has been hindered by two factors, a lack of finance, and the short-sightedness or sheer incompetence of its administrators.

Big things were promised when Super League began shelling out its millions (of dollars and pounds) from the mid-1990s. After a flurry of activity, few permanent foundations were laid. Most of the money went into the pockets of players and out of the game altogether. Real estate agents, car salesmen, boat builders and, especially, lawyers profited more than rugby league. The game was soon crying poor again.

International expansion is not possible without regular competition between countries. While the Australian National Rugby League and English Super League are permitted so much clout, their respective national bodies are rendered powerless. The club officials who have so much influence are charged with fostering those clubs and you can't blame them for looking after their own interests. But the game as a whole suffers.

In New Zealand we are perennially plagued by having opposing factions alternately clinging to power or seeking that power and prepared to use any means to win their personality clashes. They seem to think it doesn't matter what damage they do in their blind belief they can rebuild the game once they wrest control. There appears to be no order of rotation in the New Zealand Rugby League hierarchy, with people randomly coming and going, some voted in and then thrown out by the provinces, and others becoming discouraged and walking away. Unfortunately, it is usually the best ones who leave by choice to put their energies and ideas into other projects.

The situation filters down through the district leagues. Some have flourished all too briefly because a solid administration base crumbles when one or two people, or families, drop out of the game for one reason or another. It's the same at club level. Those which have remained strong over the decades are those which have been run smoothly. I have sympathy with amateur officials trying to keep rugby league's head above water in what is now a very professional sporting world. In too many cases the worthy volunteers get worn down when they could have given excellent services over a much longer time had there been more support and less destructive criticism.

Trevor Maxwell, the judge, was New Zealand Rugby League chairman when I was appointed Kiwi coach but not for long after that. During my term Graham Carden and Gerald Ryan were contrasting personalities in the chair, while Mike Knowles, Jennifer Haydock and Gary Allcock filled the chief executive or general manager positions, and there was a passing parade of board members.

I always compared Graham Carden with Ian Robson. Both were fantastic front men, great with the media, and able to hold an audience. They had silver tongues but neither could understand the word 'budget'. From my experience, Carden ran the NZRL board meetings very efficiently and was the boss at the table. Whether the board members believed what he was saying or not, no one really questioned him. Both Robson and Carden would be great for any organisation that had a bottomless bucket of cash. But we all know that every usable bucket has a bottom to it. The Lion Red Cup, which Carden put together and modelled along the lines of the Australian Winfield Cup, was a superb competition for players, coaches and referees but it lost a fortune because there was an attitude that money was no object. Until it ran out, that is.

Gerald Ryan was as honest as the day is long. He was always very supportive of me, but I know he has upset a few people on both sides of the Tasman. The Australians called him eccentric, and worse, but Gerald always kept them on their toes. They didn't know how to take him and he wouldn't back down to them. I found it good working with him. Gerald was a very bright man and had a dry sense of humour. He couldn't front up to an organisation and hold 500 people spellbound with his oratory like Graham Carden. Gerald was more from the heart and down to earth. His word was his bond. I know that even when certain people were talking about breaking my contract near the end of my term Gerald just kept saying 'a contract is a contract'. That was the lawyer in him. I knew with Gerald I could have shaken his hand and known his word would be honoured without even putting anything on paper. There aren't too many around I could say that about.

The general managers and chief executives were an interesting assortment during my time. I worked with Mike Knowles in the NZRL office when I was director of coaching. Mike had been around the joint for a long time and he was a very intelligent person. A little inconsistent, though. Sometimes you would walk into the office and Mike would welcome you like a long-lost brother. On other mornings you would greet him, and Mike would ignore you. Generally he liked company and was a good bloke to go down the road and have a beer with. That's when his warped sense of humour would emerge.

Mike had a deserved reputation for keeping much of the NZRL business in his head, which caused a stir when he took ill in England and was hospitalised while checking out arrangements for a Kiwi tour. The rest of the people back in Auckland suddenly realised that if the worst happened all the tour details would have gone with him. There was a joke going around that Mike was irreplaceable because the NZRL data base was in his head. He was a survivor and saw off a few chairmen, but eventually went in late 1996.

It ruffled many rugby league stalwarts when Jennifer Haydock became the first female chief executive. Worse, maybe, she didn't have a rugby league background either. But she won over the selection committee that interviewed the finalists for the job. It was not long before she upset Gerald Ryan, and rubbed others up the wrong way. My personal memories of Jennifer are of an efficient working relationship. As an example, I was promised a bonus if we beat Australia in the '98 Anzac test. I had heard all that before and knew how long bonuses traditionally took to get paid. The Kiwis beat the Kangaroos on the Friday night and on the Monday the cheque was delivered to my home.

But Jennifer was a very strong, aggressive woman, had a mind of her own, and no one could change it. She only lasted a year or so, and I suppose she suffered from being a female in a male world. In the end the conflict between chief executive and chairman meant she had to go.

Gary Allcock was a leading rugby league referee who came from a police background and was a breath of fresh air. He was an absolutely straight-up guy, had a good appearance and an impressive manner about him. Soon after starting the job he grabbed me and Gary Kemble and we went on a tour of South Island secondary schools. Gary Allcock and I did the talking to the pupils and it was very successful. In his short time he did a lot of fine work that he didn't get enough credit for. He added a lot of credibility to rugby league in New Zealand.

Some of my contract negotiations were fairly hard fought but I think we both enjoyed them. Sometimes I would bend a little and at other times he would concede some ground. But they were all about honesty. I knew that if I had an agreement with Gary it was set in concrete and I could get on with my job. Gary also worked smoothly with Gerald Ryan.

Administration really is a worry. Stability in a game should start in the front office, no matter what level it might be. In addition to going through three chairmen and three chief executives while I was Kiwi coach there were also multiple staff changes and one of the board members, in particular, was forever coming and going as if through a revolving door. The rapid turnover continues. In 2001 Gary Allcock's successor, Barry McAlister, stayed only a few weeks. Selwyn Pearson had been elected to succeed Gerald Ryan, and he assumed many of McAlister's responsibilities to effectively become executive chairman into the 2002 season.

We have always had good individuals but they have too often been outnumbered. That goes right back to when George Rainey was chairman. George was a man who ruled with an iron hand, but if you shook that hand you knew he would honour the agreement. George had a saying, 'It's all about results', and no coach would argue with that.

The good people need to surround themselves with other good people, but that is difficult. The problem is the New Zealand Rugby League's system of putting people on the board by means of votes from district leagues. In my opinion, and I know it is held by many others, they should have four proven businessmen contracted to sit on the board and only the other three to be elected by the districts. One of the paid members would be the chief executive.

We never seem to have a group of people who can get along with each other. Former Prime Minister David Lange touched on it when he stood down after being Gerald Ryan's deputy chairman. Lange said half of the people involved in rugby league were crooks and the other half were the salt of the earth. I wouldn't have put it quite as strongly as that but it is not far wrong. If all the good people in rugby league would band together and move in one direction, the game would be a real force in New Zealand sport. But that doesn't happen, never has, and probably never will. There are too many hidden agendas, too many egos. If they just got on with fostering the game, thought about its best interests, and worked selflessly for the game then it would be a potent force. There is too much skulduggery going on when it comes to voting time. Promises are made to district leagues just to get elected to the board, knowing those promises can never be kept. Some people get onto the board for the wrong reasons, and some have more lives than Lazarus.

Bob Haddon was the perfect board member. When he resigned it was a sad day because too many good people were going out of the game at once. Gerald Ryan and Gary Allcock had just left and Bob Haddon's departure topped it off. He was a man who made decisions with common sense and logic, came from a business background, and was honest. That is all you can ask for.

David Lange, of course, is an interesting character. He was one of the most humorous blokes I have ever met. The intelligence just oozes out of him and he was great to sit down and have a discussion with. But he also had strong opinions. While he would listen to yours, he wouldn't waver from his own. David Lange was valuable to the board while he was there and offered strong backing to Gerald Ryan. He recognised Gerald's honesty.

While rugby league in New Zealand is invariably ruled by the clique in power at the time, world rugby league is being run by Australians. Just look at the overbearing influence Australians have had on the game in Britain. They also intimidate and in their own way run rugby league in New Zealand. The Australians have a lot to answer for. Although they say they are interested in the welfare of the international game, they are not. Everything has to be bent to suit Australia.

What Australia must do is take a step back and realise the game in New Zealand is New Zealand's own game. Let's play tests over here, and get the crowds back. They knew we could compete with the Kangaroos every time in New Zealand and, as the records show, beat them as often as not.

There was talk early this year of shunting a one-off trans-Tasman test to Canberra, Newcastle or Gosford in October because they can never get anyone to go in Sydney after the grand final. Those are the sorts of venues where they usually play Papua New Guinea and Fiji. Is New Zealand now being classed as a second-rate side too? What of all those statements only two years ago about promoting trans-Tasman tests to the level of rugby union's Bledisloe Cup or their own State of Origin series?

Surely it would be sensible to play tests in New Zealand at that time of the year and get big crowds in Auckland or Wellington. But the two countries couldn't even work out the meaning of playing home and away when allocating Anzac tests. Four matches were played between 1997 and 2000 and three of them were in Sydney. The other was at North Harbour. No prizes for guessing which one we won.

The Australian players are keen to be involved in international football but their officials are content to get those pesky test matches over at the most convenient venues on Friday nights so they cause as little disruption as possible to their precious club competition.

The on-again, off-again nature of the 2001 Kangaroo tour to Britain was just another example of Australia's couldn't-care-less attitude to the international game. Sure, the September 11 terrorist attacks in the United States made a lot of sports pause and consider the safety of their players. But it didn't stop anyone else from eventually going through with tours to Britain.

The Australians simply didn't want to go. They find it a waste of time, and sometimes a waste of money, making these tours. It was only public pressure and the fact the players enjoy wearing the Australian jerseys that retrieved anything out of the shambles. By then the 'tour' had been cut from seven matches to three tests, which no doubt made the Australian clubs happier that the risk of injuries to their players had been lessened.

More importance has to be placed on test matches. They should be put up on a pedestal. The international side of rugby league is being neglected, largely because of the stranglehold the National Rugby League has in Australia and Super League has in Britain. The clubs are putting games at Bradford and Brookvale, Wigan and Wollongong ahead of international expansion.

There needs to be a strong International Federation with representatives from all countries who can make resolutions and rulings which cannot be ignored at the whims of two or three clubs jealously guarding their own interests. Other nations must have an equal say to Australia so they can come up with a fair dinkum international programme. Places like Papua New Guinea, for instance. Rugby league is their national game but they still need tours to foster it.

Wayne Bennett took the Brisbane Broncos to Fiji for a week-long training camp in February 2002 and turned both barrels on the Australian Rugby League when he got home. He was angry nothing was being done to promote rugby league in the Pacific Islands, not just in Fiji but also Tonga, Samoa, Papua New Guinea and the rest. Bennett has seen what players such as Noa Nadruku, Petero Civoniceva, and Lote Tuqiri can do in the best competition in the world and was dismayed such a rich nursery was being neglected. Clubs would be happy just to skim the cream off the top.

There were all those promises from Super League a few years back, but the work done by them and the Australian Rugby League has been allowed to crumble away to nothing. The two factions had a big power struggle in the Pacific but once hostilities ended they just packed up and sailed off home.

The lack of a proper international calendar was a major reason why players such as Jason Robinson, Wendell Sailor, Mat Rogers and Henry Paul went to rugby union. They still had everything to offer their rugby league clubs and could have retired with a stack of medals, trophies and premiership rings. But most of them had been there and done that, so by their own selfishness in not fostering international football the clubs drove their stars away.

Rugby union offered them the chance to perform on a bigger international stage in the later years of their careers, at little or no financial cost. It was ironic, though, that Sailor's first destination with the Queensland Reds was to be Greymouth for a friendly game. In days gone by he would already have visited there with the Kangaroos, but Australian tours of New Zealand don't happen any more. Greymouth missed out again when Sailor didn't turn up with the Reds either.

Rugby union might not have any decent club competitions, and blokes like Wendell Sailor and Henry Paul will wonder where the crowds went when they turn out for their new clubs. But it is a sport that puts test matches up front at certain times of the season when they play their Tri-Nations and Six Nations tournaments.

New Zealand should have a greater say on the International Rugby League Federation because of our standing in the game. Ten years ago we were a distant third behind Australia and Great Britain. Now the players have pulled us into a clear second and we should be respected for that. For some reason every dispute seems to be decided by a sub-committee dominated by Australians with only the token Englishman or New Zealander.

The International Federation is Mickey Mouse, a joke. Look what happened when it met in England during the 2001 Kangaroo tour. Gerald Ryan was still New Zealand's representative but was no longer on the New Zealand Rugby League board, which refused to pay his way. So the meeting went on without New Zealand having anyone there. No wonder the July test match pencilled in for the Kiwis was swept aside so that Australia could play Great Britain at Sydney instead.

The obvious difference between the two rugby codes is that rugby union is so much better organised. There might be fights between individual countries around their board table, usually over money, but they seem to plan their tours several years ahead and stick to them. Rugby league just reacts as things happen, with tours being hastily put together a few months out. There is no real planning or preparation and that is where mistakes happen.

We moved up the international ladder because we had stability in our teams, despite all of the hassles assembling them for mid-season test matches. Previous coaches had been saddled with selection panels that inevitably resulted in a greater turnover of players and more compromises around the selection table. Graham Lowe accused me of being too loyal to players but I don't make any apology for that. It was that loyalty and stability that actually brought the Kiwi side back on track.

Great Britain has its own problems in building a powerful and consistent international squad. There are too many overseas players in England. I believe they need a few overseas coaches and players to give them updated ideas but there are so many that good young talent is being stifled. A limit of three players to each club would be fair. Although the rule has been five, other players can qualify on residential grounds and there could be as many as seven Australian accents in any one club team. That is not counting the London Broncos, which have had virtual open slather as a special case away from rugby league's heartland. Making it worse, the foreigners are often filling specialist positions, such as scrum-half. When Sean Long was injured and could not play against the 2001 Kangaroos they could find no quality halves to replace him, despite having a far stronger player base than New Zealand.

There are plenty of players in Britain who could make it in the Australian competition, not just the one or two who are frequently mentioned. Keiron Cunningham and Terry Newton are two hookers good enough to break into the NRL. Terry O'Connor and Barrie McDermott would make an impact in the front row. Andy Farrell and Paul Sculthorpe are world class as lock forwards. Fullback Kris Radlinski would succeed anywhere in the world. Gary Connolly proved himself in Australia a few years back. Plus the Brits have any number of outstanding youngsters coming up, like Kevin Sinfield at Leeds.

Their Great Britain Academy side handed our New Zealand 18-years team a hiding in 2001. But will those kids be given a smooth pathway to the top in their homeland or have to play second fiddle to ageing Australians?

British clubs have beaten their Kangaroo counterparts to sign some good young Australasian talent in 2002, such as Lesley Vainikolo at Bradford and Ben Walker at Leeds, but plenty of older ones are still going north.

Despite that, the way the below-strength Lions performed in winning the first test against the 2001 Kangaroos, and again in issuing such a strong challenge in the third test, makes them a real threat to New Zealand. When Gary Freeman took over from me as Kiwi coach he picked a remarkable number of new guys who will need to adjust to international football in quick time.

Now that rugby league is a summer sport in Britain it is much harder to arrange even shortened tours of the sort we used to blood our younger players up until the 1990s. But it is heartening that the New Zealand Rugby League tried to put as many games as possible around the three tests to be played in England in late 2002. The Australians are even planning to resurrect their aborted 2001 tour in 2003.

But will we ever again see the Lions playing Down Under in mid-season rather than in brief glimpses when the fans are thinking of barbecues and beaches, and British clubs are persuading their players to undergo treatment for any injury niggles so they will be ready for the start of the next Super League season?

 *Chapter 18.*
Coaches and coaching

Frank Endacott was nicknamed Happy Frank by rugby league journalists in Australia and Great Britain who were variously surprised, delighted, and even sometimes amazed at the affable reception they received from the Kiwi coach. He was a welcome contrast to the generally dour and cliché-ridden coaches who abound in the politically correct world of professional sport. Endacott was so forthcoming about his team's tactics at one informal press conference before New Zealand played Great Britain in the 1999 Tri-Nations tournament that BBC commentator and former international Ray French was moved to say, 'Frank, you don't have to tell us everything.'

Media relations is an important aspect of a coach's work. I have always made it a policy that I would never walk away from the media and I never have, even on my worst days. I regard the Happy Frank tag as a tribute to my father's advice all those years ago about a smile and a kind word costing you nothing.

Sometimes media conferences can be embarrassing, at other times they are bloody hard work, but you have to do it. I have never feared the media and am fortunate to have made a lot of friends in the various countries I have coached in.

Believe me, there were times when Happy Frank was hurting inside. But you shouldn't take it out on other people and must be honest at all times. The media guys are only doing their jobs and responding to their questions was part of my job.

I hated losing as much as anybody in the world. Everyone shows their losses differently and I believe if you lose then you must lose with dignity. You don't like it, of course, but you must accept it and start thinking about the next game no matter what your emotions might be telling you.

My finest win was in the '98 Anzac test when we beat the united Australian team at North Harbour Stadium despite suffering all those injuries during the game. People who have been in the game much longer than me believe that match will go down as one of New Zealand's finest rugby league victories.

There are two games that stand side by side as my worst losses, the Anzac test in 2000 and the Warriors' defeat by Gold Coast in 1998.

We were on a hiding to nothing in that 2000 test. It was the worst build-up I had experienced, with only one training run possible. There were no excuses for collapsing to lose by more than 50 points. We played poorly and everybody admitted it. Even if there is no build-up at all, players should be able to compete when they go out in a Kiwi jersey. Such blow-outs are becoming more common under the current rules, and not only at club level. Look what the Kiwis have done to Great Britain and England, not to mention Wales, Papua New Guinea, Tonga and the Cook Islands, over the last few years.

All I could do in Sydney that night was front up to the news media and promise they would see a very different Kiwi team at the World Cup. They did.

The Warriors went to the Gold Coast in '98 knowing they had to win, not so much for the competition points but for the very future of the club. We had a team which should have beaten them by 20 points yet were down by 18 points by halftime. It happened right in the midst of all the talk about the Warriors being sold and the players knew the destiny of the club was on the line. We had prepared well and I felt good before the kick-off. It's not often I scream at a team at halftime but I went right off my tree that day.

Although we outscored Gold Coast in the second half, the loss provided further ammunition for people in Australia who were questioning why the Warriors should even exist when their competition was about to be reduced from 20 teams. I described it as 'disgraceful' and 'the most disappointing loss in the club's history'. A columnist praised me for my honesty. I would rather not have provided the theme for his column.

All coaches have their own methods, and in recent years statistics have become as much a part of rugby league as they always seem to have been in American sports. I have done my time watching video tapes and checking statistics sheets but I never went overboard on them. They were merely a means of checking on individual players to find ways of lifting their games. Gee, you can take a lot of the fun out of football by overdoing the stats analysis.

I can't say I am a great fan of employing sports psychologists either. If they have value it also is only on an individual basis. I don't believe they can get their message through to every player but in a one-on-one situation they can sometimes make a difference. Collectively, sports psychologists can be a waste of time and money. I remember one time with Canterbury I had one of these blokes in to talk to the team and when I looked around the room Wayne Wallace, our most experienced player, was asleep. Waldo had been there and done that. I regarded it as my responsibility to get into the players' heads. Every coach should be part-psychologist.

It has been well documented that Graham Lowe showed the 1983 Kiwis film of New Zealand's winning Olympic Games rowers crying tears of joy when they were presented with their gold medals, and how his Kiwis won the test against Australia at Lang Park a few hours later. But there were a couple of hard heads sitting in one corner, Canterbury freezing worker Mark Broadhurst and West Coast woodchopper Gordon Smith, who told one reporter, 'All those Aucklanders might need those mind games but not us.'

To me a happy team will get better results than a side under pressure. The coach has to do his homework on his own players and the opposition but I have never believed in over-analysing matches. A lot of coaches can fool a lot of people with their mumbo-jumbo about how they have dissected every little thing about the opposing team but I don't subscribe to that.

No matter how extensively you plan a match much of what eventually happens inevitably depends on what the other team does. You can never plan for that, just as they can only guess what your players are going to do. From a team's point of view, you need do just enough study to get a result. The rest is about having your players in the mood to produce a peak performance on the day.

As coach of the Warriors and Wigan I was matched against every first grade coach in the sport's two most professional competitions. At international level the rivalry is more fleeting and you seldom come into direct contact with the other coach.

However, there was one tense and ultimately amusing meeting with Bob Fulton during my first series against Australia in 1995. Fulton was already a legend of the game, as a great stand-off half for Manly and the Kangaroos and later as an uncompromising coach of his club and country. Matthew Ridge raved about him, and they went on to win a premiership together with the Sea Eagles. I was aware of Fulton's reputation for doing anything to give his teams an edge.

He had already been reprimanded for wishing top referee Bill Harrigan would be 'run over by a cement truck' and was not known to take prisoners. He was obviously a fierce competitor.

It was halftime in the third test match at Brisbane and the Australian coaching staff was supposed to take the lift to the dressing rooms first, with the lift to return for me and my staff. We walked around the corner and saw the lift door was open, with the operator waving us to hurry up. I thought Fulton and his two sidekicks had already gone and we ran into the lift. The lift operator was new, however, and there we were, Fulton and his two stats men on one side and me and my two stats men on the other. The Lang Park lift must have been the slowest in the world, and we all stared blankly at the doors for an eternity. Not a word was uttered until we just about reached the ground floor. Then Fulton looked me straight in the eye and said, 'Hate to fight you', and my answer was, 'Well, that would be one we would win.'

I coached against him right through until 1998, and he didn't change. Just before we beat them in the '98 Anzac test, Fulton had another go at Harrigan, claiming, 'The man's ego is out of control, he reckons he's bigger than the game.' Fulton called Harrigan the biggest showoff in rugby league, saying, 'The game has got to get rid of him unless he changes his ways.'

Fulton's Manly team had just lost heavily to the Brisbane Broncos, but he was prepared to risk a $AUS10,000 fine to get all that off his chest. Maybe he thought if he could be seen standing up to the top whistle-blower the other referees would be intimidated.

His comments were so widely published that even English referee Russell Smith, who was due to control the Anzac test in Auckland soon afterwards, could not have missed being reminded of Fulton's barbs. Fulton had lashed out at Smith after the extra-time World Cup semi-final in 1995, a game his side had eventually won. One can only imagine Fulton was indignant Smith had presided over a match in which his players needed 100 minutes to get the desired result.

Another Fulton target was New Zealand referee Phil Houston after the second 1995 test against the Kiwis in Sydney. That was another close call, with Australia ahead only 14–10 until a last-minute converted try inflated the margin. Fulton confronted Houston in the players' tunnel at fulltime and gave him the customary blast at the press conference.

Yet Houston had sin-binned Tony Iro when the scores were tied at 10-all after 51 minutes for the heinous crime of knocking the ball out of an opponent's grasp. Fulton might have had a phobia about Super League and New Zealanders but Houston, who was a very capable referee, was then involved in the ARL Winfield Cup competition and was effectively a stablemate of the Kangaroo coach.

Fulton was a sharp man with an unquestionable record of success. The longer I knew him the more we spoke and I remember having a good chat with him after a Warriors match at Ericsson Stadium. He had a rough exterior but was a nice bloke once you got to know him. He wasn't communicating too well after our last test, though, because we won that one.

With Australian national coaches you have to fight fire with fire. If they got in the gutter you had to get in the gutter with them. They used to demand meetings with test referees and I got on to that real quick. I would get a message through to the referee along the lines of 'The New Zealand camp would rather let you get on with the game but if they arrange to have any meetings I am going to be at every one of them'. The Australians cut out their meeting requests, for a while anyway.

It's going on again now. In Britain last year there was that awful stink over who should referee the third test after Englishman Robert Connolly had done the first test and Australian Bill Harrigan the second. Of course, the Lions had won with Connolly and the Kangaroos had won with Harrigan. In the week leading up to the decider there was more publicity about the refereeing stalemate than there was about the players who would decide the outcome of the series.

Kangaroo coach Chris Anderson was adamant he would have Harrigan. The Brits didn't want him at any cost but the Australians, as usual, got their way through a so-called neutral International Federation committee. Whatever happened to the old policy of bringing in referees from a third country? They had rated Frenchman Thierry Alibert as one of the most impressive referees at the World Cup only the previous year and he could have been there within a few hours. They didn't trust each other, and they didn't trust a neutral either.

Maybe Anderson and Fulton had a special reason for not wanting to be the first Australian coach to lose a test series since the 1978 Kangaroos were beaten 2–0 in France. Fulton was the captain of that 1978 team and Anderson played on the wing in both tests. The Australian media might just have dug up that piece of embarrassing trivia.

John Lang coached the Australian Super League team against us in '97, but I knew him most as a coach who had very good results with Cronulla without quite being able to break the Sharks' premiership drought. He is one of the nicest blokes in the game but has taken on a big task trying to lift wooden spooners Penrith back up the ladder. I went to Cronulla a few times to watch the Kiwi players, and Lang would always come over in the leagues club later to have a chat. He's a good coach and a good competitor but was very aware of the public relations side of things and a real gentleman.

BEING FRANK

After Fulton retired during the '98 season, with us one-up in the tests, the Australians did us no favours by giving the position to Wayne Bennett for the second and third tests after he was through with his club commitments. I knew there would be a different philosophy and a different team. Bennett got the mix right very quickly.

With Fulton you knew you would be up against a big, tough, intimidating forward pack. At that time our forwards were at least as big, tough and intimidating and we felt we had their measure up front after winning the Anzac test. We also played powerful centres like Richie Blackmore and Kevin Iro so couldn't be monstered out in the backs. We were getting to master Fulton's blueprint when we were confronted by Bennett with a new game plan and a new set of players to analyse.

Wayne Bennett is a master coach, the number one in the world, and the only Australian coach I haven't beaten on the field. He has always had a problem with the news media but I don't regard him as an introvert at all. After the third test in '98 we met for about three hours over breakfast and swapped test jerseys. He told me not to feel disappointed because the Kiwis had played very well. But his teams had been red hot that season, and many of the players were with him in a unique winning treble with the Broncos, Queensland and Kangaroos.

Bennett obviously earns great respect from his players despite having said goodbye to a few of them in his 15 years coaching the Broncos. He has the knack of knowing exactly when to get rid of those whose careers have peaked so he can retain and introduce younger players to keep the Broncos right up there. Only a few months after wishing Brad Thorn all the best in rugby union and losing Gorden Tallis to injury, Bennett had replaced them with two new Kangaroo second-rowers in Brad Meyers and Dean Carlaw and State of Origin forward Carl Webb. He knew just when to release Steve Renouf, and what he did with Allan Langer in bringing him back from Warrington to star in last year's deciding third State of Origin game was inspired.

Even a heart attack during the third Ashes test and bypass surgery early in 2002 couldn't break Chris Anderson's grip on the Kangaroo coaching job. He comes across as a dour sort of a bloke but has a very dry humour. He was the one who resurrected Fulton's requests for meetings with referees. I went along to a couple and when they found out they could not have their own cosy little chats without me butting in they gave the idea up.

Anderson took that hard-nosed traditional Canterbury Bulldogs philosophy to Melbourne and then into the Australian squad. It was one we knew well. The Warriors have always had a creditable record against the Bulldogs and Storm, which use an up-and-in style of defence. But he has maintained the Kangaroos' glowing record. We beat them in the first Tri-Nations match and the Lions won the first 2001 test, but each time Anderson and his players struck back to win the series.

Both Fulton and Anderson have proved that outstanding players can make successful coaches. Anderson won a Challenge Cup with Halifax and premierships with Canterbury and Melbourne. Coaching is obviously in Anderson's psyche, to the extent he was determined to keep his new fulltime position with Cronulla as well as his Kangaroo job after recovering from heart surgery.

Over the years the Australians don't seem to have prepared well for their opening tests of a series, probably because of overconfidence. Look at 2001, when they thought they would have the Lions on a platter. You really must get to England at least 10 days in advance of the first test so you can not only get over jet lag but also accustom yourself to the conditions. It takes about four days to flush the air flight out of your system. Whenever the Kangaroos suffer a setback, however, it doesn't take them long to get back into top gear.

I noticed when I first started coaching against the Australians that they had a real sense of arrogance, as if they just had to take the field to beat us. But that attitude soon changed as was evident from the nervousness on their faces before the 2000 World Cup final. The fear of losing must be weighing more heavily on their shoulders the longer they extend their sequence of World Cup and test series victories. Brad Fittler frequently mentioned the teams he captained didn't want to be the first to drop one. It will happen. They have a right to be arrogant with their record. But they are not unbeatable.

Parramatta's Brian Smith is the best technical coach in Australia. He has been guilty in the past of playing a few mind games that undid him at vital times of the season but I believe he is destined to win a grand final. He was desperately close in 2001. Smith's a real good bloke, a deep thinker, and good to have a discussion with. I could talk to him all day about football. Some people don't like him, maybe because he's so honest and says what he thinks. Smith could also take credit for setting up the systems at Bradford for Matthew Elliott, who went on to win a Challenge Cup, while Warriors coach Daniel Anderson was one of his assistants at Parramatta.

Some environments don't seem conducive to success, though. Tim Sheens had been one of the most highly respected coaches in Australia while he was at Canberra and, before that, Penrith. Then it all fell apart in Townsville. He had strong teams to coach at Canberra and went up to North Queensland where no one has done any good. Sheens was probably the highest paid coach in the NRL but never got results with the Cowboys and was eventually ushered out the door.

There is a never-ending debate about whether good players make good coaches, or whether good coaches make good players. I think it's a bit of both. You can't get the results you want, however, unless you have players who can do the job for you. You might be the general leading them in the right direction but you must have soldiers who can overcome the flak fired back at them. If the environment you have created is right the chances of that happening are much greater.

Sometimes a head coach becomes more of a co-ordinator than a coach. You give them the game plan and tell them what you want. But once they run over that white line you are relying on their ability, their knowledge and their application of your game plan to win it for you. If you do not have the players who can do that then you are not going to win.

Old style English coaches, such as Dougie Laughton at Leeds, were legends but I was told by several players that they never saw him at training. Star player Ellery Hanley used to run the training sessions. Laughton was a man who sat in his office, occasionally came out with a big cigar in his mouth to see how things were going, then ducked inside again. He and his type were more managers than coaches in our meaning of the word.

Craig Innes told me that all the time he was at Leeds he never had any advice from Laughton on how to play rugby league. Apparently the only thing Laughton said to Innes was, 'How's your flat, lad?' It also happened to another converted All Black, John Gallagher, at Leeds. Innes went on to better things at Manly, while Gallagher dropped out of the game.

I mention Laughton as one example but there were plenty of former coaches in Britain who were like that. That has changed since the introduction of Super League, and the influx of many Australian and a few New Zealand coaches. Super League has actually been good in raising the standards of British rugby league. The coaches over there are now coaching, including the English ones when they can get a look in.

Once again, Bradford sets the standard. When they had Brian Smith his apprentice was Matthew Elliott, who took over for about four years and began to get results. In turn, Elliott's lieutenant was Brian Noble, a former Great Britain captain and hooker. Noble is a lovely bloke who deserves success, and achieved that in last year's grand final. He should be set there for years to come because Bradford has the stability that other clubs lack.

As I know only too well, Wigan has been averaging one coach each year for the last seven or eight years and they are not alone. The turnover unsettles the players, who don't know where the instructions are coming from one season to the next. If a coach is appointed for two or three years then he should be allowed to complete that term. If a club has faith in a coach at the start of a season then he should be judged on his results at the end of it, not by a knee jerk reaction midway through.

It happens in every sport. Look at netball's Yvonne Willering, the Football

Kingz with their coaches, Graham Henry and the Welsh Rugby Union. English sports are the worst example, especially soccer. But at least the soccer coaches tend to go from club to club.

In rugby league sacked coaches usually disappear out of the game, which cannot afford to lose so much experience and so many knowledgeable men. It is unbelievable how many coaches in England have defected to rugby union. Ellery Hanley, Joe Lydon and Phil Larder are all with the English Rugby Union. Then you have a real league legend like Shaun Edwards slumming it at club level. Billy McGinty, who was my assistant at Wigan, has helped take Sale right up the ladder as defensive coach. Midway through the 2002 first division season Mike Ford left Oldham to take up a post with the Irish Rugby Union, just after they sacked New Zealander Warren Gatland.

Another example is Clive Griffiths, who coached Wales at the last two rugby league World Cups. Wales made the semi-finals both times, drawing a big crowd to Old Trafford against England in 1995 and then frightening the daylights out of Australia in 2000. Griffiths had to take up a rugby union contract to earn a decent wage between those tournaments and is now virtually a fulltime rugby union coach. Another good coach, and good bloke, gone. There are others too. I blame the administrators, who really have to look at themselves.

Phil Larder was the first Great Britain coach I opposed at test level, in New Zealand in '96. His background was in development, and the word I got from the Lions camp was that he was a very efficient technical and theory coach but not really a practical man. Yet I see he has been doing a great job with the British Lions since he changed codes. He didn't have the best of results against the Kiwis and suffered after that '96 tour. But there were a lot of things going on which didn't help his cause, like players being sent home to save money.

The other Lions coach I came up against was Andy Goodway in the '98 series in England and the '99 Tri-Nations. Goodway had been a great second-rower for Wigan and Great Britain but always seemed to be skating on thin ice as his results against us got progressively worse. He was never popular with the news media over there and from what I heard he wasn't popular with the players either. He wouldn't communicate with them and ruled more by fear than co-operation. In '98 Goodway got offside with officialdom by not leading his players onto the field for the tests. Instead, he ignored that time-honoured British tradition and sat up in the grandstand. Goodway lost his job at Wigan before I took over and was also bypassed by England for the 2000 World Cup.

John Kear coached England. He was similar to Larder in that he had been a director of coaching and development. Kear is a very passionate man, and was devastated with the 6–49 loss to the Kiwis at Reebok Stadium in the World Cup semi-final. He was always destined to fall, or be pushed, onto his sword after that.

So the British have done what would have been unheard of a decade or so ago and appointed an Australian, David Waite, as their international coach. It's far less surprising now because of the deep Australian influence within the British game. The Aussies had a boys' club over there and looked after each other. Waite's name was bandied about as a candidate for every position in the rugby league world, including the Kiwis and the Warriors. You expected him to be mentioned whenever the local supermarket needed a new trolley boy. He started off coaching England against Wales and struggled to beat what was nothing more than a reserve grade team. I noticed Waite was very nervous during that game and rightly so. In his first Lions series he silenced the traditionalists by upsetting Australia first up, but got hammered in the second test and beaten in the third. How he goes against the 2002 Kiwis could make or break him in what promises to be a very even series.

Of the British club coaches, Brian Noble is the one really making an impact. He's on a winner at Bradford. Another mover is Shaun McRae, who began as a trainer at Canberra, then assisted Bob Fulton with the Kangaroos in pre-Super League days and was on my staff at the 1995 World Cup. McRea had great success at St Helens before becoming another victim of the English system. Now he is coaching Hull and has got them into the top bracket. He is a really likeable bloke who enjoys his wins. Players respond to him but he is not frightened to make a tough call.

I was at Wigan when Gary Freeman was appointed Kiwi coach but heard there was an uproar among the local coaches because they had brought in someone from Sydney who had not fulfilled any previous national duties. There had been a defined route, through club and provincial football, the Junior Kiwis, and then onto the Kiwis, and that chain had been broken. Coaches within the New Zealand system were annoyed Freeman had swooped in over their heads when they believed they were doing all the right things by attending elite camps and the like. Even the selection process changed, with former Kiwi coach Graham Lowe, retired Kiwi Jarrod McCracken, and then NZRL board member Bob Haddon interviewing candidates and making their recommendation. Freeman then returned serve by including McCracken on his selection panel.

By rubber stamping Freeman, the NZRL overlooked people like Gary Kemble, Gerard Stokes and Graeme Norton. Kemble had coached the Junior Kiwis and is now with the Warriors again, and Stokes has been heavily involved in the Bartercard Cup with Canterbury and Wellington as well as coaching New Zealand Residents teams on tour. Norton was at a disadvantage because he had not coached regularly for a while but had still been made

New Zealand Rugby League big
guns during my term as coach of
the Kiwis. Graham Carden (top left)
was succeeded as president by
Gerald Ryan (top right), while Gary
Allcock (bottom left) took time out
from his police career to serve as
NZRL general manager.

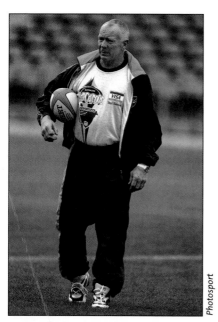

Bob Fulton. This Bozo was no clown.

Wayne Bennett. Top of the coaching tree.

Chris Anderson. Literally put his heart into coaching the Kangaroos.

Top ten

My toughest ever selection task was to name the top 10 Kiwis of my era. These players represent so many outstanding men who wore the Kiwi emblem from 1994 to 2000.

Matthew Ridge, just the man to lead the troops from the trenches.

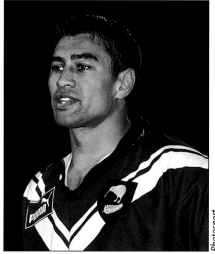

Richie Barnett, a perfect role model for the game.

Stacey Jones, the face of New Zealand rugby league.

Henry Paul, a budding champion from his junior days.

Jarrod McCracken, always had a certain aura about him.

Kevin Iro, larger than life, a player for the big occasion.

Stephen Kearney, the epitome of
the modern professional.

Craig Smith, trained his way into
the test team.

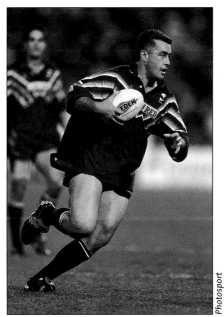

Quentin Pongia, an 80-minute man
in the interchange era.

Ruben Wiki, unwavering loyalty to
club and country.

The Endacotts at the wedding of Gary and Shelley. From left, Wayne, Joan, Gary, Shelley, me, Frank and Shane.

Gary takes the ball up during a president's grade match for Linwood against
Halswell.

Shane helped Sydenham reach the 1992 Canterbury grand final before
embarking on his professional career.

Another mission accomplished. Gary after finishing one of his four New York City marathons.

project manager for the 2000 pre-World Cup camps.

At least Freeman did appoint Stokes as assistant coach and there should be a good chance that he will take over some time in the future. The signs for Stokes are promising and it is a good way to do it. Stokes had a solid background at club and provincial level.

From my experience, Freeman can't afford any slip-ups. He doesn't want to lose a test in Papua New Guinea or a series to Great Britain. No one has the right to win every game and the tour to Britain will be a real test. It's not easy. In fact, it's bloody hard work. I wish him all the best and will support him and the Kiwis to the hilt.

Despite all my moments with the hierarchy I seem to be the only coach to have put away the Kiwi clipboard without first being sacked in the last 20 years. Ces Mountford didn't want to go when he found out they were ignoring other New Zealand-based coaches (shades of 2001) and bringing Graham Lowe home from Brisbane. Lowe got the chop because he wanted to coach the Kiwis and Wigan at the same time, and in turn Tony Gordon, Bob Bailey and Howie Tamati were all replaced when still adamant their work was unfinished.

As the old adage goes: 'There are only two types of coaches, those who have been sacked and those waiting to be sacked.' Aussie Jack Gibson came up with: 'Winning a match only means you're champion for a week.'

And there was that great quip from Bob Bailey when comparing his treatment to that of British coach Malcolm Reilly after both experienced 1–2 series losses to Australia: 'Reilly won one test against Australia and got an MBE. I won one test against Australia and got sacked'.

Chapter 19.
Gary

Although Frank Endacott left Christchurch to further his professional coaching career after the 1993 season, the family name was soon back in the headlines down south because of the extraordinary deeds of Gary, the second youngest of his four sons. Despite suffering from cerebral palsy, Gary Endacott has taken part in several strenuous sports, completed four New York City marathons, and has even scaled Africa's highest mountain.

Joan and I had two health scares with our boys. When our second son Frank was six months old he was diagnosed as having meningitis. We were called to the hospital and told Frank would not get through the night, and had accordingly been christened by the hospital chaplain.

As a last resort, one of the doctors mentioned a new experimental drug, and asked if we were prepared to use Frank as a guinea pig. We accepted. We just couldn't face the near certainty of him dying overnight, of not seeing him next morning. There were no guarantees. Far from it. They told us later that Frank 'died' three times in the night, and that they kept bringing him back. They called him the Miracle Baby, and that drug is still in use today. Frank himself is now the proud father of three children.

All our kids are equal in Joan's and my eyes, but when you sit down and think about it Gary is something really special. His brothers agree with that totally.

Gary was born in 1968, premature but okay. However, Christchurch was then experiencing a rash of power cuts. In the split second between the electricity cutting off and Christchurch Women's Hospital switching over to auxiliary power an airlock occurred in Gary's incubator. We were told that by the nurse in charge of the ward or we would never have known.

It affected Gary's muscles. To feel them they are like iron; they're not flexible at all. We knew something was wrong when he should have been crawling and wasn't. When he finally got mobile he was crawling backwards. Then he showed no inclination to walk. Gary didn't walk until he was in his fourth year, and that was only after Joan had taken him to doctors who diagnosed he had cerebral palsy and were of the opinion he would never walk at all.

Joan would not accept that. She persevered by putting pegs on the kitchen floor, made Gary lift his feet to get over them, and started him walking. He would fall over every second step, bounce back up, then fall over again. At kindergarten and school he wore special boots with wheels on the front to stop them from rapidly scuffing out.

Gary entered every race on one sports day at Gilberthorpe School, and a well-meaning teacher suggested that he should receive about 300 metres start in the 400 metres race. But he refused and said he wanted to start with the other kids, which he did. The others ran like crazy and finished in a bunch. About 10 minutes later Gary came around the final bend, falling over every five or 10 paces, and received a standing ovation from parents, teachers, pupils, the lot.

It was evident from an early age that Gary wanted to be treated as an equal, to do things other kids could do, and to finish whatever he started. On that same sports day he wanted to go in the high jump even though he couldn't lift his feet off the ground more than an inch or two. So they lowered the bar to a few inches. Gary charged in for his high jump, fell on the bar, and smashed it. They spent half the day looking around the school and beyond for another bar. Gary found it tough at school but he never gave in.

No one ever thought of him playing football, and we were grateful when coach Kevin Woodham and manager Maurice Kerr, two great Hornby stalwarts, gave Gary the job of assistant manager of their premier team. They would offer to help him with the heavy gear bag but he would always refuse and struggle along with it. Gary loved the game and was always there when I was coaching Canterbury.

Our oldest son, Wayne, had played some social rugby with his mates for the Hornby club. Frank was a premier grade rugby league player for Sydenham, and, of course, Shane became a very fine footballer for the Junior Kiwis, Canterbury, Hull and the Warriors.

With all that going on around him, Gary was never going to be satisfied with pulling a gear bag behind him. When he was 19 he started playing for Linwood in the president's grade. After that team folded, he joined Hornby but wasn't happy with the amount of time he was spending on the sidelines. So he switched to Kaiapoi and enjoyed a few wins at Hornby's expense.

I remember Gary coming home one night and saying to Joan and me that he really wanted to achieve something in sport. Tennis was his choice and representing New Zealand was his goal. He went down to Wilding Park and won the Canterbury disabled standing title against a guy who was expected to beat him easily. Gary then went on to win the New Zealand singles and was twice selected to play in Tokyo. He brought home gold, silver and bronze medals from Japan Open singles and doubles championships. Mission accomplished.

When Joan went to watch Gary playing at Wilding Park she was horrified because he would never give up chasing the ball and threatened to wipe himself out. There was a row of wheelchair athletes at the side of the court, watching the game. When Gary gets going he can't stop like an able-bodied person. He took out two or three wheelchairs in one hit. Gary would arrive home with no skin on his forearms, elbows and knees, but we couldn't stop him being so competitive.

In 1996 Gary was approached by the Achilles Track Club of New Zealand, which provides support for disabled athletes, and was asked if he wanted to compete in a New York City marathon. Until then he had never considered long distance running because of the number of shoes he would literally go through. In his eighth week of training he was on his sixth pair, about $850 worth of footwear.

The New York organisers estimated that someone with his disability needed 12 hours to cover the course. Gary would have none of that. He predicted he would finish in between eight and 10 hours. It took him 7 hours 55 minutes the first time, and he lopped almost an hour off his personal best by his fourth trip through the streets of New York City.

Remembering that at school he would crash every few paces, Gary was thrilled to run that first marathon among 30,000 people without falling over once. But one year they made the disabled athletes start with the main bunch and that was a real struggle. The able-bodied runners threw their paper cups onto the road after the drinks stations and they were like hurdles to Gary. Fortunately he had Aaron Whittaker with him as his support crew.

I reckon the proudest moment of our lives, Joan's and mine, was in 1997 when we flew to New York to see Gary in the marathon. We were sitting there in Central Park about 100 metres from the finish watching all the competitors come around the bend and up the straight. There were dozens and dozens of able-bodied runners who had tried to beat their predicted times by going out too hard and were so disorientated that they were collapsing, even turning back and not knowing where they were. Then all of a sudden around the corner comes Gary, and he absolutely powers to the finishing line. I'll never forget that beaming smile he gave us as he went past. I looked at Joan, she looked at me, and there were tears streaming down our cheeks. Considering what Gary had gone through as a kid it was bloody unbelievable. After the race they packed Gary in ice up to his neck to cool him down and help his recovery.

When Gary was getting up to all these things I was always the more protective one. Joan would just tell him to do anything he wanted but I would worry about the possible consequences. Then one day in 1996 I was in Sydney with the Warriors reserve grade team on the day before a match when Gary rang and asked, 'Dad, how would you feel if I did a parachute jump?'

I don't know why but for once I just said, 'Gary, if you want to do it then do it.' There was a silence on the phone before he came back with, 'You really mean that? You don't want to think about it first?' I told him no, to go and get on with it. 'Oh, that's good,' he said, 'because I did the parachute jump at three o'clock yesterday.'

I have to say, though, that I wasn't too happy when I heard Gary was planning to scale Mount Kilimanjaro last year while Joan and I were in England. I thought it would be too much for him. I had heard Kilimanjaro was the highest freestanding mountain in the world, and some people who had climbed it reckoned he would have no chance. I tried my utmost to talk Gary out of it but he had made up his mind and was practising for it by charging up the embankments and grandstands at Rugby League Park back home in Christchurch.

It worried me even more that he was travelling to and from Tanzania on his own. They wouldn't give him enough funding to take Auckland firefighter Alan Barr with him as a support climber because the people who control the sponsorship money said the community would not benefit as a whole. That was an absolute joke because Gary has become a role model for children, and not just the disabled ones. He goes around schools talking to and helping kids and they get plenty of positives from his visits. It was one of the lamest excuses I had heard. However, Gary's achievement was all the more remarkable because he did without special assistance.

It's an inspiring story how he got up that mountain. Seventy people started out and only 32 made it to the top. Gary was the only disabled person in the group and became the first cerebral palsy sufferer to conquer Kilimanjaro. All of those who turned back were able-bodied.

They have a rule up there that if your nose bleeds due to altitude sickness you must turn back. Well, Gary had three nose bleeds, but the inside of his jacket was red and he was hiding the blood by wiping his nose on the red material. When the guides eventually spotted what he was doing they tried to persuade him to give up. He told them there was only one way he was going and they were welcome to accompany him if they wanted to.

Then he hit the scree nearer the summit and had to crawl to make any progress. Gary staggered and crawled for hours, until he could rise no more on the loose surface and crawled all of the last two hours to the top. On the way down he found it impossible to maintain any balance so he slid on his backside through the scree until they put him on a stretcher and carried him the rest of the way. His body had seized up. I hope he never tries anything like that again.

I know it meant a lot to Gary when he was named Canterbury Sports Personality in the Sport Canterbury winter awards late last year. He had been nominated by the Canterbury Rugby League; local rugby union legend Todd Blackadder was among his rivals. The awards dinner was held the night before Blackadder's big farewell in the provincial final at Jade Stadium, in a week when the Christchurch news media had gone Blackadder mad, and that made it all the more memorable. He had climbed his mountain in more ways than one.

Not bad for a kid who a few years before had told us he wanted to achieve something special and went out to buy a tennis racquet. Gary has been the real achiever in the Endacott family. Not me. Not Shane. It's been Gary.

Appendix I – The Endacott file (statistics)

Club – senior

1982   Addington: won minor premiership, won grand final.

1983   Addington: third in minor premiership, semi-finalist.

1985   Hornby: won minor premiership, beaten grand finalist, won Thacker Shield.

1986   Hornby: won minor premiership, won grand final, won Thacker Shield.

1987   Hornby: runner-up minor premiership, beaten grand finalist.

Club – junior

1986   Hornby: won 15-years minor premiership, won grand final.

1987   Hornby: won 16-years minor premiership, won grand final.

1988   Hornby: won 17-years minor premiership, won grand final.

Canterbury

1989   played 8, won 3, drew 0, lost 5, points for 178, against 184.

1990   played 9, won 6, drew 0, lost 3, points for 283, against 205.

1991   played 6, won 4, drew 0, lost 2, points for 177, against 116.

1992   played 7, won 3, drew 1, lost 3, points for 133, against 127.

1993   played 8, won 7, drew 0, lost 1, points for 230, against 85.

Total: played 38, won 23, drew 1, lost 14, points for 1001, against 717.

Average result: 26–19.

Junior Kiwis

1992   v Australian Schoolboys: lost 24–26 (Rotorua), won 36–14 (Auckland).

1993   tour of Britain and France, played 12, won 11, lost 1, including three tests, v Great Britain Academy: won 30–22 (Wembley), lost 12–34 (Wigan), and v France Juniors: won 26–4 (Carcassonne).

Auckland Warriors Reserves

1995   played 23, won 12, drew 0, lost 11, points for 602, against 472.

1996   played 25, won 19, drew 0, lost 6, points for 520, against 277.

1997   played 8, won 4, drew 2, lost 2, points for 146, against 151.

Total: played 56, won 35, drew 2, lost 19, points for 1268, against 900.

Average result: 23–16.

BEING FRANK

Auckland Warriors First Grade

1997 (Aust)   played 9, won 4, drew 0, lost 5, points for 189, against 204.
1997 (WCC)   played 8, won 7, drew 0, lost 1, points for 346, against 118.
1998 (Aust)   played 24, won 9, drew 0, lost 15, points for 417, against 518.
Total: played 41, won 20, drew 0, lost 21, points for 952, against 840.
Average result: 23–20.

Wigan

2000 (SL)   played 31, won 25, drew 1, lost 5, points for 1032, against 500.
2001 (SL)   played 10, won 6, drew 1, lost 3, points for 295, against 152.
2000–01 (Cup)   played 4, won 2, drew 0, lost 2, points for 148, against 42.
Total: played 45, won 33, drew 2, lost 10, points for 1475, against 694.
Average result: 33–15.

New Zealand – Test Matches

1994   New Zealand 28 Papua New Guinea 12 at Goroka
        New Zealand 30 Papua New Guinea 16 at Port Moresby
1995   New Zealand 22 France 6 at Auckland (Ericsson)
        New Zealand 16 France 16 at Palmerston North
        Australia 26 New Zealand 8 at Brisbane
        Australia 20 New Zealand 10 at Sydney (SFS)
        Australia 46 New Zealand 10 at Brisbane
        New Zealand 25 Tonga 24 at Warrington (World Cup)
        New Zealand 22 Papua New Guinea 6 at St Helens (World Cup)
        Australia 30 New Zealand 20 at Huddersfield (World Cup)
1996   New Zealand 62 Papua New Guinea 8 at Rotorua
        New Zealand 64 Papua New Guinea 0 at Palmerston North
        New Zealand 17 Great Britain 12 at Auckland (Ericsson)
        New Zealand 18 Great Britain 15 at Palmerston North
        New Zealand 32 Great Britain 12 at Christchurch (Lancaster)
1997   Australia 34 New Zealand 22 at Sydney (SFS)
        New Zealand 30 Australia 12 at Auckland (North Harbour)
1998   New Zealand 22 Australia 16 at Auckland (North Harbour)
        Australia 30 New Zealand 12 at Brisbane
        Australia 36 New Zealand 16 at Auckland (North Harbour)
        New Zealand 22 Great Britain 16 at Huddersfield
        New Zealand 36 Great Britain 16 at Bolton
        New Zealand 23 Great Britain 23 at Watford

1999	Australia 20 New Zealand 14 at Sydney (Stadium Australia)
	New Zealand 24 Australia 22 at Auckland (Ericsson)
	New Zealand 74 Tonga 0 at Auckland (Carlaw)
	New Zealand 26 Great Britain 4 at Auckland (Ericsson)
	Australia 22 New Zealand 20 at Auckland (Ericsson)
2000	Australia 52 New Zealand 0 at Sydney (Stadium Australia)
	New Zealand 64 Lebanon 0 at Gloucester (World Cup)
	New Zealand 84 Cook Islands 10 at Reading (World Cup)
	New Zealand 54 France 6 at Castleford (World Cup)
	New Zealand 58 Wales 18 at Cardiff (World Cup)
	New Zealand 49 England 6 at Bolton (World Cup)
	Australia 40 New Zealand 12 at Manchester (World Cup final)

Total: played 35, won 22, drew 2, lost 11, points for 1046, against 632.
Average result: 30–18.

Kiwi Tour Matches

1994   beat Cairns XIII 44–16 at Cairns, beat Port Moresby Vipers 40–4 at Port Moresby, beat Northern Zone 34–2 at Lae.

New Zealand Residents

1994 tour   beat Western Division 54–20 at Blayney, beat Sydney Metropolitan 36–24 at Parramatta, beat Northern Rivers 22–12 at Ballina, beat Australian Residents 39–28 at Brisbane (Lang Park), beat Western Samoa 64–2 at Auckland (Carlaw Park).

Other Appointments

1984	Canterbury B, Southern Provinces.
1987	New Zealand Elite squads.
1988	New Zealand Elite squads.
1989	New Zealand Elite squads, New Zealand trial team.
1990	New Zealand trial team, Canterbury women's touch team.
1991	Kiwi Colts, New Zealand Elite, Canterbury women's touch team.

Awards

1970   Addington Rugby League Club, Sportsman of the Year.

1988   Hornby Sports Awards, Coach of the Year.

1992   Canterbury Westland Winter Sports Awards, Outstanding Winter Sports Coach.

1993   Sir Richard Hadlee Sports Trust Awards, Most Outstanding Coach or Administrator.

1994   Sir Richard Hadlee Sports Trust Awards, Most Outstanding Coach or Administrator.

1997   Alac Sports Awards (Halberg Trust), Coach of the Year finalist.

1999   Canterbury Westland Winter Sports Awards, Outstanding Winter Sports Coach, Overall Outstanding Winter Sports Coach and Administrator.

1999   Sir Richard Hadlee Sports Award, Nomination for Sportsperson of the Decade 1990–1999.

2000   English Super League, Coach of the Year.

Certificates

New Zealand Rugby League, Level III Coaching

New Zealand Rugby League, Level II Coaching

Australian Rugby League, Level II Coaching

New Zealand Coaching Qualification, Sfrito Level III Coaching

New Zealand Rugby League, Director of Coaching 1994–95.

Frank Endacott's Kiwis 1994–2000 (55 players)

Stephen Kearney 32 tests (of possible 35): once injured, twice suspended

Ruben Wiki 30 (of 35): missed five through injury

Richie Barnett 26 (of 28): missed two through injury

Quentin Pongia 26 (of 35): missed eight through injury, once rested

Stacey Jones 25 (of 28): twice injured, once rested

Joe Vagana 25 (of 25): replacement 13 times, started in 12

Sean Hoppe 24 (of 24): then dropped out of international football

Henry Paul 23 (of 33): twice injured, once rested, seven unavailable

Gene Ngamu 21 (of 28): once injured, six not selected

Robbie Paul 19 (of 20): once rested

Logan Swann 19 (of 24): once injured, once not selected, twice rested

Matthew Ridge 18 (of 19): once injured

Syd Eru 18 (of 22): twice injured, twice suspended

Tony Iro: 17 tests

Richie Blackmore, Nathan Cayless 16

Jason Lowrie 15

Jarrod McCracken 14

Richard Swain 12

Daryl Halligan, Craig Smith, Nigel Vagana, Lesley Vainikolo 11

Kevin Iro, Matt Rua, Willie Talau 10

Tony Puletua, John Timu 9

Gary Freeman, John Lomax, Tyran Smith 8

Brendon Tuuta 7

David Kidwell, Brent Stuart, Grant Young 6

Marc Ellis, Mark Horo, Hitro Okesene, Jason Williams 5

Tonie Carroll, Terry Hermansson 4

Logan Edwards, Brian Jellick, Tony Kemp, Tasesa Lavea, Tawera Nikau, Tony Tatupu 3

Ali Lauiti'iti, Duane Mann, Aaron Whittaker 2

Tea Ropati, Anthony Swann, Whetu Taewa, Tony Tuimavave, David Vaealiki 1

Also: Halligan was a non-playing reserve in one test match

Appendix II – Kiwi coaches

In days of old Kiwi coaches were somewhat shadowy figures working away in virtual anonymity. That all changed with television and over the last 20 years the men with the clipboards have been put under the closest media and public scrutiny.

The accompanying table details the test records of New Zealand's coaches since the Second World War. Frank Endacott is clearly the longest serving coach in terms of tests (35), 10 more than legendary Aucklander Snow Telford, who had three terms between 1955 and 1965.

Comparisons, however, are near impossible. Until the late 1970s, the Kiwis' traditional rivals were Australia, France and Great Britain. Papua New Guinea then joined the established nations, and the number of matches against emerging nations increased with the expanded World Cup tournaments of 1995 and 2000. Whereas the Australians have dominated the international scene in the last quarter-century, they frequently bowed to the British before then.

For many years New Zealand battled the handicap of fielding amateur sides against the professionals from Australia and Britain. Yet Jim Amos had the distinction of coaching the 1952–53 Kiwis to four consecutive test triumphs over Australia in home and away series, and fellow Cantabrian Lory Blanchard masterminded the 1971 Grand Slam Kiwis' victories over Australia, Great Britain and France in one year. Many of the coaches listed below won or drew home series against the Kangaroos and Lions.

Endacott has easily the best record against Great Britain (six wins and one draw in seven matches), plus decisive World Cup wins over England and Wales. His teams were unbeaten in test series against the Lions at home in 1996 and away in 1998. Only Graham Lowe (at home in 1984) had previously achieved that in a three-test series, but his 1985 Kiwis were held to a drawn result on English soil.

Against Australia, Endacott enjoyed three victories from 11 attempts, the losses including the extra-time semi-final at the 1995 World Cup. By comparison, Telford won three of 12 trans-Tasman tests, and Lowe won two of his eight. Endacott was unbeaten in his 24 tests against all other nations.

Records of post-war coaches

Coach	Years	Won	Drew	Lost
Scotty McClymont	1947–48, 1949–52	6	0	9
Jim Amos	1952–54	5	0	7
Harold Tetley	1955–56	2	0	4
Snow Telford	1955–58, 1961–63, 1965	8	3	17
Travers Hardwick	1959–60	4	0	4
Des White	1961	1	0	1
Maurie Robertson	1964–65	4	0	1
Lory Blanchard	1966–67, 1969, 1970–72	6	1	11
Des Barchard	1968, 1972	0	0	6
Morrie Church	1970	0	0	3
George Menzies	1974–75	3	2	6
Ron Ackland	1977–78	2	0	5
Ces Mountford	1979–82	6	1	8
Graham Lowe	1983–86	10	1	8
Tony Gordon	1987–89	7	0	6
Bob Bailey	1990–91	6	0	5
Howie Tamati	1992–93	4	1	6
Frank Endacott	1994–2000	22	2	11
Gary Freeman	2001	1	0	1

About the Writer

John Coffey is a West Coaster who has spent most of his working life at *The Press* newspaper in Christchurch since joining as a cadet reporter in 1963. He covered the first of his 99 rugby league tests at 17, and celebrated his 21st birthday in Sydney on the last night of his first (1967) tour with the Kiwis. Other assignments have included 10 years of test cricket, which happily coincided with New Zealand's golden era of the 1980s, international boxing and yachting, and various sports at Commonwealth and New Zealand Games. His previous books include *Canterbury XIII* and *Modern Rugby League Greats*, and he has been a contributor to overseas rugby league and cricket books and magazines. Coffey's hobby is harness racing, as a breeder and owner. He is married to Shirley, and they have three teenaged children, Nadia, Gina, and Shaun.